BEYOND THE IMAGE

Ronald Holloway

APPROACHES TO THE RELIGIOUS DIMENSION IN THE CINEMA

film oikoumene

WORLD COUNCIL OF CHURCHES
Geneva 1977

in co-operation with INTERFILM

The author, in completing this research, wishes to acknowledge grants from the Rockefeller Foundation and the World Council of Churches. He is particularly grateful to John Taylor, Hans-Rudolf Müller-Schwefe, and Rune Waldekranz for help and assistance.

Cover: John Taylor
Cover photo from Ingmar Bergman's "Seventh Seal", Svensk Filmindustri
ISBN 2 8254 0538 8

Printed in Switzerland by Imprimerie La Concorde

For my mother.

oikoumene

CONTENTS

A WORD OF INTRODUCTION

Christian Graf von Krakow humorously commented that a theologian is a man in a dark room looking blindfolded for a black cat that is not there — and who suddenly cries out: "I've got it!" I had somewhat the same experience when writing this book: when even the word "religion" is a bone of contention today, how is one to interpret the religious dimension in the cinema?

However, since few will deny that movies are erotic or political, at least in the eye of the beholder, let us assume too that the cinematic image has a theological implication. *Beyond the Image* offers ten approaches to the religious dimension in the cinema — a modest survey of a broad field. It owes a great debt to film historians and critics who have covered much of the same ground before, albeit from other angles. Many philosophers, theologians, and other academics have prepared the way for this book with related studies of literature, theatre, and the arts. I have only tried to tie together some of the loose ends related to cinema.

Be aware that certain loaded concepts, such as "pietism" and "propaganda," are used in a broad, generalized context — thus "propaganda" means "information of a persuasive nature," the sense in which it is often used and applied in European circles. Film titles, too, differ from country to country and continent to continent: "Cries and Whispers," for example, is the title given to Bergman's film at European festivals.

Some confusion may be caused by the ambiguity of the book's title. *Beyond the Image*, like meta-physics and meta-music, attempts to look "beyond" the immediate image to the traditional, the historical, the religious (there, I've said it) in the seventh art, in order to find the deeper meaning in film esthetics and a better appreciation of the contemporary human condition.

RONALD HOLLOWAY
Berlin, January 1977

I. A THEOLOGY OF THE CINEMA

The history of the cinema is the story of man in the age of technology. It is an art completely born out of the industrial age, and since its arrival it has been the chief witness of the passing of one epoch and the beginning of another. A theology of the cinema is therefore essentially related to a theology of technology.

But herein lies a difficulty. As Prof. Hans-Rudolf Müller-Schwefe points out in *Technik und Glaube*, the change-over into a new epoch has brought unrest and underscores "a permanent challenge" between technology and belief:

The revolution now in progress changes the position of man to nature. Mother Earth, who bore and nourished mankind, now becomes matter which man processes. In the place of integration into a higher order, and instead of the pious cultivation of nature, order is disturbed by this violent break-in, which brings with it challenge and experiment.

In responding to this challenge, the theologian must overlook the major controversies separating the nineteenth from the twentieth century and rearrange his thinking to focus on the origin of technology, instead of the consequences of it. Thus, when placed into a single package, the social polarities between yesterday's order of kings-and-manners and today's style of living in the world village, as well as the theological differences between liberalism and neo-orthodoxy in Protestant circles (to mark the dates: between Adolf von Harnack's 1914 *Manifesto of Intellectuals* and Karl Barth's 1919 *Epistle to the Romans*), tend to fade quickly into the background. Indeed, the future may eventually judge that much of today's theological squabbling has been the direct result of man's inability to comprehend the great technical power God has seen fit to place in his hands.

The permanent challenge between technology and belief may never be satisfactorily resolved, for it is one toward partnership and not dominance. That partnership was ultimately brought about by the movie camera, not at all accidentally, but in a very blasphemous way. Cinema as art and the moving picture as documentation were the chief witnesses to the demise of the gods of nature: it was that small mechanical instrument accompanying mountain expeditions and space flights, raising up man as the idols fell. For a time man trembled before his power, forcing God to remain safely in the heavens as the miracles were accomplished by his minions on earth. Cinema documented the mistake of this venture too, for technology on the loose had a way of making a mess of things. Man discovered to his sorrow that alone, without faith, he could not effectively control his fate. A partnership between technological man and an immanent-but-transcendent God was inevitable. And I think cinema has also documented that partnership in our own time.

The history of the cinema has three divisions, reckoning from the usual date of the *paid* Lumière exhibitions in the Grand Café in 1895. The first, between 1895 and the First World War in Europe and the Stock Market Crash in America, documents the end of the nineteenth century and the final period of transition from the previous nature-centered epoch. The period still accents the former mystical bond of holiness between man and the soil, and it tries as a whole to place man within the safe, secure embrace of the universe. The second division, signaling the birth of the sound film and carrying up to the Second World War, traces the rise of the propaganda film and the use of technology to manipulate the thinking of the public and control the masses under a form of hypnosis. This is not to say that the public was completely fooled, or that the cinema of the thirties and forties did not also faithfully reflect the subconscious of the mass public. The emphasis, however, in both the Hollywood Dream Cult and the Nazi propaganda film, was no longer on a form of active participation, but passive identification. The third division, from the Second World War to the present, marks the breakaway from the captivity of the star system and the development of the mature theme. Dialogue with the audience was fostered, and the film artist, the individual director, was set free to come into the market-place of philosophical and religious discussion. Mystical participation, passive identification, theological dialogue — these are the three main areas of influence a theology of the cinema has to contend with.

But there is a pre-history of the cinema too: the origin of the age of technology. An examination of this period is important not only to catch the spirit of the age in relation to the previous one, but also to demonstrate the fundamental reason why theology has conspicuously avoided cinema as a worthy dialogue partner (while all the other art forms were perfectly acceptable). The origin of the motion picture reveals too that this phenomenon belongs to the very essence of technological thought.

Pre-history of the cinema

Cinema, or the motion picture, is the outer expression of a philosophy of procession. In theological terms, grace in the motion picture is related to personality instead of to nature. The cinema is more an existentialist phenomenon than an essentialist one. It belongs to the same process of technology that turned matter to energy.

The year 1829 marks the date the conversion to energy and movement was felt in the public's consciousness, and it thereby formed the threshold between the two epochs. A new term was coined in Massachusetts physician Jacob Bigelow's book-title *Elements of Technology*. That year Stephenson's Rocket vividly proved the superiority of steam locomotion over the horse, and the first American railway began operation. It was the same year the Belgian scientist Plateau conceived the idea that pictures could be made to move; he perfected his shutter apparatus and began optic experiments with the sun (resulting in eventual blindness). Twenty years later, in 1849, he demonstrated to a seated audience a genuine motion picture show: his invention, the Phenakistiscope (deceitful vision), employed painted drawings on a glass disk, which, when projected, demonstrated the wonders of an animated cartoon. Plateau recommended photographs in future experiments.

Very few of the primitive inventors of cinematography (drawing motion) were scholars in any sense of the word, and as primitives they would have little interest in the present form their inventions eventually assumed. The driving search behind the photograph, the phonograph, the motion picture was "integral realism", that is, the recreation of the world in its own image. They were guided by the in-depth illusions of the nineteenth-century stereoscope; in André Bazin's words, they would settle for nothing less than "the reconstruction of a perfect illusion of the outside world in sound, color and relief."

The real primitives of the cinema, existing only in the imaginations of a few men of the nineteenth century, are in complete imitation of nature. Every new development added to the cinema must, paradoxically, take it nearer and nearer its origins. In short, cinema has yet to be invented!

In the context of the previous epoch, this might have been classified as blasphemy.

In responding to the challenge of technology, the cinema's first theologians arrived on the scene before the fact. Poet-philosopher Ralph Waldo Emerson, sensing the full significance of the industrial age, left the Unitarian ministry in a weary state of mind in 1832 for a year of travel in Europe; when he returned, he chose the "secular pulpit and secular wisdom" to found the Transcendentalist movement, a mediative philosophy "between Unitarian and commercial times." Like Existentialism to follow, it was basically a religious movement, a style of life, a way "to build your own world" in a climate where everything was on the move and growing more and more impersonal. George Ripley took the message back into the churches to call for a revision of theology based on a new study of human consciousness. Emerson preached a discarding of worn-out religious symbols, the acceptance of the torment of "Unbelief, the Uncertainty as to what we ought to do," and a greater role for love to help us find the way into the future. The outlines of today's theology of secularity are clearly visible.

Not all the Transcendentalists had Emerson's courage to face the future, and for this reason the movement as a whole tended to gaze with nostalgia on the "lost innocence" of the past. The best they could do as a group was to formulate spiritual principles: (1) the rejection of all external authority, particularly as known in the Puritan heritage; (2) the strict dependence on an intuitive perception of truth; and (3) the existence of a divine immanence in the world. Their favorite form of expression was the diary and the journal; the most gifted turned to poetry, self-analysis and "nature mysticism" to bring a fresh breeze into arts and letters. Henry David Thoreau, the Nietzsche of New England, turned to Walden Pond and "radical paganism" as his form of self-expression; Walt Whitman's "erotic mysticism" was equally at home in urban Brooklyn; the movement moved backward instead of forward, a Puritanism turned upside down. At the turn of the century the poet-troubadour, the ballad-singer, the banjo-player, and the movie cameraman supported mysticism in everything: open roads and apple trees and new towns and electrical advertising signs. In other words, they shifted the focus of attention from nature as *existence* to nature as food for reflection. Man-on-the-move stopped to gape.

Throughout the nineteenth century and into the twentieth, the steady roll of impersonal urban industrialization stripped away the mystical bond of holiness between man and the soil. Seen in this light, Transcendentalism can be viewed as a prophetic mission raised to prevent man from falling into the conditions of existential estrangement; it concerned itself chiefly with man's loss of innocence. Socialism and Marxism (later Communism), the other major ideologies rising out of the nineteenth century, understood the process of industrialization far better, but were to have a lesser impact on the arts, particularly the motion picture, than the heirs of the Transcendentalist movement. One has only to measure the distance between the dream-cult popularity and the public's distaste for the social-political documentary in the silent film: the great masses had to live in an industrial society, but didn't necessarily like it. The Transcendentalists stumbled on the discovery that "God *is*, not was," but, stunned by the news, immediately substituted a metaphysical idealism of "mind over matter" to continue living in communion with the cosmos. Man was on the move, but God had to stand still.

It is significant to note that although science accepted the challenge of motion, philosophy and theology were bewildered by the discovery — up to the present. Bergson became overnight the most popular philosophical thinker on the international scene in 1906 with his publication of *Creative Evolution*, but he had to confess to an impasse. The human intelligence, as a matter of course, comprehends the outer form of matter but misses energy; we are sure we know what matter is; still when energy is found at the center of the atom, we are bewildered and our categories fall into disarray. "No doubt, for greater strictness, all considerations of motion may be eliminated from the mathematical processes; but the introduction of motion into the genesis of figures is nevertheless the origin of modern mathematics." Nineteenth-century mathematics eventually produced Einstein's theory of relativity; but Bergson himself was unable to allow the intellect to conceive the phenomenon of motion; it was there to "think matter." He used the analogy of the motion picture to prove his point! The moving picture does not really move; it is only a series of static photographs flashed before our tired eyes to create the illusion of continuity. But it is an illusion all the same.

The philosophies of procession in the thinking of Teilhard de Chardin and Ernst Bloch in our time have radically changed this static view of matter and motion, although the conversion from essence to existence is not yet fully a reality. Bergson's view of the motion picture had at least lifted motion out of the past into one of "present consciousness." Bloch went a step further. He postulates that not only is there energy in the atom, but that all of matter contains an inner restlessness, a longing for form. Like Chardin, he believes we are moving ahead into history, into the future, toward some unknown. For Chardin, this "pull" is God, no longer radically separated from the world; for Bloch, it is a vacuum, an area still unfilled in time. He uses the analogy of the cinema screen to pinpoint this moving point in advance of human history. Formerly this screen contained religious projections; today it merely serves to demonstrate something beyond even existence, a constantly withdrawing entrance into the future, into a new essence, a quest that can never be satisfied here on earth.

Here we have something closer to an authentic theology of motion based on a philosophy of procession. Unlike the Transcendentalists at the origin of technology, God does not remain static in a moving world and the motion picture does not photograph the past in a sense of mystical yearning. Motion is also not reduced to substance to fit into the human consciousness as a separate category; Bergson's delusion was only being at home with the inert world. Instead, we are moving toward a belief in the future and "a future of belief." A theology of motion must have both a past and a future. A theology of the cinema not only records and documents; it projects into the future.

Cinema in the age of technology

The cinema has witnessed technology in motion. It has seen and felt the conversion in philosophy from the Transcendentalists to the Empiricists to the Phenomenologists to the Existentialists to the "Pull of the Future" Processionalists. It has documented the long view of the present epoch; it affirms that everything is in motion. Substance is process, evolution, activity; the motion picture is motion. Around these concepts the beginnings of a theology of the cinema can be constructed.

Process on the broad time scale implies a beginning and an end, a birth and a death. Being is no longer static, but in relation to something else; in Tillich's terms, it is in relation to the "Ground" of our being. Modern thought is historical, time-filled, biblical; theology takes the long view of salvation history. The total historicization of the world is secularization: not only man and the world, but man's thought about the world, become radically historical. Man becomes responsible to the world that belongs to him. The accent is on giving as well as receiving: man accepts God's love and returns it in equal partnership. The universe is placed in a context of love, instead of justice. The virtues of faith, hope and love take on an existentialist character.

In terms of the cinema, this leaves us with a number of options. If the very nature of technology and history is movement, cinema of course plays a key role: the motion picture is no longer the bastard of the arts, but a royal consort. Motion becomes an esthetic principle, the handmaid to philosophy and theology. When the moving object on the screen is man, and this experience is assimilated into the consciousness, a theology of secularity has one of its prime targets.

We must first view motion in the cinema as an esthetic principle, then draw relations to the three divisions in film history. The men-in-motion — the Keystone Cops, the Thomas H. Ince Westerns and action films, the young Chaplin and Keaton, Doug Fairbanks, Fred Astaire and Busby Berkeley, James Cagney — take precedence over the "great profile" lovers of the screen; indeed, their reputations increase as the others decrease. D. W. Griffith's suspense-filled chase sequences in *The Mother and the Law* and *Orphans of the Storm*, photographing seconds of blurred images, remain immortal. The secrets of the Great Chase in terms of advances in film technique — not only editing and speeded-up camerawork, but hundreds of little tricks to fool the eye and brain — comprise the lost, buried treasures of this century. As just one example, we may never know just how much the French Pathé company contributed to, and may still be in advance of, the present art form. Nearly all of cinema as we presently know it was perfected before the First World War, but we have yet to construct a theology of the pie-in-the-face.

Poet-missionary Vachel Lindsay, a direct heir to Emerson and Whitman, wrote the path-breaking *The Art of the Moving Picture* in 1915. The first half was devoted to the period's fad for the mystical elements in the action and intimate photoplays and the wonders of crowd, patriotic and religious splendor: innocent material as "food for reflection." Then he subjected these same elements to the sensitivities of motion, as found in paintings, sculpture, technological inventions and architecture, arriving at perceptive conclusions: "I desire in moving pictures, not the stillness, but the majesty of sculpture." And "here (in Manet's Girl With the Parrot) continence in nervous force, expressed by low relief and restraint in tone, is carried to its ultimate point." These were Lindsay's guidelines to the all-too-often left-footed action films and the mushy melodrama of the day; they are still accurate guidelines.

The subtleties of motion are refined gestures and relationships between objects and ideas. Asta Nielsen, Lillian Gish and Greta Garbo could effortlessly transcend the surface trappings of the trite melodrama. Garbo was less a goddess than a human of extraordinary psychic dimensions. Kenneth Tynan has pointed out: "Garbo alone can be intoxicated by innocence. She turns her coevals into her children, taking them under her wing like a great sailing swan." An original, authentic gesture can never be imitated and seldom repeated. The imitators of Charlie Chaplin were blown off the screen like leaves.

Hollywood in the sound era soon found that the essence of the film script was movement. Directors resorted to stealing Howard Hawks's scripts to discover his secret of imbuing a story with restless energy. John Wayne built a career on "moving" instead of acting; and many a good actor, such as Gary Cooper and Marlon Brando, have achieved their reputations as exemplars of compact, restrained, pressure-cooker, "motion-less" nervous energy. Under the Hitchcock thriller runs a swift river, cutting deep, critical gorges into the subconscious of the middle-class. Max Ophuls's endlessly moving camera is a moral instrument tracing a relentless course of tragedy amid lost illusions. Miklos Jancso's mathematically conceived tracking shots manifest a powerful fatalistic character. The list is endless: the talented director nearly always resorts to motion of some kind to solidify the cinema experience. But even after the film is "in the can," relationships extend out to other expressions in the cinema and real life. For example, the hard-shell of the Hawks action film is best understood in relation to the soft underbelly of his comedies. Hawks's view of the world is from the American standing position; Ozu's view is from the Japanese kneeling position. A theology of the cinema must take its cues from a theory of relativity.

The history of the motion picture itself demonstrates an evolutionary process; it reflects history, the history of philosophy and theology. In the first era of the cinema, the travelling Lumière cameramen made it a point to put man in the center of creation. The first audiences were frightened by the mystical kingdom of ghosts and shadows set before them, but were quickly calmed by a "self-portrait" of their own city with a recognized citizen walking innocently through the grey, shadowy kingdom. The next step was to bring the infinite into the finite: mountain peaks and exotic places were immediately accessible. Within the first cinema decade, Sidney Olcott conceived the idea to tramp across Ireland and Palestine and bring back tales of epic grandeur. The Swedish directors bypassed Impressionism, Romanticism and almost Naturalism to open up a passage into the demonic depth of the human soul: Stiller and Sjöström, Sjöström particularly, were chiefly concerned with the endless struggle between the divine and the demonic in human nature; in Tillich's terms, the negative side of Romanticism, the Schelling-Schopenhauer-Freud line. That magnificent chapter in film history, Swedish Naturalism, had therefore two poles: nature and man. Sjöström's *The Wind* is an apt description of this vertical line.

In D. W. Griffith the horizontal line of history is manifest. In the nineteenth century many movements were under way — Darwinism, Socialism, Marxism, Protestant Liberalism, the mystical-romantic side of Transcendentalism — they all have a share in Griffith's art; he was an eclectic who swallowed everything whole, digested it, and spewed it all back again. The "universal Deity" form of Mysticism, an all-pervasive concept, was coined at the turn of the century, and it aided him greatly in striking unforgettable lyrical images in several of his masterpieces. But he was mostly interested, Pauline Kael notes, in experiments of time.

He was living in an era of experiments with time in the other arts, and although he worked in a popular medium, the old dramatic concepts of time and unity seemed too limiting; in his own way he attempted what Pound and Eliot, Proust and Virginia Woolf and Joyce were also attempting, and what he did in movies may have influenced literary form as much as they did. He certainly influenced them.

If time can be viewed in a mystical way (for the mystic, time is viewed as unreal and reality is eternal in the sense of being "out of time") in the cinema, it is certainly to be found in Griffith's view into the past in *Birth of a Nation* and, more significantly, into the past (Griffith's), the present and the future in *Intolerance*. Griffith is the most historical of movie directors. In his hands cinema ceases to be strips of single photographs; he has plugged into a universal Time-Machine.

Before the movies began to speak, they shouted! The horrors of the First World War were reflected in Expressionism; arts and literature shook the foundations of nineteenth-century culture; the year that saw *The Cabinet of Dr. Caligari* saw also Karl Barth's "expressionist" *The Epistle to the Romans*. Expressionism, like Romanticism and Mysticism, is a much abused term: it is better explained by what it did, than what it was. It broke through the barrier between the artist-writer, or filmmaker-theologian, and his object in real life, so that artist and work form a single unity. Naturalism, implicit in Impressionism, is thrown overboard in search of a simplified style carrying, theoretically, a greater emotional impact. Exaggerations and distortions, reflecting in this case the tortured condition of the soul, become the main rule of thumb; time and history are abandoned to highlight a single moment of truth.

For Barth, the truth eventually to be highlighted was the Incarnation, the Virgin Birth, Christmas, the single time and place God alone chose to meet man and the world. The "distortion" is tempered by belief. The cinema underwent a similar "standing-still" during the period between the two wars, an outgrowth of the expressionist movement toward a "distortion" in nature: the reflection of the supernatural in man and the universe, the pointing to something beyond nature. Expressionism gave way not only to New Objectivity, the return to the concrete in search of more constructive and enduring values, but also to the capturing of a "sense of the holy" on the screen. Barth's parallel in the cinema was Robert Flaherty, who accepted the universe as mysterious, secretive and holy: man was nothing more than its privileged chalice. When *Nanook of the North* appeared in 1922, with its new, indescribable vision of life on the screen, the words "sublime" and "mystical union" entered the film critic's lexicon.

Flaherty's documentary-minded, "realist" friends were as disturbed by this news as Barth's colleagues: few had the courage to follow him through *Moana, Man of Aran* and *The Louisiana Story*, films that approached the secrets of man, of life, of living with an open mind. The timeless quality in his films was the shaping of the film into the thinking of an already existing social structure. He went beyond outward, physical appearances to the inner, psychological reality. He reached out to touch the finger of the hand touching the universe: no director has tried that with such foolish magnificence since. But cinema has profited from somewhat similar excursions "into the unknown" in the European films of Renoir and Rossellini (the stream before and after the rise of the propaganda film), in the Indian director Ray's unique communion with nature in the Apu trilogy, and in Ozu's view of the universe through the microcosm of the Japanese family. These outlines of the timeless in the universe, of the unhistorical in the historical, of revelation reaching man in the only form in which he is capable of receiving it, whether in a religious (Barth) or secular (Flaherty) sense, are religion in its purest, and as religion are always human distortion. Cinema is thereby raised to a high art: the camera ceases recording life; it takes its pulse.

Barth's *Epistle to the Romans*, a great prophetic work, aimed its attack at religion in its common form. He pointed to the crisis in theology: the absoluteness of God reduced to an object of human knowledge and study; religion thus maintained and practised was idolatry. Barth's prophetic voice continued to ring out between the wars, virtually saving the German church and theology from disaster, but at the cost of denying the whole of natural theology. Barth and Flaherty might not agree on fundamentals in their views of the eternal, but each could fully understand what the other was up to. As Barth struggled to rescue theology from disaster from his perch in Basle on the German border, Flaherty's *Man of Aran* scaled the cliffs jutting out of the Atlantic to prophetically warn mankind of the dangers facing it in the approaching war. They were of course not alone, as prophecy was rampant in the arts in the interregnum period. Another striking example was Bertolt Brecht, whose powerful "parables" on the times — *Mother Courage and Her Children* and *The Good Woman of Setzuan* — had their premières in Zurich well into the war years and long after Brecht himself had departed for America. These were eloquent voices crying in the wilderness.

Prophets also rose up inside the controlled hothouse atmosphere of the growing, centralized film industry. Resistance is to be found every step of the way in the rise of the Hollywood star system and the European propaganda film, both pushing cinema deeper and deeper into the Babylonian Captivity of civil religion. On one side of the Atlantic, the Dream Cult stretching over a half-century, approximately from the erection of architect Thomas Lamb's dream-palace, the Regent, in New York in 1913 to the death of Marilyn Monroe in 1962, slowly stifled the public's active, participatory powers of judgment and analysis; patterns of rhetoric and the principle of identification reigned supreme. On the other side, Eisenstein and Vertov developed the "Kino-Fist" and "Kino-Eye" as political weapons with broad propagandistic value, supplemented in turn by the loud speaker. The churches dropped their moral charges against the cinema and blessed it as "an instrument of the apostolate." Mussolini turned saint biographies into fascist ones; Hitler resurrected the legends and ghosts of the Teutonic past; cinema became enslaved to the will of the state. Everywhere censorship, pressure groups and classification systems supported the cause of civil religion in the consciousness of the public.

The prophets of the cinema began to speak in parables: the crises, the perils of the moment were described in no uncertain terms in form and content. In Hollywood W. C. Fields's humor became brutally human in expression; Hitchcock's detective thriller, once the rhetoric is stripped away, contains scathing attacks on puritanism; Ernst Lubitsch taught a battery of directors how to shoot "between the lines" and thus leave the naughtiest tidbits just outside camera range; Josef von Sternberg invented the "mystique" ruse to cover up his playful decadence — these, and others, argued eloquently for the right to present moral problems in their proper light. John Ford was at his best when he set his sights on the dignity of man, but from a different angle: his insights transcend the flesh and focus on the heroic qualities in behavior; a superb storyteller, like Griffith and Hawks, he is in the horizontal line, an Old Testament prophet urging man to search for a truth that may never be found. On the broader scale,

Fritz Lang's leitmotiv of "the world in flames" derived from his faithful reading of the morning papers. Jean Renoir's *The Rules of the Game*, made in 1939, and Orson Welles's *Citizen Kane*, in 1941, are favored by critics in today's polls primarily because of their historical relationships to European and American history. A handful of writers and directors (plus Fields and the Marx Brothers, who were essentially writers) kept Hollywood honest. And if we care to look hard enough, we can find traces of this honesty in the state-controlled propaganda films — for instance, in Ferdinand Marian's humanizing of a medieval Shylock in the Nazi film *Jud Süss* (an acting role), and Eisenstein's horrific portrait of Stalin in the second part of *Ivan the Terrible*. In a closed society the devil's lines are the nearest to the truth.

After the Second World War theology shifted from the rediscovery of the deity of God to an acknowledgement of the worldliness of the world. Barth's Incarnation gave way to Bultmann's Cross and Resurrection and Tillich's Pentecost: Existentialism viewed not just as revolt but as a style of life. The individual and human existence took stage center; but here again, in Bultmann as in abstract painting, radical subjectivity led to a distortion in detaching the human condition from its situation in the world. In Tillich, the movement is allied with Freudian psychology: the conscious and the unconscious are given equal status, so that deep-rooted moral questions are raised to the level of theological thinking. Theology is thus held to a sense of responsibility for the social conditions in which man exists. A path of dialogue is opened up to the world. The world in turn is open to the future.

Cinema has experienced its moment in communion with modern Existentialism: it is the needed tool to describe existence without resorting to language. It has recorded revolt, the distortion in existence, but it is more at home in simply sketching life as it is and thus raising the fundamental questions. In theology, the questions of faith, hope and love take on existential character in the movies. The essence of God stands in partnership with the existence of the world.

The European directors were the first to take Existentialism seriously, due to the catastrophe of a second war and the slow death of the star system in America. The director regained his footing; he found he could, on a cheap budget, control his film from start to finish. The cinema began to think. The films of Carl Dreyer, Luis

Bunuel, Federico Fellini, Ingmar Bergman, Pier Paolo Pasolini and
Robert Bresson, to name just the front line of the postwar period,
all focused on the human traits of intention, purpose, desire, will,
choice, commitment, witness — the very elements formulating progress in history. And insofar as they are in the line influenced by
Pascal, Kierkegaard, Dostoievsky and Kafka, with loose connec-
tions to Barth, Bultmann, Tillich, Marcel and Jaspers, their films on
religious topics form the nucleus of a Christian existential cinema.
They have constructively added to a more developed concept of
history in the world, of self hood and human personality, and of
responsibility.

Cinema has been at the service of theology in modern times without
the latter sometimes being fully aware of it. It has joined, for instance,
in the renewed quest for the historical Jesus, less involved however
than Bultmann and the Marburgers. Bunuel's *Nazarin*, Pasolini's
The Gospel According to St. Matthew, Bergman's *Winter Light*,
Bresson's *Balthasar*, and Dreyer's *Ordet* reflect the disintegration of
the person Jesus to the point where nothing is left but his teaching:
the Christ figure is presented as sign, myth, symbol, allegory and
finally word. The "word-event" becomes for both Carl Dreyer and
Gerhard Ebeling the neck in the hour glass through which an evolutionary, twentieth-century understanding of history and the Christian
message is interpreted; it is an event of speaking, of language, through
which the speaker communicates himself in love. Faith comes to man
as he receives the Word: that is the central theme of *Ordet* (Danish
for "word") and the message in Ebeling's *Word and Faith*.

In the light of *Ordet* it becomes illuminatingly clear that the whole
of Dreyer's career, spanning the same half-century that saw the rise
and fall of Hollywood, was concerned with the problem of faith in an
existential context. He is a key figure in film history. Luis Bunuel is
also concerned with a new form of existential faith sprouting out of
the ruins of past religion. The best of the allegorical, "dialogue"
cinema of East European directors — Polish cinema in the 1950s,
Czech and Yugoslav cinema in the 1960s, the Hungarian and East
German cinema at present, as well as the Third World Marxist cinema
in the future — takes its roots from the existential need to believe in
some truth of life and living; the underground river of faith runs
deep in socialist countries, but every so often it surfaces like a
geyser.

Ernst Käsemann views the preaching of Jesus as determined by his eschatological understanding of himself; it is the parables in particular which contain this orientation toward the future, and accordingly the Apocalypse in the early church is accepted as "the mother of Christian theology." The person and message of Jesus are thus viewed as a single unity, bound by the eschatological orientation of his mission. It is thus not theologically necessary to know the specifics of Jesus's career; the kerygmatic function of a believing church preaching its belief is, in the modern context, more important. In this light, the Christian trilogy of Ingmar Bergman — *Through a Glass Darkly*, *Winter Light* and *The Silence* — depicts the journey of modern man in search of belief, but *preaching* the equivalent of it in spite of his unbelief. Bergman still clings to a thread of hope in the future. Bergman, as Ford, underscores the necessity of search in life, above and beyond what is found here on earth. They are as eschatologically oriented as Christ was.

Ernst Fuchs finds in Jesus's parables, particularly the Good Samaritan, the central, driving force of love directing all his words and actions. We have a parallel between this view and the cinema of Robert Bresson. Just as Jesus's behavior in receiving sinners is clarified by a parable of putting himself in God's place, and his behavior is thereby transposed into preaching itself, so Bresson fundamentally contends that *how* we conduct ourselves determines who we are as Christians, and also how worthy we are of God's grace. For Bresson, unlike Dreyer and Bergman in the realm of belief, is not an outsider looking in but an insider looking out; his vision of the world is from the standpoint of a man of faith fully aware of God's grace working in it. It is only through grace that he arrives at the profoundest understanding of spiritual and physical death in the cinema.

Today, both theology and cinema are at a stage of rich diversity and specialization. It is difficult and easy to match various strands together, but this is a sign of hope rather than confusion. It means that existence is no longer the accident of essence: history has drawn even with nature; man shares the responsibility for the world with God. The point of departure to God is man; in Peter Berger's arguments, it is through the elements of order, play, hope, damnation, and humor in human life. We have gotten over the postwar scare of existentialist pessimism, and we have passed the heady optimism of the "God-is-Dead" theologians. Tillich's mediative thinking still commands attention on the vertical line between theology and psycho-therapeutic psychology, but a cluster of "Theology-of-Hope" thinkers have gathered on the horizontal, historical line. The future might prompt a synthesis between the two.

The young filmmakers are also gathered mostly on the historical line. With good reason: unless one has the depth of a Dreyer, this is where the action is. Directors in America, Europe and Latin America are more political-minded than ever before, as are the younger theologians; but as they become more radicalized, they tend to uproot themselves from the emotional side of human nature. The most interesting directors are those who can balance history and nature. In America Kubrick and Cassavetes command attention by standing, respectively, at the horizontal and vertical lines; but Bogdanovich with a foot in both camps has more appeal. Britain's Ken Loach is at his best in analyzing the loss of personality in the technological world; Werner Herzog's metaphysical parables on broken lives in isolated places reach far beyond the German experience, and he is as fiercely human as apocalyptically oriented. Europe has two of cinema's best storytellers in Rohmer and Widerberg, whose moral and political starting points have their roots in the subconscious of French and Swedish society. Bertolucci has bypassed Godard by including the protagonist himself, the author, in auto-biographical cinema. Dusan Makavejev in Yugoslavia has posed the serious question whether Socialism can accept the blame along with the responsibility for its present position in the world order. If there is one word that characterizes these directors as a whole, it is "awareness" of the problems besetting *them* as individuals and responsible agents in the world process. The cinema is the instrument to work these problems out.

The future of cinema lies in its openness to problems. In this openness lies transcendence. Transcendence is thereby related to belief rather than certainty. This is the message of the New Testament: the kingdom of God is here, but it is also to come. The present is focused on the future, and the future reflects the present. The beyond is played out in our empirical experience. In our awareness of the reality of the present, we are aware of God. Such is the task and glory of the filmmaker.

II. TOWARD A RELIGIOUS CINEMA

Much has been written about the cinema, classic and modern, so that little question remains today of its legitimacy in the arts. Its cultural contribution to society is even less disputed; indeed, no other artist is analyzed and interpreted with greater scrutiny than the contemporary film director. Nevertheless, and regardless of widespread interest, theologians and church leaders have contributed little to religious dialogue in the marketplace of the cinema. More often than not, because of the moral and ethical questions involved, they have studiously avoided it.

The abrupt change in modern theological thought has suddenly brought attention to the religious significance of the cinema. It has always been important in the past for the same reasons that religious implications in literature, drama, architecture, painting and the arts in general are important to the theologian without special justification. The cinema is more significant today because much of the talent of our age, formerly associated with the expression of stage or novel, has turned to it as *the* art of the twentieth century. Some candidly admit to drawing the source of their inspiration from the font of modern religious debate (one has only to think of Bergman), although many theologians are not yet fully aware of the theft much less responding to the challenge. This seems all the more tragic as cinema is being frequently lauded as the richest avenue of cultural expression available for examining the complex values and problems of the contemporary world.

The reason for this neglect? Why are church leaders slow to measure the religious depth of the cinema? The answer appears to lie in the muddled image of the so-called "religious" film, as well as the unwillingness of churches to deviate from traditional practices to confront openly the arts. A cinema of pietism is still by and large the only acceptable form. But now that a major shift in theology is taking place — as the anxiety-centered thinking of Barth, Bultmann and Tillich a few decades past gives way to the responsibility-centered searching of Hamilton, Cox and Moltmann — the feeling arises that modern theology should take another look at cinema as a mirror of today's immediate and ultimate concerns. So as times change, and censorship and classification fall by the wayside and pressure-group tactics diminish, what was once fodder for the poor man's gristmill has come to contribute to the progress of philosophy and theology.

A cursory view of the history of the cinema should make this development clear.

In the era immediately following the Lumière paid screenings of 1895, religious themes the world over exploiting the favorite legends of deities became immensely popular with illiterate audiences on fair grounds, at music halls and in store-front theatres. In Western civilization at the turn of the century, the Life and Passion of Christ (modelled on the Catholic Way of the Cross) was considered the highest expression of cinematographic art. Churches were often used as movie theatres for the high-paying "spectacles," until Pope Pius X forbade this desecration in 1910 among Catholic offenders. In Protestant circles the revival tent often featured a reel of the Passion after the preacher's warm-up exhortations. In the populous urban, industrialized communities, particularly among the poorer communities, the first silent movie palaces were constructed along the lines of the architecture of nineteenth-century Catholic churches. The poor in effect had two cathedrals to harbor their cares, sorrows and dreams, but the movie palace also offered escape from the surrounding drabness.

After the First World War destroyed most competition, Hollywood flooded the market with dream cults and pietistic moralizing. The gods of the screen were Valentino and Garbo, and the high priest of the religious genre was Cecil B. DeMille. The melodrama, extending back beyond Napoleonic times to the French Revolution, continued its long reign in the movie cathedral. The only people in the film world with both feet on the ground seemed to be the silent comedians and documentary filmmaker Robert Flaherty. In the era of sound between the wars, the cinema of Chaplin and Dreyer,

Bunuel and Renoir can be viewed as a partial revolt against the domination of the international market by a puritan Hollywood system.

In other hemispheres the first fifty years of cinema history was not much different. The world's religions flashed across the screen on nitrate prints destined for disintegration and seldom rescued for today's audiences. In Japan period films dealing with religious legends and historical personages made up half the productions at the coming of sound. Indian audiences in 1913 prostrated themselves before images of Rama and Lord Krishna, and even today ten percent of film production is given over to the same mythological formulas. The religious character of the cinema could not have been much different in other cultures. When Robert Flaherty arrived in Samoa in 1923 to shoot *Moana*, he showed a copy of Henrik Galeen's *The Golem* to the natives. The impression was so strong, they insisted on seeing this giant figure over and over again and named their children after the Golem.

The pietistic formula found its chief expression of sentiment and emotion in the religious spectacle, whose architect was Cecil B. DeMille. It is so familiar little needs to be said about it, save to mention that DeMille's *King of Kings* and Victor Sjöström's *The Phantom Chariot* in Sweden were not only huge box-office successes in the silent era but are screened today at catechetical gatherings. DeMille's *The Ten Commandments* aptly suited the wide span of the drive-in theatre in 1956, and it is often revived for Easter services in Negro ghettos. Henry Koster's *The Robe* introduced CinemaScope in the 1950s to gross 13 million dollars on its initial run. Considered collectively, the spectacles *The Sound of Music*, *Ben Hur* and *The Ten Commandments* in the wide-screen era grossed over 150 million dollars, although each was essentially a successfully re-worked "pietistic" formula. In short, the majority of the box-office winners from *Birth of a Nation* to *Love Story* can be traced directly to the staying-power of the melodrama. In this regard it should be kept in mind that Hollywood was nourished by the flood of immigrants flowing into America at the end of the nineteenth century (among them many of the future movie moguls), and that the mores of these peoples from Ireland, England, Germany, Southern and Eastern Europe were primarily puritan.

As the country's poor responded eagerly to a cheap form of entertainment, Hollywood developed into America's fourth largest industry and became more and more the concern of banks and politics. The advent of the loud speaker and sound in films opened the door to propaganda of all sorts. Lenin was the first to recognize the cinema as a power to mold the masses, but he was soon followed by large religious bodies who proclaimed it as "an instrument of the apostolate". In the 1930s religion mixed well into the government propaganda films of Mussolini and Hitler, while the Vatican went far out of its way to promote a Christian cinema along the guidelines of Pope Pius XI's encyclical *Vigilanti Cura*. Mussolini founded the first film festival at Venice in 1933 to promote his own ends: a few years later, by no coincidence, religious propaganda films dealing with past African missionaries were released at the same time as the invasion of Ethiopia. Distinct parallels can be found between Russian, Catholic, Fascist and Nazi films on the European continent, particularly in the use of religious symbols and rites. Striking contrasts with the same are to be found too in the Hollywood propaganda film; indeed, the concept of formula productions in the Hollywood dream factory was in effect propagandistic (as the McCarthy Hearings point out) and fundamentally at the root of its own self-destruction.

The aftermath of the war brought the first refreshing traces of a new humanism on the screen in the Italian neo-realist films, stemming partially from the prewar tradition of realism in the French school headed by Jean Renoir. Festivals at Venice and Cannes provided an important meeting ground of international dialogue and exchange, although anything dealing with religious pietism or propaganda was now suspect. In fact, it was evident that De Sica's *The Gate of Heaven* and Delannoy's *God Needs Men*, among others, were partially made to square accounts with the erring tradition of the religious propaganda film. Church authorities and classification groups had to mobilize again to prevent their constituencies from being exposed to too forthright human and moral problems, as a result of which pressure from individualist film directors was applied all the harder. Eventually cracks in the moral façade of Catholic rating offices were detected, particularly in the disagreement between countries and rating agencies on the moral character of certain key films. Fellini's *La Strada*, for instance, was awarded a major prize at a meeting in Havana of the International Catholic Film Office in the mid-1950s, although it had already been rated unacceptable for the general public by the national Legion of Decency in the United States. Even though

Catholic rating offices were strong religious censorship bodies, it was only a matter of time before the moral evaluation of a particular film was left up to the judgment of the individual. A new era in motion picture history was dawning.

From the 1950s to the present the churches and a small body of educators and theologians have molded a new approach to a more sophisticated cinema. The past concept of cinema as "instrument of the apostolate" was gradually modified or dropped, replaced by an ever-increasing interest for "dialogue with the world through cinema." Religious bodies of various faiths began to foster a new Christian humanism on the screen, in which life's moral dilemmas were exposed to the core for reflection and answer. Film education programs multiplied, and special religious juries were sent to major festivals to participate in international dialogue with secular critics and film-makers themselves. This served in turn to soften church leaders on treatment of moral and ethical problems in the cinema, increasing at the same time ready acceptance of more provocative material on the screen. Numerous religious awards were given to the films of Bresson, Bergman and Fellini, although the outright anti-clericalism of Bunuel and Pasolini proved more and more impossible to deal with. Eventually a storm erupted: Pasolini's erotic-orientated *Teorema* was offered the grand prize by the Catholic jury at the 1968 Venice festival; this was followed by a hurried condemnation of both film and jury by the Vatican. Dialogue reached an impasse.

Parallel with the decline of church censorship a new sophistication for film art developed, hastened in turn by the departure of the mass audience for television. The audience coming to the cinema now is liable to be younger, critical and better prepared to accept a serious, contemporary theme for study and reflection. The 1960s pointed to a rash of film courses on American campuses, inter-faith film forums in church halls and community centers, and occasional "happenings" and multi-media programs. The attractiveness of these meeting places was that they brought the film artist into dialogue with the academic community. For the first time the theologian and the film-maker began to discuss the possibilities of an honest religious cinema.

The 1960s saw the rapid fall of the major censorship bodies in America. The production of *Anatomy of a Murder* in 1959 first stirred the waters of controversy with the introduction of two new words into movie vocabulary: "rape" and "contraceptive." Vittorio De Sica's

Italian film *Two Women* (1960) then depicted the rape on American screens for the first time. Fellini also presented a startling survey of contemporary sexuality in *La Dolce Vita*, followed by Ingmar Bergman's fruitless search for God in his famous trilogy: *Through a Glass Darkly*, *Winter Light*, and *The Silence*. Two exposures of the middle class from different points of view were tested on audiences in Bryan Forbes's *The L-Shaped Room* and William Wyler's *The Collector*. Most challenging of all to the morals of the previous decade were the secret agent pictures, *The Silencers*, *Goldfinger* and *In Like Flint*, whose titles hinted at hidden pleasures offered inside the theatre. Finally came the three surprises on the screen that suddenly put Hollywood's old-fashioned production code out to pasture: Sidney Lumet's *The Pawnbroker*, Mike Nichols's *Who's Afraid of Virginia Woolf?*, and Lewis Gilbert's *Alfie*, all appearing in the mid-1960s.

The result? Confusion. Old standards no longer applied. The laws of the land were being challenged, dissected, changed, patched up and thrown away. The watchdogs of society, censor boards, were attempting at their peril to interpret the moral fibre of the community. Churchmen, sociologists and educators were discovering new *rationales* and exploring new approaches to an already extremely segmented society. Self-styled radicals of both extremes were to be found in the middle of the foray. About the only way to police the American movies in the 1960s, many observers agreed, was through parental censorship.

The word "censorship" was to come under heavy scrutiny. For our purposes, we can divide the issue into three categories: censorship by law, self-regulation and classification.

Censorship by law

In the United States, this means the prior determination by a duly appointed board under a statute or ordinance of a film's suitability for exhibition. Such boards included customs censorship (under the Department of the Treasury), state censorship (formerly four states), city censorship and occasionally police censorship. Although in many places censor boards were not actually constituted for reviewing and licensing of films, nevertheless obscenity laws were on the books of forty-seven states and innumerable cities and towns. Normally prior restraint was exercised by a board, which meant that a film had to be submitted for review before a license was given.

Self-regulation

The Hollywood industry preferred to regulate itself, so for this purpose it set up an administrative office to police its own product. The standards were to be found in the production code, written in 1930 and revised in 1956 and 1966. The code applied to both film scripts and the completed picture. If a member company of the Motion Picture Producers and Directors of America (MPPDA) did not receive code approval for a movie, the ruling could be appealed to a Board of Review or the company could risk exhibition without approval. Foreign films were almost never submitted to the Production Code Administration (PCA).

Classification

Films could be classified according to the audience for which they were suitable, either by the industry itself or by people outside. Two types of classification were differentiated: first, compulsory classification, with mandatory powers of enforcement; and second, voluntary classification, applying to its free acceptance by a constituency. Unlike other countries the United States has no form of government classification, which is considered by the industry as too close to suppression of rights.

It is well to note that these are simplified terms. When censorship is discussed in a group, any number of imprecise terms and phrases can be used, as: governmental censorship, customs censorship, police censorship, pressure-group censorship, industry self-censorship, obscenity regulations, police obscenity regulations, pressure-group regulations, governmental classification, industry classification, voluntary ratings, distributor-exhibitor ratings and publication ratings. One might even include parental censorship.

The most important issue in film censorship is that of prior restraint, enforced by law through state and local censorship boards. It is one thing to say that free press and free speech are impeded by prior censorship. It is yet another to claim that the motion picture, as a medium of free expression, is entitled to the same freedom.

The first city to establish a censorship board for the purpose of viewing and determining the moral fitness of films before exhibition was Chicago in 1907. The board was placed under the direction of the police department, where it still exists today in a somewhat modified form. Nearly every city and a few states (New York, Kansas, Virginia and Maryland) followed suit. In the beginning the film producers did not object vociferously, until the realization came that the boards presented constant problems of time, fees and harassment. The first challenge arose in 1915, when an Ohio distributor argued that movies had the same rights as free speech and free press. The Supreme Court however disagreed, stating that the exhibition of motion pictures was a business pure and simple and was not to be considered a medium of free expression. For the next forty years this decision held. Naturally, censorship boards thrived.

The picture began to change in 1948. The major movie companies saw their monopoly structure of theatre ownership crumble and fall, again by decision of the Supreme Court. This led to a weakening of restraints because theatre owners could now choose the product they themselves desired, and what they came to desire were movies with more provocative themes. Moreover, the influx of foreign movies led to a new era of screen appreciation — the impact of Italian neorealism, particularly *Open City*, *Paisan*, *Bicycle Thief* and later *La Strada*. Since these films did not seek code approval, the self-regulation system of the industry was open to challenge. The issue of freedom of the press with its distant application to the film medium came again to the fore, particularly after some of the justices on the Supreme Court (William O. Douglas) expressed in the industry monopoly case their view of the motion picture as included in the freedom guaranteed by the First Amendment.

Four years later, in 1952, "The Miracle Case" provided the breakthrough. *The Miracle* was made in Italy by Roberto Rossellini and presented the story of a simpleton girl seduced by a passing vagrant whom she believed to be St. Joseph. The pregnant girl was played by Anna Magnani and the script was done by Federico Fellini (who played the tramp). An independent importer, Joseph Burstyn, sent the film to the New York Censor Board; it was approved and licensed for the Paris Theatre. Two weeks later, the New York City Commissioner of Licenses threatened to suspend the license on the grounds that the film was "officially and personally blasphemous." He was supported by a public outcry of offended groups, notably Cardinal Spellman of New York. The film was reviewed again and the censors this time ruled it "sacrilegious." When the Supreme Court handled the case, the decision was reversed unanimously. But the Court stated that "sacrilege" was simply not a valid judicial guide under which a censor board could operate, while it made no decision on whether censor boards could operate at all under law.

In the cases to follow, other standards by which censor boards acted were called into question and eliminated. Examples are *Pinky*, a film dealing with the relationship between a Negress and a white man ("prejudicial to the best interests of people"), *La Ronde* ("immoral"), *The Moon Is Blue* ("tending to corrupt morals"), *M* ("harmful"), *Native Son* ("contributing to racial misunderstanding"), *Lady Chatterley's Lover* ("adultery as proper conduct"), and *The Garden of Eden* ("indecent"). This left only the term "obscenity" as grounds for censorship.

An attempt was then made to rule out the constitutionality of all censor boards. A film called *Don Juan*, an innocent variation on the classic Don Giovanni theme, requested a license from the Chicago censors without preview. The 1961 decision of the Supreme Court on this "Times Film Case" was to prove extremely important and is still relevant to the situation today. By a close 5-4 decision the Court ruled that the city of Chicago had a right to inspection beforehand on the grounds that government could select the remedies it deemed most effective for the welfare of the community. However, the dissenting justices felt that the same licensing scheme could therefore be applied to newspapers, books, periodicals, radio, television, public speeches and every other medium of expression. As a result of this historic case, the issue of prior restraint still remained defensible in a limited manner, applying particularly to those movies that violated "obscenity" laws.

A final case for consideration was "Freedman vs. Maryland" in 1965. In a situation slightly different from that in Chicago, a Baltimore exhibitor played a non-obscene film, *Revenge at Daybreak*, without bothering to apply for a license. He was arrested and convicted for violation of a state law, but contended that prior restraint of his film was unconstitutional in itself as an infringement of free speech. Again, the Supreme Court ruled against the defendant on the grounds that the case was substantially the same as "Times Film" and that films did differ from other forms of expression. But the Court then proceeded to strike down the Maryland state statute that prevented the defendant from receiving a prompt judicial ruling by court of law (instead he was merely impeded by administrative action). In effect, the tables were now reversed. It was up to a court now to rule promptly on each individual film as it was contested. As a result, this decision provided the burial ground for most state and municipal laws which didn't formally guarantee the defendant the freedom of the courts. The censor boards of New York, Virginia and Kansas also went out of existence.

To summarize, the bite of the legal watchdog had been severely reduced by the mid-1960s. Statutes had to be rewritten to be effective, and the sole standard of "obscenity" with immediate judicial response was the only pillar on which they could stand. It was only a matter of time before the word "obscenity" would be challenged.

The famous "Ginsberg Case" in 1966, in which the publisher of *Eros* magazine was convicted for the distributing of "obscene" material, received wide and unfavorable attention. The Supreme Court ruled that "obscenity" could be defined as (1) constituting hard-core pornography, (2) having no redeeming social value, and (3) offending community standards of public morality. The problem went much deeper than this, but the issue we are treating here is movie censorship. As far as the courts in America are concerned, freedom of the motion picture is not the same as freedom of the press.

Some note must be made of the establishment of appeal boards, which provided a safety-valve mechanism for the film distributor who wanted to work with the censor boards indirectly without having to lose time in the courts. Before the Maryland case stipulated immediate court action, for example, the exhibitors in trouble with the Chicago censor board usually preferred making some changes and/or re-submitting their films to the appeal board made up mostly of academic people. In most cases they came away satisfied.

With the courts making possible more daring film material on the screen, it fell to the Hollywood film industry to regulate itself in some new form of self-censorship or self-classification. In actuality, this could be done only if the motion picture was solely a "home product." And since movies are an international and independent medium of expression, it was inconceivable that the American film industry could ever police itself totally. The only alternative was classification, either compulsory or voluntary, that would meet the temporary needs of society. To some, all proposals for classification are untenable and they would prefer a system of checks and balances that would allow the audience to choose for itself (thus indirectly determining the quality of most film fare). The majority in the industry opted for self-control in the traditional spirit of the founding of the Production Code Administration, but with a revising once again of the code itself.

The history of the code dates back to the first manifestations of self-control in the industry shortly after the First World War. The introduction of a bolder type of entertainment (that was paying off commercially) and the headlines caused by Hollywood scandals aroused the public to protest. The industry replied by forming its own organization for protection and public relations, known originally as the MPPDA (changed later to MPPA, the Motion Picture Producers of America) but for all practical purposes as the Hays Office, after its czar, Will H. Hays, former Postmaster General in President Harding's cabinet. With the growing clamor caused by angry censorship boards across the land which didn't always agree with the medium's increasingly sophisticated ways, the industry was finally prevailed upon to adopt a code of morals in 1930. The production code was written by a Jesuit, Daniel Lord, and a trade journalist, Martin Quigley; both were Roman Catholics. After the code (which was voluntary) went unheeded for a few years, the Production Code Administration (PCA) was set up to handle affairs more efficiently as an enforcement agency. This was done reluctantly, because the newly formed Legion of Decency showed that the Catholic Church in America could easily bring about a boycott of offensive films on request. The code was to be revised twice, first in 1956 and again in 1966.

It is important to note that the PCA examined scripts too before production and could suggest cuts afterwards in the final print as well as just handing out a seal of approval. It was in the full sense of the term an advisory agency agreed to by the member companies. If a film was contested it was brought before a Board of Review (consisting of producers, directors and theatre owners), where the final determination was made as to whether it was to receive approval. The code itself suffered from a wide assortment of ambiguities and misleading inferences. This can best be illustrated by the accentuated moral tone of its opening paragraphs under "General Principles":

I. No picture shall be produced which will lower the moral standards of those who see it. Hence the sympathy of the audience should never be thrown to the side of crime, wrongdoing, evil or sin.

II. Correct standards of life shall, as far as possible, be presented. A wide knowledge of life and of living is made possible through the film. When right standards are consistently presented, the motion picture exercises the most powerful influences. It builds character, develops right ideals, inculcates correct principles, and all this in attractive story form. If motion pictures consistently hold up for admiration high types of characters and present stories that will affect lives for the better, they can become the most powerful natural force for the improvement of mankind.

III. Law — divine, natural or human — shall not be ridiculed, nor shall sympathy be created for its violation. By natural law is understood the law which is written in the hearts of all mankind, the great underlying principles of right and justice dictated by conscience. By human law is understood the law written by civilized nations.

The code then goes on to make particular application to crime, murder, brutality, sex, seduction or rape, vulgarity, obscenity, blasphemy and profanity, costumes, religion, special subjects (bedroom scenes, hangings, drinking, childbirth, etc.), national feelings, titles, and cruelty to animals.

It would be correct to say that although the treatment of certain subjects should perhaps be moral and meaningful, it should not on the other hand depict life as an unnatural, vicarious experience. This, indirectly, was what the code was doing and trying to do, thus frequently robbing the audience of an encounter with its own environment and conditions. For this reason, as films began to mature (especially in the 1950s and 1960s) the code ran into serious trouble. The awkward circumstances leading up to the code's second revision in 1966 were reflected in editorials appearing in the *Motion Picture Herald* in the summer of that year:

"*Virginia Woolf* and the Code"

The crisis in the Motion Picture Association (MPA) over *Who's Afraid of Virginia Woolf?* has been resolved — as had been widely predicted — by the appeal to the Review Board. As constituted the Board is unlikely to deny a Code Seal to any film brought before it. In the case of *Virginia Woolf* an "exception" was granted. This was the way the appeal of *The Pawnbroker* was handled over a year ago. In its statement explaining the "exemption" the Review Board made three points: 1) The film is not designed to be prurient; 2) Warners (film studio) wants no one under 18 admitted unless accompanied by a parent; and 3) The exemption is specific and "does not mean that the floodgates are open for dirty language or other material." The statement ended in these words: "We desire to allow excellence to be displayed and we insist that films, under whatever guise, which go beyond rational measures of community standards will not bear a Seal of Approval." If the Code system is to be preserved, immediate action is required to forestall any more Code Seals issued by "exemptions." If the Code system is not worth preserving, let's give it a quick burial.

"The Code Is Dead"

While the causes of the Code's long sickness are many, the cause of death is one. The Code died because of *Who's Afraid of Virginia Woolf? Who's Afraid of Virginia Woolf?* got its exemption on the grounds that the film is of high quality, made at a great cost by people of consummate talents. Certainly the members of the Review Board did not take the position that blasphemy is not blasphemy, that profanity is not profanity, and that verbal obscenity is not verbal obscenity. Here is the issue between the handling of *The Pawnbroker* and *Virginia Woolf*. *The Pawnbroker* did not kill the Code. *Virginia Woolf* did. Many have held that "good taste" is the ultimate standard. *Virginia Woolf* kills this approach. There certainly is a question of "good taste" in handling nudity, violence and many other matters. There is no such thing as "good taste" in blasphemy, profanity and obscenity.

"And Now — *Alfie*"

Now, having passed blasphemy, profanity and verbal obscenity — all barred by the Production Code — the Motion Picture Association is confronted with a film which treats abortion beyond the limits imposed in the Code. The film is *Alfie*, made in England on a small budget and a remarkable success at the box office there. The MPA has two alternatives: 1) The Production Code Administration may ignore the plain and flagrant violation of the Code (as has been done from time to time in the past but never so blatant a case); or 2) The PCA may refuse to grant a Code seal until ordered to do so by an interpretation of the Review Board. Should Geoffrey Shurlock (head of the PCA) deny *Alfie* a Code approval, Paramount would immediately appeal. Given the present membership of the Review Board and the record of the body's past actions, the outcome is a foregone conclusion — *Alfie* will get by, either through an overriding of the PCA or by a Code exemption. The *Alfie* situation again raises the question of the proper function of the PCA and of the Appeal Board. Everything expressly prohibited in the Production Code apparently is to be approved, one way or another.

The editor's angry feelings can be readily understood in light of the fact that his father, Martin Quigley, was the co-author of the original code. They point out two facts: first, the editor's fears that the code was dead were well founded, particularly in the light of the uselessness of the third revision; and second, the Appeal Board was having as much of a problem defining "good taste" as the courts were trying to define "obscenity."

A few side comments are in order on the subject of the industry's desire for self-regulation. Ostensively, the MPA has made a good showing of wanting to police itself but it goes little beyond that. When Otto Preminger released *The Moon Is Blue* (1953) and *The Man With*

the Golden Arm (1955) without code approval, he benefitted finan-
cially from the notoriety the films caused. The producers were aware
of this. In another light, the PCA had often been referred to as the
"right arm of the Legion of Decency" because of the Legion's historical role in calling it into being. When the Production Code
Administration passed Billy Wilder's *Kiss Me, Stupid* in 1964, the
Legion of Decency accused the PCA of a "betrayal of trust." A year
later an embarrassing situation developed for the MPA when the
New York Times ran an article suggesting that the code be revised,
with the industry answering that it was planning to do that; yet when
questioned further, it responded with befuddlement. Within a year
Jack Valenti, ex-Special Advisor to President Johnson, was appointed
the new president of the MPA. Shortly thereafter a new code was
adopted.

Approved by both the National Association of Theatre Owners
(NATO) and the two major religious bodies, the National Catholic
Office for Motion Pictures (formerly the Legion of Decency) and the
Film Commission of the National Council of Churches, it went into
operation in 1968 with a Rating Program.

The basic dignity and value of human life shall be respected and upheld. Restraint
shall be exercised in portraying the taking of life.

Evil, sin, crime and wrongdoing shall not be justified.

Special restraint shall be exercised in portraying criminal and antisocial activities
in which minors participate or are involved.

Detailed and protracted acts of brutality, cruelty, physical violence, torture and
abuse shall not be presented.

Indecent or undue exposure of the human body shall not be presented.

Illicit sex relationships shall not be justified. Intimate sex scenes violating common standards of decency shall not be portrayed. Restraint and care shall be
exercised in presentations dealing with sex aberrations.

Obscene speech, gestures or movements shall not be permitted.

Religion shall not be demeaned.

Words or symbols contemptuous of racial, religious or national groups shall not
be used so as to incite bigotry or hatred.

Excessive cruelty to animals shall not be portrayed, and animals shall not be
treated inhumanely.

It was tongue in cheek. The industry stood little to gain and
much to lose by enforcing the new regulations. Only the Armed
Forces cinema service and television required the old Seal of Approval,

and theatre owners were more likely to look at surveys or follow various rating sheets on their own to judge public opinion on the product they were exhibiting. Hollywood super-productions suddenly began to lose money, and the old formulas were no longer reliable. Keeping faith with the audience was becoming more and more out of the question: what sold was all important. Family magazines, like the *Reader's Digest*, began printing surveys showing that the vast majority of their readers were opposed to themes dealing with sex, suggestiveness and veiled pornography. The trade journal, *Variety*, began to challenge the exhibitors' sincerity in preaching their desire for family-style pictures, when their receipts proved otherwise. From inside the industry itself came complaints, particularly over the repulsive and dishonest advertising practices that accompanied even decent-minded material. They predicted the downfall of a strong and experienced organization if the abuses were allowed to continue.

Where the industry particularly failed was in not sponsoring research into the influences and effects movies have on children and adolescents. Such research was always sparse in the history of the industry: only the Payne Fund Studies of the 1930s (helping to establish the Legion of Decency) and the 1956 Hearings of the Kefauver Committee on Juvenile Delinquency stand out as notable attempts in this direction. The industry usually responded that the total impact on society and its youth from all the media was immeasurable, so it would be unfair to blame the trouble only on the motion picture. Further, film education (now the domain of several college programs) was never actively supported to raise the standards of the young audience, despite enormous amounts of money spent on public relations.

The best the industry did was to introduce in 1968 a Code and Rating Program, in which "G" and "GP" rated films could generally be seen by the entire public and "R" and "X" were restricted to adults. Nevertheless, abuses were widespread. In a survey of 13,000 questionnaires NATO sent out to determine if children were being admitted to "R" and "X" rated films, only twenty-five percent were answered. *Variety* answered the question in another way:

The problem with X is that it lends itself to exploitation by distributors who would like to give their films that far-out identity in behalf of the rapid dollar. It's no secret that some lesser-scale companies are submitting their pictures to MPA for evaluation for the sole purpose of getting the X, which they regard as an advertising lure.

The beginning of the 1970s saw the Film Commission of the National Council of Churches and the National Catholic Office for Motion Pictures jointly making a statement that the Code and Rating Program was a failure. However, they maintained that a voluntary rating system was still preferable to the exercise of this responsibility by the government. Possibly such an opinion was accompanied by the knowledge that compulsory classification would be ruled out by the Supreme Court as a violation of the First Amendment.

Statutory classification of movies on the state level has a myriad of interpretations and thus has met with constant trouble. One example is a classification statute adopted by the State of Pennsylvania in 1959, which provided for the classification of films and their suitability for adolescents under the age of seventeen. But the law also made it a criminal offense to exhibit a film that had been classified as "completely unsuitable for all." Basically, this amounted to censorship and the statute was declared unconstitutional by the Pennsylvania Supreme Court as a violation of free speech. Other statutes have encountered similar difficulties.

On the level of the federal government, Senator Margaret Chase Smith sought support to introduce a bill in Congress that would provide for a form of government classification. Nothing has come of the idea, despite the recognition that every government has adopted a classification system except the United States. Two questions come to the forefront in an argument for compulsory classification by the government: (1) what standards would be employed; and (2) should provision be made for the constitutional rights even of minors to have ideas freely disseminated. Moreover, it seems to be the right of parents alone to decide what is suitable for their children. So far as the industry itself is concerned, the MPA is always fearful a compulsory classification system would result in the loss of revenue in the long run. (In this respect, it is significant to note that the MPA hired one of the country's leading lawyers at an enormous salary to handle the industry's complex legal problems: it far exceeded that of Jack Valenti, the industry's president.)

The tactics of pressure groups are also extremely difficult to pin down. A simple explanation is that whenever a moral influence — political, national, religious, educational, ethnic, racial, etc. — is brought to bear on a community, there exists a pressure group of some sort. These have the most influence on small communities, schools, libraries, and the like, where the media of communication are often prejudged for their "worth" or "harmfulness." This of course amounts to a form of censorship: censorship by fear of intimidation. The movie industry has acted numerous times out of fear of a strong, well-organized pressure group.

Formerly the rating system of the national Legion of Decency fell under legal scrutiny. That many a film could lose money if it was rated "B" or "C" (i.e., morally objectionable) was seen by some as "restraint of trade." The argument has some validity and was discussed widely in the 1950s, as the PCA and the Legion of Decency were waging a losing battle to save the "morality" of the movies. The difficulty was to prove that the Legion acted out of "intended malice" and not for the general good of the public, a premise that could hardly be supported. Another argument of "censorship by boycott," meaning that studios and distributors feared the threat of the Legion to invoke its pledge against the movies and acted accordingly, disappeared when the Legion lost its constituency in part or whole in the maturing 1960s.

Probably the most important realization today is that controls or guidelines of some sort must exist and that censorship as a way of life has a way of turning up in the most liberal of communities. The wave of sex and violence on the screen has dulled the sensitivities and awakened the public to seek a *modus vivendi* with the liberties that have been granted.

Some proposed guidelines:

First, cinema, like all the arts, is an expression of the mind and spirit. It has a right to be viewed in the light of what it does best rather than what it does worst. Nothing should obscure the primary purpose of film art, which is to hold up a mirror to humanity and reflect the world in which men live. Cinema in its honest portrayal of life is a matter of great concern for churches.

Second, the church as an institution is rightly concerned with all aspects of life and culture. The development of a responsible audience is part of that concern. What is particularly needed today is an audience that expects and demands cinema of good quality, an audience that will support the filmmakers who provide it. Out of this educational process could emerge a cultural richness we have yet to experience, namely, a cinema geared to stimulate as well as to entertain.

Third, the day of the pietistic film has passed. In retrospect, the limitations of supporting piety in the cinema are now obvious. Religion in this guise was more often than not offensive. (One has only to consider the treatment of Jews in the Christ films.) The history of the pietistic film is, for the most part, the story of escapism and propaganda in the cinema.

Fourth, if religion is ever to be relevant in the marketplace of the cinema, dialogue with filmmakers must be fostered as a matter of policy. Such dialogue will challenge filmmakers to respond to theological questions, or at least to create the proper cinematic climate for the study of these problems. Out of this mutual concern could develop a new tradition of so-called "religious" cinema, a cinema of theological search and discovery.

Fifth, the religious film today is recognized by its relationship to the message of the gospel, the message of Christian hope through faith, the message of love and tolerance. Films dealing with man's search for his identity are very close to biblical man's search for the same truth.

Sixth, all depictions of life worthy of the name of art involve selection and interpretation. The important factor in viewing a film is the interpretation of life and values set before the audience by the filmmaker. In his depiction of truly human situations and character, whether they be comic or tragic, the artist confirms his conviction as to whether Christian values and virtues are ultimately worthwhile. Any film which possesses the power to elevate the spirit, deepen compassion for the human situation, and broaden the borders of understanding deserves the church's full attention. The subject matter itself is not the first nor the primary consideration, but how it is interpreted by the artist.

Seventh, whether a film should be praised solely for its "moralizing" or "humanizing" qualities is a sticky area of debate. It is as dangerous as looking upon the subject matter alone as a reliable guide to the religious dimension of the cinema. The critical approach to interpreting the film's meaning as a whole is much safer, especially in praising or recommending a film.

Eighth, the argument that a film should be wholesome and unobjectionable must be laid aside. It is illusory and superficial to think that a suitable religious cinema can be fostered in this way; in the past it has been proven that such an approach leads to greater problems. The possibility of portraying reality honestly on the screen must never be denied. If the lost character of modern man is allowed to be covered up, then the relevancy of the gospel largely disappears.

Ninth, an artist with a conscience is an integrity unto himself. If he has no apparent conscience, he should at least be looked upon with compassion as one worthy of redemption. This is where dialogue between the theologian and the filmmaker plays an important role.

Tenth, classification and censorship of films by religious bodies seldom reach the goals they are intended for. A positive approach to the cinema founded on education wins more converts to a good cause than a negative one directed toward prevention. Just as the filmmaker should be granted the freedom of integrity, so should the potential viewer be allowed the liberty of his own conscience.

III. FROM THE *PASSION PLAY* TO *INTOLERANCE*

The nineteenth century found the rationalism of the previous age rapidly disappearing into a compromise with Christianity. England under Victorianism agreed to support the Anglican church. The melodrama prospered under Napoleon. The Deism of the founding fathers in America gave way to a religious revival.

The dawn of the movie age was breaking. The Magic Lantern Show at the end of the eighteenth century seated its public before a white sheet, upon which was back-projected eery phantasmagoria. Often an audience was frightened into a faint by these supernatural "happenings." Much of this magic and superstition was carried over into the "shadow world" of the movies. It was the origin of the horror film, as well as adding considerably to the evil mystique of the "vamp" in the early history of the motion picture.

The nineteenth-century melodrama, with its curious blending of sexual fantasy and religious ecstasy, was a more immediate fore-runner of the cinema. Its monumental war between good and evil, virtue and sex, the powers of heaven and the agents of Satan, evolved into the movie prototypes of Mary Pickford and Theda Bara. Sweet little Mary — the girl with the golden curls, surrounded by puppies, kittens and bunnies — was the personification of the Victorian ideals of virtue, loyalty, duty, kindness, self-sacrifice and love. Theda Bara — an anagram for "Arab Death," surrounded by skulls, snakes and skeletons — was the incarnation of evil, spiritism, the deadly female, the woman who uses her charms to make passionate love while humiliating, debasing and impoverishing the unsuspecting male (following the general outline of Rudyard Kipling's poem "The

Vampire," on which was based a number of melodramas at the turn of the century). Through these two personages the melodrama was permitted to live long into the twentieth century.

The melodrama was molded and nourished by the "new moral attitude" fostered in the reign of England's Queen Victoria (1837-1901). As a result of the revolutions convulsing Europe between 1789 and 1837, religion was resurrected as the only solution to put down the radicalism of the poor (Napoleon remarked that religion kept the poor from murdering the rich). A proselytizing zeal swept over the ruling classes of Europe, but few were more ardently dedicated to keeping the hands of the working class busy than Queen Victoria and her prime minister Gladstone. The motto that "respectability leads to profit" was not only accepted by the ruling class, but the working class responded with an even greater fervor of its own. A passionate, rigid puritanism spread like fire in England between 1830 and 1850, dedicated to penny-pinching and a war on liquor. The outer expression of this puritanism was the "temperance revolution," which was subsequently to have more success in America than in England. Its inner expression was a dogmatic, sentimental and obsessive preoccupation with virtue and sin, a self-righteousness equating fine manners with morality. Historian J. H. Plumb's assertion that at the core of Victorian morality stood a fear of sex, which it refused to accept in resolutely pursuing purity and respectability, aptly explains why Victorianism disguised its failures either by taking refuge in silence or by resorting to the double standard.

The Victorian double standard was reflected in the era's numerous paintings, photographs and literary works. Queen Victoria hung a huge composite photograph, "The Two Ways of Life," dated 1857, in the study of Prince Albert. As an allegory on Dissipation, Repentance and Industry, a bevy of semi-naked girls arranged in erotic poses occupies one side of the picture, while a madonna sheltering a half-dressed convert to religion is in the middle, and people busily engaged in various trades take up the other side. Plumb underscores it as the epithet of the age. The theme is echoed in the life of Laura Bell, London's celebrated courtesan, who turned to religion at the height of her fame, to become an evangelical preacheress. It is to be found too in the Art Academy's "stories-in-paintings," which turned to real life for inspiration while unveiling the bitter truth in the process. These paintings became the models for one-reel movie sermons a half-century later. Between 1908 and 1914, the years the American cinema moved to the forefront, the motion pictures preached with a passion Victorian attitudes contained in the poetry of Browning and Tennyson and the novels of Charles Dickens.

A common practice, as the narrative in cinema evolved, was to copy appropriate motifs in art and literature, particularly the "stories-in-paintings" of the Academy. Thus, the inspiration for Theda Bara's *The Forbidden Path* (1918) likely stems from Ford Maddox Brown's painting "Take Your Son, Sir," in which a young unwed mother holding her new-born child is "halo-ed" by a mirror, which also reflects the figure of the guilty seducer. In the movie version Theda Bara is depicted as an innocent living in Greenwich Village who becomes a dissolute artist's model for a painting of the Madonna. She assumes the pose in Brown's painting. Later, after succumbing, she slips to the depths, then returns to the same painter to pose for a portrait of the Magdalen. She wreaks her revenge.

The early filmmakers were fascinated by the double standard in the melodrama. It is said that Russian director Sergei Eisenstein once found two postcards of the same model while touring Mount-Saint-Michel: in one, she posed as "The Little Flower," St. Thérèse of Lisieux; in the other, she nuzzled languidly in the arms of a sailor. Such contrasts became a hallmark of his cinema.

December 28th marks the birthday of cinema. On that day in 1895 the Lumière Brothers projected a series of films in the Grand Café of Paris for a *paid* admission. Cinema is in fact much older than that; fully a decade before this business adventure, motion pictures had been similarly projected by Louis Aimé Augustin LePrince, Thomas A. Edison, W. K. L. Dickson, Jean Acme LeRoy, Birt Acres, Robert W. Paul, Woodville Latham, C. Francis Jenkins and Thomas Armat, among others. (In the process of development from the Magic Lantern Show to cinema, the name of the Reverend Hannibal Goodwin, Episcopalian pastor, should not be bypassed: the invention of the photographic film was his.)

After the passing fad of the Lumière projections in the salons of the rich, the cinema grew up on the fair grounds of Europe and in the nickelodeons of American cities. The public quickly tired of realistic city scenes, so newspaper-style reportage and popular themes took their place. The "Passion Play of Oberammergau" was the longest and most popular of these themes, save for an occasional prize fight. The first Passion was sponsored by a book company, La Bonne Presse, in the summer of 1897. It was shot on a vacant lot in Paris, substituting actors for children at the last minute; it made enough money to transform a religious publishing house overnight into a film production company. About the same time Lumière cameramen were negotiating unsuccessfully with the city of Oberammergau for a special performance before their cameras; they settled instead for a fake Parisian reproduction of the Horitz (Bohemia) Passion in September of 1897. The Lumière Passion was a rather lengthy 15-minute version arranged into 13 tableaux-scenes of about a minute each, far superior to the Lear production for La Bonne Presse. It was offered for immediate sale in America to Richard G. Hollaman's Eden Wax Museum in New York, but the price of $10,000 was considered too high and Hollaman felt that he would be better off making his own Passion. He did so on the roof of the Grand Central Palace as winter was approaching (there is snow in the Garden of Olives!), hiring stage director L. J. Vincent to arrange the tableaux and William C. Paley, a British cameraman, to do the shooting (after Vincent had left). Meanwhile the Lumière Passion was bought by theatre entrepreneurs Klaw and Erlanger for a Lenten presentation on Broadway; Hollaman had to race against time to get his version shown before that. The première of "The Original Oberammergau Passion Play" was on 31 January 1898.

The Hollaman Passion of 20 tableaux was 700 meters long, three times the length of the Lumière Passion, and was accompanied by a full orchestra with chorus and commentator. Mixed in with the Eden Museum's other merchandising of mysterious wax figures, death's heads and various oddities designed to send shudders up the back, the Passion Play had just the right touch to draw a wide audience. Many visitors to the Eden were in tears or on their knees. Upon protest from Klaw and Erlanger (who even produced a bishop's affidavit trying to prove their Passion Play was real), Hollaman had to retract "The Original Oberammergau" part of the advertisement and he substituted instead "The Cinematographic Passion Play"; the change brought more customers! An evangelist preacher then bought a copy to take to revival meetings around the country, the first time the rather suspect "shadow world" was used as a power for religion. Pioneer filmmaker Sigmund Lubin of Philadelphia made his version in 1898, which was followed by scores more during the following decade. Film historian Terry Ramsaye referred to Hollaman's Passion as "the screen's first step toward conscious art."

Through the world-wide distribution offices of Charles Pathé the Passion Play spread around the world. Pathé hired Ferdinand Zecca, one of cinema's great primitive artists, to direct a series on the Life and Passion of Christ between 1902 and 1906, the first movie serials. They were beautifully tinted in color, subsequently bought by Adolph Zukor for presentation as a feature-length film. Occasionally an organist and singers accompanied the projection. It ran for months in four different theatres: Zukor credits it as the start of his financial empire. It also dispelled the lingering fears of church leaders that darkened cinemas were disreputable places to visit.

The Passion Play wasn't the only popular religious theme. Humorous "anticlerical" films featured jolly monks and boisterous devils making merry in peek-a-boo eroticism and drinking scenes meant to be scandalous. Robert W. Paul made *The Monks* in 1898 for the peep-show market in penny arcades. The paper prints in the Library of Congress show a collection of Biograph "monk" films (*The Jolly Monks of Malabar*, *The Simple Life*, and *Wine, Women and Song*), made in 1906, which were obviously designed for an appreciative audience. Of greater interest in the paper print collection is a cleverly constructed, quite erotic interpretation of *The Temptation of St. Anthony*, dated 1902 without crediting a director. From a single camera position it shows a monk turning the pages of a manuscript; then a naked woman appears before him. He leaves his seat and moves toward her, but suddenly he is amazed to see her turn into a skeleton. He falls penitently to the floor. The film was evidently an American adaptation of Georges Méliès's *La Tentation de Saint Antoine*, made in 1898.

Georges Méliès of Paris had an incredible flair for the cinema. He outdistanced between 1896 and 1908 every artist in the cinema world (at this time it included such large movie capitals as New York, Chicago, Philadelphia, London, Copenhagen, Stockholm, Berlin, Rome, as well as large distribution centers scattered around the globe). He was copied by Edison's Porter and Pathé's Zecca, but no one could match the poetic gaiety of his unique style. Already established as a well-known magician, mechanical inventor and proprietor of the Théâtre Robert-Houdin in Paris, he added to these accomplishments by buying a camera from the Lumière Brothers to turn out in rapid succession one-reel fantasies snatched from his child-like imagination. His stories were filled with mischievous devils, full-bosomed dancing girls, magic rockets, fairy-tale castles and whatever could tickle a laugh out of the young clientele at the Robert-Houdin. The devils wore dumpy costumes, but the dancing girls were real, and the settings for both were traced from medieval church missals.

Méliès's reputation as an artist stems from his discovery of the double exposure, stop-motion photography (thus playfully replacing figures at will), changes in speed of motion, fades, dissolves and various forms of animation. He controlled his material every step of the way from conception to delivery. The charm and execution of his ideas and fantasies quickly put him on top, while the merry pranks of his artistes (some from the Folies-Bergère) kept him there. He was copied by everyone; when that didn't work, the prints were simply stolen and presented under another name. Because he did not capitalize on his investment and preferred production to rental exchanges, he was gradually nudged aside by the Pathé company and went bankrupt in 1914.

Besides the energetic, flamboyant figures of the primitive artist Zecca (Pathé credits him as "the most prolific director working before the First World War") and the artistic magician Méliès, a third director brought cinematic art another giant step forward — the American Sidney Olcott, an actor-writer who entered filmmaking in 1904 to give the small Kalem company in Chicago its finest hour.

Historian Lewis Jacobs recounts that Olcott found it too confining to work inside a studio; he turned instead to outdoor grandeur and the romantic folk hero. He preferred local color to give his melodramas authenticity, travelling anywhere for the right folkloric background: the New Jersey hills for Westerns, Florida for Civil War history (with a Southern viewpoint), Ireland for quaint "rebel" legends, Europe for folk tales, Egypt and Palestine for the first "authentic" Life of Christ. In his hands, more than any other's, the motion picture "toy" grew up. He dumped exciting world snapshots into the laps of the urban poor, the immigrant, the tenement-dweller — all for the price of a nickel.

Recognizing the importance of myth and fantasy in Méliès's *Christ Walking the Waters* (1899), *Joan of Arc* (1900), and *Gulliver's Travels* (1902), he first made a name for himself by adapting Lew

Wallace's popular novel and stage play, *Ben Hur* (1907), into an epic costume drama. It attracted copyright action from the Wallace Foundation and Klaw and Erlanger, who owned the stage rights. In 1911 the case went before the Supreme Court, Kalem lost, and the movies went legitimate thereafter. The $25,000 fine may have soured Kalem on Olcott, who at this time was on the actual Via Dolorosa in Jerusalem shooting his Passion Play. The finished film, *From the Manger to the Cross* (1912), was considered too expensive and out-of-fashion (despite Zukor's success with the Zecca *Passion Play*); so Olcott was fired. When Kalem did decide to release the film, it was an instant success and was hailed by critics and churchmen alike as a masterpiece. The Bishop of London, where the film ran non-stop for eight months, proclaimed it superior to the Oberammergau Passion. Legends sprang up around the film, one that scriptwriter Gene Gauntier wrote the script while in a delirium from an attack of sunstroke. Released again in 1938 with added soundtrack and close-ups, the film has maintained its popularity down to today.

The importance of Olcott can be measured by the number of features made in the mold of *From the Manger to the Cross*, mostly European productions to challenge the time length of the two-reelers on the American market. The reason was simple: the American market had grown to such huge proportions in 1907 that its gross income was larger than that of the legitimate theatre and vaudeville combined. In 1909 the eight largest companies in America and the French firms of Pathé and Méliès (with offices in New York) combined under Edison to form the Motion Picture Patents Company, on the belief that together they held air-tight patents on the making and sale of camera equipment. Its distribution arm, the General Film Company, looked upon its public as largely illiterate and undeserving of anything better than cheap entertainment. Two-reelers fitted the system fine — despite the growing suspicion that audiences in crowded urban communities wanted bigger and better movies, instead of the low-quality fare General Film was dishing out. The awakening came when smaller American and foreign companies heeded the times, made feature-length films along the lines of Sidney Olcott's "mad experiments," and pulled the rug out from under the Patents Company and General Film. By 1914 both were wholly ineffective, and they were abolished by law a year later.

Olcott's counterparts were the Italian "Grand Opera" directors: Enrico Guazzoni's *St. Francis* (1911), *Quo Vadis* (1912), and *Fabiola* (1913); Giovanni Pastrone's *Cabiria* (1914); and Giulio Antamoro's *Christus* (1914). Antamoro followed Olcott to Egypt to film *Christus*, modelled it after famous paintings, and had great success with the film all over Europe. Its leading attraction was the selection of famous actors in the main roles, a trend that began with Sarah Bernhardt appearing in the four-reel *Queen Elizabeth* (1912) and Maria Jacobini in *Joan of Arc* (1914). Adolph Zukor imported *Queen Elizabeth* to America, founded the enterprising "Famous Players in Famous Plays" (attracting stage actors and a sophisticated public to high-class movie houses), and went around the policies of the Patents Company to start a "feature craze". Built on a "states' rights distribution" plan, the feature-film supply from Europe was the doorway to success for many of Hollywood's future moguls. The key film was the nine-reel religious "spectacle", *Quo Vadis*, opening on Broadway for a $1.50 admission fee. The nickelodeon was dead.

The inventive age of cinema between 1895 and 1915 had its mystical side for audiences new to the magic of the seventh art. Zecca's tinted Passions in the manner of Sulpician art calendars were sent around the world by the Pathé company, popular attractions both artistically and commercially in the cinema world in 1912. Méliès and his raucous devils, fairy lands and fantastic voyages opened up a world of breathless imagination. Olcott's epic stories of grandeur and folklore created new myths greater than the ones he built on. The grand-scale Italian spectacles of Pastrone and Guazzoni recast the whole history of the birth of Christianity. Young film companies in Germany, Denmark and Sweden dug below the surface of melodrama to tap the legends of long ago, the tales of vampires, ghosts and golems, the phenomenon of the inhuman in human form. India's D. G. Phalke exploited the mythological tales featuring Rama and Lord Krishna, before whose images audiences prostrated themselves. In Japan the trick films of Shozo Makino, director, and Matsunosuke Onoue, star, were costume pictures constructed around a wizard or a supernatural hero overcoming all obstacles with magic or bravado. Working without a script to speak of, these filmmakers created a new world of dreams and fantasies in a climate of freshness and spontaneity. Nothing was quite like it before in the age of technical invention; nothing may ever be so engagingly fresh again. Least of all, the movies.

But the cinema was more than just a new cultural expression of the twentieth century. It was an art form. In 1915 poet Vachel Lindsay devoted more space in *The Art of the Moving Picture* to the "Photoplay of Splendor" (Fairy, Crowd, Patriotic and Religious Splendor) than to action films or psychological dramas; in a sense, his whole book is stamped by the "mystical" nature of the cinema. When he proclaims his view of Religious Splendor he is pointing to the crowning achievement of the young art form:

The real death in the photoplay is the ritualistic death, the real birth is the ritualistic birth, and the cathedral mood of the motion picture which goes with these and is close to these in many of its phases, is an inexhaustible resource.

And in summarizing the aesthetics of cinema art, he dedicates his book "as an open letter" to the achievements of D. W. Griffith.

The art of film language originated with an itinerant actor and playright, who signed "Lawrence" Griffith to his Biograph productions between 1907 and 1910 for fear of being recognized by friends in the theatre world. Like Méliès he had a fantastic flair for the cinema, instinctively sensing it had a manner of expression all its own. He devised a film grammar to fit these expressions, drawing from Victorian poets and Charles Dickens poetic justification for the use of close-ups, lighting and the radical selection of young actresses — thin, quivering, wide-eyed, some still in their teens — to personify the ideal of these poets. Unfortunately, he was also saddled with Victorian self-righteousness that convinced him his audience should think and feel the same as he. This self-deception ultimately played a major role in his downfall.

He had matured as an artist in three short years, when he signed his 1910 contract under "D.W." and left for the sunlight of California (a favorite winter location) to make a popular series of film sermons (*The Unchanging Sea*) and stories of old Americana (*The Thread of Destiny*). Here he gave more attention to the atmosphere and setting of a story, composition, editing and technique, molding the melodrama and its twin, the adventure play, into a personal style. Striving to build suspense or sustain mood he forced Biograph to allow him to make two-reelers of a half-hour length in 1911, which placed him solidly in the forefront as cinema's leading director. He lost ground nevertheless when the European "feature craze" swept the American industry, overshadowing his own star-less productions of *The Battle*

(1911) and *Man's Genesis* (1912). Not to be outdone by the four-reel *Queen Elizabeth* and the seven-reel *Quo Vadis* of 1912, Griffith presented a biblical spectacle of his own, *Judith of Bethulia* (1913), a four-reeler based on Thomas Bailey Aldrich's stage play but freely adapted. It starred 17-year-old Blanche Sweet (already a veteran of some fifty one-reelers!) and was a much finer psychological drama than anything of its day, in addition to being packed with more skillful action, suspense and narrative technique than the European product. But he was still ignored in the excitement over Adolph Zukor's "Famous Players in Famous Plays."

Dropped from the Biograph Company on the pretext of being too expensive (it signed a contract with Klaw and Erlanger to photograph stage plays) and refusing to sign with Zukor (who knew Griffith's value as he did Mary Pickford's), Griffith joined the young Mutual Company, bided his time on a few minor features, saved his money, and launched out in 1914 on the monumental epic in the history of motion pictures, *The Birth of a Nation* (1915).

Griffith, as *The Battle* had shown, savored the thought of making an historical epic on the American Civil War, based on the memories of his father fighting for the Confederacy and his own knowledge of the painful Reconstruction years. The images growing out of these stories were burned into his head from youth, which accounts for the beauty, clarity and rightness of so many of the scenes; indeed, the film has as much power as the Brady photographs of the war, upon which many of the war sequences seem to be based. These elements, and others tied to Griffith's passionate views on justice and intolerance, form the basic integrity of the film. His mistake was to wed this fervor to the dogmatized bias of the Reverend Thomas Dixon's novel-melodrama *The Clansman*, which provides the framework of the story, plus an insensibility to the hate being engendered nationally by Tom Watson's politically-oriented Ku Klux Klan movement at that time. His social sense for the cinema was admirable, but on political issues he was, regrettably and fatally, a naive.

Still, *The Birth of a Nation* as it stands is its own vindication. It has the customary moral flip-flopping and bad Victorian taste Griffith liked, but at the same time it is relatively free of the preachy, the nearsighted and the provincial contrary to claims of his severest critics. There is at the beginning of the film more of his father, Colonel Jacob Wark "Roaring Jake," than anything or anybody else.

There is also, as the story unfolds, little prejudice against the Negro himself (he is more often than not treated with patronizing kindness and affection). But there is a great sense of outrage against the Negro's exploitation by white carpetbaggers and congressional leaders. It is a rural, Southern view of the Negro and Reconstruction days, hardly in keeping with the urban formation of America taking place at the turn of the century. Watson's Ku Klux Klan movement — anti-Negro, anti-Catholic, anti-semitic, anti-intellectual — reached its height of political power in 1915, using the Dixon prejudice and the Griffith sentimentality in *The Birth of a Nation* as a rally-cry for membership (as the Ku Klux Klan still does today). How much a public, squeezed by social unrest, political intrigue and a coming war, cared to understand the feelings of a Southerner reliving the past is a mute question. *The Birth of a Nation* was not only a box office champion (in total number of viewers up to the present it is probably *the* box office champion), but it provoked a public outcry and riots in a number of Northern cities by its one-sided view of the Negro and Reconstruction. After its showing at the White House President Woodrow Wilson commented: "It is like writing history with lightning, and my one regret is that it is all so terribly true." Today, in light of the Civil Rights movement's progress, the film can be viewed with greater fairness and objectivity; Griffith's strongest critics would be hard pressed for evidence proving the film clearly supports hate, although prejudice is clearly there.

Recognizing his mistake, Griffith spent the rest of his life trying to catch up with the public. After *The Birth of a Nation* he managed to stay on top for only five more years, working out of wounded pride while remaining an incurable romantic whose emotions embraced all of mankind. His second great epic, *Intolerance* (1916), grew out of these hurt feelings: an enormous four-part super-spectacle to prove he wasn't the bigot some claimed. The theme was "a protest against despotism and injustice in every form," tracing hypocrisy back through history from modern slums to Renaissance France to the Christ story to ancient Babylon. The four stories were edited into the single, flowing form of a fugue, tied by a poetic symbol of a mother rocking a cradle which drew its inspiration from Walt Whitman's lines "Out of the cradle endlessly rocking..." *Intolerance* turned out to be a colossal production costing nearly two million dollars, running some 400 reels in negative, 13 reels in final form (about three hours in length): it was a colossal failure. Griffith had made and lost a fortune in a matter of months. The failure of a masterpiece perhaps greater in scope and power than *The Birth of a Nation* stems from the gigantic proportions of the theme, the difficulty in following the edited narrative, and the unacceptable note of pacifism in the midst of a great war. Nevertheless, in the process Griffith laid the foundation for another goliath: Hollywood, sprouting up around the ruins of Belshazzar's Babylon on Sunset Boulevard.

Creative sparks continued to charge a few Victorian "tales of tears" bought and recast by Griffith, but the calculated success of these productions, taken less and less seriously by the public, did little for his reputation other than paying his debts. This is not to detract from the delicate spirituality of *Broken Blossoms* (1919) and the passionate defense of the Christian ideal of marriage in *Way Down East* (1920), condemning at the same time clerical hypocrisy and the double standard in Victorian morality: these are strong assets and Griffith at his best. But while he was exhausting his considerable poetic powers in turning them into gold, the condescending cuteness of the melodrama kept peeking through. He still felt bound to defend an ideal hardly needing defense in *Orphans of the Storm* (1921), subtitling it "Love Conquers Tyranny," in which he even reached for the cliché of a crown of thorns for Lillian Gish as she passes on the way to the guillotine during the French Revolution: it worked! It was his last critical success in the old school of filmmaking, marked by many such tender moments in an otherwise uneven work. Thereafter we find him subordinating his poetic powers to realism; and when the cause was right — *America* (1924), *Isn't Life Wonderful* (1924), *Sally of the Sawdust* (1925), *Abraham Lincoln* (1930), and *The Struggle* (1931) — he was as consistently good as he ever was. *Abraham Lincoln*, in particular, was a major contribution to the sound era, perhaps the best-made talkie up to that time.

During the last fifteen years of his life he could find little work, and died alone in a Hollywood hotel in 1948 at the age of 73. He had made 432 movies; *The Birth of a Nation* alone grossed about $50 million; but there was no room for him in an industry he created. A fitting epitaph by James Agee in *The Nation* analyzed the key to Griffith's genius: "he was a great primitive poet, a man capable, as only great and primitive artists can be, of intuitively perceiving and perfecting the tremendous magical images that underlie the memory and imagination of entire peoples." Griffith's own choice of epithet might have been: "Above all... I am trying to make you see." About Griffith's epic masterpiece Agee wrote:

This was the one time in movie history that a man of great ability worked freely, in an unspoiled medium, for an unspoiled audience, on a majestic theme which involved all that he was; and brought to it, besides his abilities as an inventor and artist, absolute passion, pity, courage, and honesty. *The Birth of a Nation* is equal with Brady's photographs, Lincoln's speeches, Whitman's war poems; for all its imperfections and absurdities it is equal, in fact, to the best work that has been done in this country. And among moving pictures it is alone, not necessarily as "the greatest" — whatever that means — but as the one great, epic, tragic film.

It was the one film to speak for a bygone age.

Griffith and the early filmmakers had much in common with the nineteenth-century American mystical poets. Mysticism — or "transcendental idealism," as Emerson called it — was a protest against the lack of belief in the Christian world, thus a major witness to the hypocrisy of the Victorian standards of morality.

Nineteenth-century mysticism is rather suspect. The academic slogans of the Naturalists and the Humanists a few decades ago preferred to tag Ralph Waldo Emerson (1803-1882) as a philosopher-essayist instead of a preacher in search of a pulpit. With him they bypassed or minimized the tradition of the mystical poet from 1850 to the turn of the century: from Walt Whitman (1819-1892) and Emily Dickinson (1830-1886) down to T. S. Eliot, from Emerson to William James's "Pragmatism and Religion" on the one side to Vachel Lindsay's troubadour (the forerunner of the folk singer) on the other. From Lindsay to Griffith, as already noted, is but a short jump. Emerson and Whitman are the only American poets mentioned in Lindsay's "Litany of Heroes," while "in the photoplay world, as I understand it, D. W. Griffith is the king-figure." Griffith's *Intolerance*, as the central motif indicates, is dedicated to Whitman.

Critics are reevaluating Emerson today, aware that he developed his religious idealism out of a loss of faith in traditional, Puritan Christianity. They recognize that he was committed, in the name of a deeper and truer religion, to making life meaningful once again, believing that revelation was, and is, continuous and universal. It was only a question of perceiving God, of finding him in experience, of learning how to look for him. Using vision as the key to all experience, Emerson developed his own method of transcendence through sharpened consciousness and expanded sensitivity to nature as an affirmative way to God. His idea of the continuous process of revelation is reflected in the Puritan psalm book he turned to for guidance: "O taste and see, the Lord is good." At the deepest level of motivation, American critic Hyatt H. Waggoner points out, Emerson's thought was not philosophic but religious.

The affirmative way to transcendental idealism differs radically from the negation practised by the medieval Western mystic, withdrawing from the world into the self to proclaim the goodness of God. He simply states that the *true* poet *is* a mystic, that he can find his "way up" to union with God by negating the superficial self and opening his humanity to the "affirmation of images." Moreover, the poet-mystic was not bound by the religious traditions and beliefs of the past, but shared in the communion of all mystics, past and present, East and West. Further, there were no rules or practices to reach this level of mysticism: one had to learn to value the authentic response to sensory experience and become a seeker after the light.

Walt Whitman was the first and the greatest of the religious poets to follow in Emerson's footsteps, insofar as his poetry can best be understood if taken as religious. The humanist critic R. P. Blackmur concedes the same religious basis to the poetry of Dickinson, Frost, Eliot, Stevens and Lowell, but Waggoner would extend the assertion to embrace the prophetic nature of all that is best and representative in American poetry. Whitman's "Song of Myself," arguably *the* American poem, is a direct translation of Emersonian thought, recognized and praised by Emerson himself. It is often cited as an epic poem; Waggoner contends it is mystical in the preacher's transcendental manner, praising the goodness of the created world from the start; to contend it is nothing more than an expression of secular humanism or a form of inverted medieval mysticism is to skirt the issue. Emerson did not believe mysticism ended with the Middle Ages or was only confined to Christianity, and Whitman was not prepared to rule the erotic out of the mystical experience. "Song of Myself" is both mystical and erotic, in which the author opens his humanity to the fullest in taking the plunge to the depths of his experience to reveal all. By piercing to the truth of the self, the poet-mystic turned the weakness of his nature into a source of strength and faith. Thoreau characterized the poem as "very brave and very American."

Between Walt Whitman, the archetypal American poet, and D. W. Griffith, the archetypal Americal film director, there existed a mystical communion in the Emersonian sense. As Whitman unlocked the doors to the self to lay himself open to scorn and ridicule, so Griffith sought in *The Birth of a Nation* to reveal his personal feelings and attitudes. As Whitman was brave enough to test the validity of his experience by pushing its truth to the point of absurdity, so Griffith placed honesty before all other virtues in telling the truth as he knew it. And as Whitman transformed his own passion and love into strength and faith of a higher order, so Griffith's own passion and pity supported the inner strength and integrity of the film's theme. Furthermore, to his lasting credit, Griffith never deviated from the truth of his vision in the uproar that followed this revelation of honesty.

His justification lies not only in the strong probability that *The Birth of a Nation* has been seen by more people than any other motion picture. This film has also served as a model, if not an inspiration, for the world's great filmmakers.

IV. THE IMPORTANCE OF CHAPLIN

R. J. Broadbent in *A History of Pantomime* describes the most popular of all the harlequins: "His costume consisted of a jacket fastened in front with loose ribbons, and pantaloons of wide dimensions, patched with various coloured pieces of cloth sewn on in any fashion." Through the magic of Chaplin's *The Rink* (Charlie impersonates a waiter) the antics of Arlechino can readily be imagined.

Italy is the mother and the nurse of the harlequin race, stemming from the *Lazzi* and improvised comedies at their zenith at the close of the seventeenth century down to the Giorgio Strehler production of Goldoni's *The Servant of Two Masters* at the Piccolo Theatre in Milan. Both the *Lazzi*, comical by-play of gesture and action to add to the effectiveness of a scene in progress, and the improvised comedies had their roots in satirical Greek drama and the *Fabulae Atellanae* (derived from the town of Atella) of early Roman entertainment, in which the whole gamut of emotions was run through for large audiences. The style was mainly burlesque, the actor's gestures corresponding with the sense of words, but the harlequins of the Italian theatre under the reforming hand of Goldoni and the character of the great harlequin Sacchi possessed lively and brilliant imaginations in an art form imbued with constant freshness and unexpected twists. The harlequin gradually shifted from a buffoon into a wit, then a moralist and a philosopher (roughly the apotheosis of Chaplin himself), ending in the creation of a complete national character representing an age and a people. Harlequins dined at the tables of kings in France and Italy of the seventeenth and eighteenth centuries, invented such legendary characters as "Scaramouch" and "Pierrot" (often created and acted by literary men), and formed the inspiration for Molière's *Médecin malgré lui* and *L'Avare*. The characters of

Italian pantomime became so numerous that every village had its own harlequin favorite, while men of genius became the votaries of the harlequin.

The Carné-Prévert evocation of the actor and the mime of nine-teenth-century French theatre in *The Children of Paradise* (1945) brings us closer to the movie age; it also underlined the great loss of the silent pantomimist's contribution to cinema since the coming of sound. In the Belle Epoque the acrobats and pantomime artists at the Folies-Bergère were suddenly in great demand at newly estab-lished movie studios, as more "life" and less "reality" was needed on the screen. The first to achieve fame seems to be André Deed, who supplemented his Folies earnings by appearing in the films of Méliès in 1904. Lured to Pathé soon after, he contributed to the development of the famous French chase and slapstick films under directors Ferdinand Zecca, Louis J. Gasnier (who later directed *The Perils of Pauline* serials in America), Lucien Nonguet, Georges Monca, Albert Capellani and René Leprince. At the height of his fame in 1907-08 he was known around the world under such sobriquets as Boireau, Cretinetti, Bilboquet, Gribouille and Foolshead, depending on which country his films were being shown in. The British Film Institute catalogue lists a typical Deed production: *Foolshead, Architect's Apprentice* (1908), directed by Gasnier, a one-reeler in which the clumsy hero makes a mess of things in helping to build a house. Twenty years later, Laurel and Hardy were reworking the same gags in *The Finishing Touch* (1928).

When André Deed (1874-1935) quarrelled with Pathé over money and left for Italy to make films, he was already outdistanced by the lesser acrobatic and mime skills but greater artistic inventiveness of Max Linder (1882-1925). Linder was a theatre actor in melodramas and farces as well as a nightclub entertainer, when in 1905 he showed up at the Pathé studio to earn extra money during the daytime hours. With Louis Gasnier's help (a theatre acquaintance who directed his first films at Pathé), he quickly learned cinema's repertoire of tricks (speeded-up chases, reverse action, invisible strings) and began intel-ligently to build on the gags provided by the Deed comedies. Two years later he was so fascinated with the possibilities of cinema he quit the theatre altogether, and he scored his first big success in *The Skater's Debut* (1907) (a Deed re-make that was the forerunner of Chaplin's *The Rink*). His major contribution thereafter to the young art form was to take a single situation or idea, set it solidly in the public's imagination, and build gag after gag on it for the entire length of the film. He was also the first to impersonate a single, unvarying character, trying a bellboy, a railway conductor and a near-sighted man among others before hitting upon the role of a dapper man-about-town. A moustache, a cane and neat tailoring were Linder's trademarks. By 1907 he was directing his own films, on his way to becoming the first international star.

Linder contributed to the cinema world a style of "restraint" in 1907. He argued that for a comedian on the screen to be successful he must think more; accordingly, he subordinated chases and slap-stick to a carefully planned gesture or expression. An example of his technique is *The Would-Be Juggler* (1908), directed by Linder, in which he plays a gentleman alcoholic visiting a vaudeville show featuring a juggler on stage. Max's behavior gets him thrown out, whereupon he sets out on a series of misguided juggling acts of his own, building one gag on another. Another, *Max, Victim of Quin-quina* (1911), is one of the best of Linder's Pathé comedies. The gag line is constructed on misunderstanding. Max, again getting drunk on a doctor's prescription, unwittingly provokes duels among the nobility as his flirtations with girls and petty quarrels get him deeper into trouble. At the end of the film a number of mistaken-identity duels take place as the result of Max having passed on an insulting card to another person, while he himself is being blissfully comforted by a general's wife. Between 1907 and 1914, during the height of Linder's fame, he made 360 comedies: most of the originals are lost, but the "copies" are the stable gags of comedians a decade later in the Golden Age of Comedy.

At the opening of the First World War Linder was internationally famous, earning $85,000 a year from Pathé and again as much from world tours. Dropping everything he patriotically entered the war as a private, was wounded on the front (the German troops mourned as much as the French), and suffered the first of a series of breakdowns. He was never the same again, despite brief success in America at the beginning of the 1920s. Obsessed with the idea of death, he committed suicide with his young wife in 1925.

Linder's experiments at the Pathé studio are the root of inventive film comedy. His best pupil was Charlie Chaplin, who paid him respect by imitating his frock coat, silk hat and moustache in his first film, *Making a Living* (1914) (the year Max interrupted his career to join the army). But his direct heir was not Chaplin so much as Mack Sennett. They were both masters of the "art" of slapstick: namely, the refinements, the freshness, and the unexpected twists to turn plain buffoonery into subtle wit. Linder described his approach to slapstick in 1916:

I prefer the subtle, but it is a mistake to say I do not use slapstick. I do not make it the object, I do not force it, but I use it when it comes naturally. For slapstick to bring laughter there must be sudden action, a quick turn of events, something unexpected.

Sennett, in a 1959 interview, said practically the same thing:

Comedians must think funny and feel funny in order to be funny. The key is comic motion, which is something like lightning. You see it, but you don't hear the thunder until seconds later. Take W.C. Fields. Bill would do his routine up to the punch-line but would seldom speak the topper itself. Instead, he'd pantomime it. That's comic motion. A wise guy once asked me, "What exactly did you have to know to be a good Keystone Cop?" I said, "You have to understand comic motion." He said, "You mean, make funny faces?" He was standing near a pool, so I pushed him in. When he came up I told him, "That's comic motion."

Whether or not either of them knew where his inspiration came from is not important. James Agee rightly credits the tradition itself:

(Sennett) took his comics out of music halls, burlesque, vaudeville, circuses and limbo, and through them he tapped in on that great pipeline of horsing and miming which runs back unbroken through the fairs of the Middle Ages at least to ancient Greece. He added all that he himself had learned about the large and spurious gesture, the late decadence of the Grand Manner, as a stage-struck boy in East Berlin, Connecticut and as a frustrated opera singer and actor. The only thing he claims to have invented is the pie in the face, and he insists, "Anyone who tells you he has discovered something new is a fool or a liar or both."

Sennett was twenty-two years old when he went to New York to try out for the Metropolitan Opera, but ended up instead doing routines in burlesque shows and wedding choruses; from 1902 until he joined the young Biograph studio in 1908 (a few months after Griffith) he never got beyond "extra" work on the legitimate stage. Biograph then was not especially known for its comedies, but Sennett quickly saw his chance to star in and direct his own brand of slapstick by imitating the French one-reelers and studying Griffith's technical advances. Mrs. D. W. (Linda) Griffith in *When the Movies Were Young* notes the Linder influence in *Father Gets in the Game* (1908) and *The Curtain Pole* (1909), in which Sennett plays the role of a Frenchman in slapstick comedy. He performed in 23 films in 1908, seven of them comedies, followed by roles in 58 dramas and 35 comedies in 1909 (according to Kemp Niver's cataloguing of the paper prints registered at the Library of Congress). In 1910 he was one of Griffith's principal assistants, writing and acting in as many comedies as dramas, but he realized he was incapable of imitating the subtleties of Linder's art. He was Griffith's director of the second unit in 1911 (when Frank Powell, later the discoverer of Theda Bara, fell ill), starting with a tale of two hoboes, *Comrades*; it was an instant success. That year Sennett directed 51 comedies and an additional 44 in the first eight months of 1912, his popularity rising to rival Griffith's (possibly earning more money at the box office). Suffering under Biograph's stringent policies Sennett signed a contract in January 1912 with Kessel and Bauman to set up the Keystone Company, and he used his last remaining months at Biograph in a frenzied effort to master all the ropes of cinematic comedy. He made a star out of Mabel Normand, whose trim figure and fun-loving antics were put to good use in *The Diving Girl* (1911) (she was the first Sennett bathing girl) and whose other assets in *Oh, Those Eyes* (1912) charmed a public longing to learn her name. He also knew the value of speeded-up chases, runaway fire engines and frantic cops (they first appeared in Biograph's *The Would-Be Shriner* in 1912), as well as those masterly conceived absurd touches that could turn laughter into a belly ache.

The best of Biograph's comic talent — Mabel Normand, Ford Sterling, Fred Mace — joined Sennett at the Keystone studio in August, 1912; in less than a year they were on the top of the cinema world. By 1915 his "fun factory" was world famous for custard pies, pretty girls, exploding buildings, careening cars, flattened pedestrians and the most motley-looking collection of madcap cops imaginable. To these were added the physical abnormalities and inspired by-play of Ben Turpin, Roscoe "Fatty" Arbuckle, Louise Fazenda, Mack Swain, and Chester Conklin, to name but a few, who flocked to Sennett in those rich, formative years of comedy between 1912 and 1915. Seven directors were working at an unbelievably torrid pace to meet the demands of distributors and a fickle California sunshine at the end of 1913. In 1914 an unknown English pantomime artist arrived at the studio to replace a departing Ford Sterling, made 35 films non-stop (directing his own after the twelfth), and could command a salary elsewhere at $1,250 a week. But even minus the name of Charlie Chaplin in 1915, Sennett's roster of stars reads like a Who's Who in screen comedy. In the decade to follow nearly all the great silent comedians — Chaplin, Keaton, Langdon, Lloyd, Normand, Fields — and a score of others — directors Capra, McCarey and Stevens and actors Wallace Beery, Gloria Swanson and Marie Dressler, were to owe Sennett more than he owed them, whether they were directly associated with him or not. And what he taught them was that nothing, absolutely nothing, was sacred. Not even the movies.

Charles Spencer Chaplin was the son of a third-rate English music-hall balladeer team, who at the age of six took his mother's place singing when she was ill. She was often ill, in and out of mental asylums; his father died of drunkenness before he had the chance to go to school. He and his half-brother, Sidney, lived in a poorhouse for a while, until he took to the music halls with dreams of becoming an actor. He got as far as Fred Karno's pantomime troupe, which at least offered a three-year world tour and the chance to visit America. There, between 1910 and 1913, he was seen in his role of a drunken "swell" in "A Night in an English Music Hall," and Adam Kessel hired him to work for Sennett at the Keystone studio in California.

Chaplin's year with Sennett was the best schooling he could have asked for: he soon outdistanced the absurd slapstick routines of Keystone, the rough cutting techniques carried over from Griffith's Biograph days and the subtleties of Max Linder's intellectual gags. He perceived the irritation of too much slapstick and motion; almost from the beginning he leaned toward Linder's visual restraint and expression for its own sake. By his fourth film, *Between Showers* (1914), forty-five prints were being ordered by distributors, double the number for the average Keystone: Sennett could hardly resist Chaplin's growing demands to direct his own films.

The figure of The Tramp appeared in rough form in the early Sennetts. Legend has it that Chaplin drafted the moustache and cane from Linder's Dandy, the oversized shoes from Ford Sterling, the baggy pants from Fatty Arbuckle, and the tight-ribbed coat from the music-hall routine. Much more to the truth is that he drew it out of his natural intuition as a pantomimist; the costume (and everything about the tramp) was an outer expression of himself.

That costume helps me to express my conception of the average man, of almost any man, of myself. The derby, too small, is a striving for dignity. The moustache is vanity. The tightly buttoned coat and the stick and his whole manner are a gesture toward gallantry and dash and "front." He is trying to meet the world bravely, to put up a bluff, and he knows that too. He knows it so well that he can laugh at himself and pity himself a little.

As actor and director, he refined the tramp and his gags during a short, fruitful apprenticeship at Keystone (1914), Essanay (1915) and Mutual (1916-1917), the richest gag years in his entire career. One of his best acts was a skating routine, borrowed from Linder, which reached a zenith of grace and clumsiness in *The Rink* (1916). He was then earning $10,000 a week, while sinking every ounce of his energy into perfecting his craft. Imitators sprang up in his wake: the mathematical Harold Lloyd in the "Lonesome Luke" series (1915-1918), reversing Charlie's costume; the clever Billy West, whose amateurish copying burned him out in 1918 as Chaplin's gags grew subtler and more difficult to grasp. After his Mutual days, Charlie found himself visited by the famous and hailed by the world's intellects as a genius. Not since Pierrot had a harlequin so many votaries.

In Chaplin's next series for First National (1918-1922), a contract that was to run originally for eighteen months, he acted as his own producer with the stipulation that he would later have complete control over the films after their commercial run. The films are filled with deep, personal, tragic memories, both past and present (Chaplin's marriage to and divorce from Mildred Harris, his first wife, was on the front pages of newspapers), and perhaps for this reason he hesitated later to re-release them. Yet they contain two or three of his first major masterpieces, and there is little doubt that he was greatly influenced by a number of scenes in Griffith's *The Birth of a Nation* (1915) (whose technical artistry had already been handed down through Sennett). Pathos, mood and atmosphere were heightened as he zeroed in on the foibles and strengths of human nature. He planned and executed every important detail of his films from beginning to end, resisting the "factory" atmosphere of Hollywood "formula" pictures. He became the cinema's first great moralist.

The cycle opens with *A Dog's Life* (1918) and closes with *The Pilgrim* (1922), both of which are superb examples of pathos and laughter interlaced with social criticism. In between are *Shoulder Arms* (1918), fantasy and realism amid the horrors of war (it was released before the armistice was signed), and *The Kid* (1921), a far more personal recollection of his wretched childhood in London than *A Dog's Life*. Both *A Dog's Life* and *Shoulder Arms* were greeted with great enthusiasm by the public, but neither matches the genuine pathos and emotional intensity of *The Kid* or the acute powers of observation and mimicry in *The Pilgrim*. *The Pilgrim* is Chaplin's ultimate condemnation of narrow-minded, puritan fundamentalism; it was also condemned in America's rural communities. One scene, the sermon on David and Goliath, is Chaplin's pantomime at its finest, but the whole is a distillation of his art and personality.

Charlie as an escaped convict in stolen minister's clothes arrives in a small Texas town near the border; immediately he is mistaken by the congregation at the railroad station as the visiting preacher. The ladies are stern Carrie Nation champions against alcohol, but the elder is a hypocrite with a flask in his hip pocket. At the church Charlie professionally supervises the collection, eyes the choir nervously, as if it were a court jury, and tries to put off giving the sermon. When he hits by chance on the biblical account of David and Goliath, he pantomimes the text by picking out key phrases. He does it with the sharpness of a music-hall routine. Goliath was very tall (broad gesture), with a big moustache (gesture), and a big sword (gesture); while David was a little guy (small gesture), but with a sling-shot (wind-mill wind-up). Goliath is quickly downed, head off, tossed over Charlie's shoulder and back-kicked away. The "pilgrim" takes his music-hall bows to an icy reception, save for one kid in the audience wildly cheering.

A central characteristic of the film is the absence of the tramp's clothes. It had happened before, but never in a feature film (this was his second, after *The Kid*). The First National period as a whole is a shift away from the limitations of a particular outfit, reaching now for a more rounded, determined personification of the human condition. Whereas Jackie Coogan in *The Kid* was an extension of Chaplin's own personality, now *The Pilgrim* was to assume universal, historical and religious proportions. Charlie was the mythical traveler on a long journey to some sacred place. He was trying to imitate us.

Nowhere is this more evident than in the ritual of Sunday afternoon following the church service. Charlie as the minister is invited to a widow's home for tea as the guest of honor. He tries his best to fit in. He clumsily puts on a show before the widow's daughter. He fends off the attacks of a brat kid, finally getting even with a graceful back-kick. He burns his fingers transporting a hot teapot from the kitchen. He puts icing on a derby hat instead of on the cake it was meant for. He jabs his nose into the same icing at prayer time around the table. When he has to cut the derby-cake, his carving-manners run the gamut from a nervous, delicate stroke to frenzied onslaught. He is defeated at every turn.

Purgatory gives way to redemption in the events of Sunday evening. An old prison buddy shows up, passes himself off as a friend of the minister, and plans to steal the widow's rent money that night. Charlie must guard the treasure and maintain his dual role at the same time. The shyster wins, until Charlie modifies his minister's uniform into a Buffalo Bill disguise to steal the money back in a saloon hold-up. The sheriff grants him his freedom, although Charlie at first doesn't understand why he has been placed on the Mexican border. Finally catching on, he breathes fresh air rapturously — until a shoot-out on the Mexican side sends him straddling the border into the distance at the fade-out. He is the eternal pilgrim on the road of life, alone, defenseless, harried from all sides.

After *The Pilgrim* Chaplin formed his own production company and set out on a personal pilgrimage in search of the dignity of man in modern, industrialized civilization. Chaplin assumed the role of moral propagandist in the tradition of the Greek dramatists. Two other moralists of his day, T. S. Eliot and Bertolt Brecht, were cut from the same mold.

The foreword to *A Woman of Paris* (1923) may be taken as a Chaplin credo:

Humanity is composed not of heroes and villains, but of men and women, and all their passions, both good and bad, have been given them by God. They sin only in blindness, and the ignorant condemn their mistakes, but the wise pity them.

It is the story of an unfaithful wife: not a comedy and not starring himself, but an intimate dramatic piece he wrote and directed for his co-star since Essanay days, Edna Purviance. Ahead of its time, it didn't bow to heavy emotionalism and was relatively free of "selling" a moral message. It drew its tone from Griffith, whom he greatly admired and studied during this period. *The Gold Rush* (1925), one of Chaplin's most enduring comedies, was a parable on man's inordinate lust for money, referring to the Klondike Gold Strike and the Donner tragedy but also aimed at the excesses of Hollywood. *The Circus* (1928), made as his private life was undergoing another upheaval, is his most personal, realistic, truthful and tragic film, loosely constructed around circus lore and the old Victorian melodrama; it's the closest he ever came to a projected film on Christ.

With the coming of sound, Chaplin could have put his stage experience to good use in *City Lights* (1931); he deferred instead to the universal art of pantomime. It was the last film in which he used his powers to the fullest: actor, writer, director, composer. After the Stock Market Crash, we find Chaplin opening the film with the tramp sleeping in the lap of an unveiled statue, under which is inscribed: "To the people of the city we donate this monument: Peace and Prosperity." *Modern Times* (1936) found him drifting into a social and political whirlpool, this time fashioning a universal damnation of industrial de-humanization. The scenes on the monotony of factory labor, done in pantomime, are classic examples of the evolution of his art. Like the best of the harlequins, he is both a moralist and a philosopher. The social messages and deep humanity in *The Great Dictator* (1940), *Monsieur Verdoux* (1947), and *Limelight* (1952), as well as the breadth of these performances, kept him ahead of the critics and movie intelligentsia of the day. But he was losing ground with his devoted public.

In 1952, when Chaplin took his family on a trip to Europe (where his films were better appreciated), he was refused re-entry (he is a British citizen) until he submitted to an examination of his political beliefs and moral character. McCarthyism, the Red Scare and pressure groups had risen against him because of his leftist sympathies, and were ready to pounce when he was out of the country for the European première of *Limelight*. Chaplin was deeply hurt, as his last two films give evidence. Made in England, *A King in New York* (1957), a satire on the American way of life, is timely yet warm, meant to show where his heart is. *A Countess From Hong Kong* (1967), the second film in which he didn't star, is but an echo of his former self. At the 1971 Cannes festival Chaplin was honored by the French government and Hollywood took this as a favorable sign to invite him back for a special Academy Award in April, 1972. The *New York Times* editorialized:

If a nation could collectively blush, the United States had good reason to do so when its officialdom ruled two decades ago that Charles Chaplin could not come back to these shores until he offered proof of his "moral worth." Happily, the guardians of this country's virtue appear to have matured sufficiently not to fear for America's political and moral safety when, on April 4, the creator of the beloved, pathetic and funny tramp returns from his exile. Only drab and limited minds could ever have sought to banish Charlie Chaplin, the genius whose films have helped millions understand the human race by allowing them to laugh and cry over the human condition. A new generation, perhaps tiring of the violence and pretensions of the mod screen, is currently rediscovering the sensitive artistry of the little man in baggy trousers and battered bowler. The honors that await "Charlie" here and in Hollywood may add little to the already firmly established popular if long-delayed victory of art and humor over bureaucratic rigidity.

The *Times* editorial underlined two fundamental truths of Chaplin's art: (1) its moral worth is indisputable, and (2) a new generation could well do with his sense of humor to defeat the pretensions and excesses of modern life.

Critic André Bazin classified Chaplin's art as "anti-sacred":

Religious or not, the sacred is everywhere present in the life of society and not only in the magistrate, the policeman, the priest, but in the ritual associated with eating, with professional relations, and public transportation. It is the way that society retains its cohesion as if within a magnetic field. Unknowingly, every minute of our time we adjust to this framework. But Charlie is of another metal. Not only does he elude its grasp, but the very category of the sacred does not exist for him. Such a thing is, to him, as inconceivable as the color of a pink geranium is to someone born blind.

Bazin defined "sacred" as "the various social aspects of the religious life." In this sense, "Charlie's old films add up to the most formidable anticlerical indictment imaginable of provincial puritan society in the United States." Bazin took pains to point out that Charlie was in no sense guilty of "anticlericalism" — it was "rather what ought to be called a radical a-clericalism."

Today, with the element of play creeping back into religious life and ceremonies, there is a need to reanalyse Chaplin's relationship to traditional Christianity. Chaplin and the silent movie pantomimists bear a close affinity to the clown-Christ figure in Georges Rouault's expressionist paintings, as well as the contagious playfulness of Sister Corita's religious-orientated pop art. The rediscovery of festivity and fantasy, culled out of the deep roots of Christian tradition, has resulted in a kind of religious rebirth in (what Harvey Cox calls) "our secularized, post-Christian era."

Cox, the prophet of playful, religious secularism, underscores the importance of Chaplin in *The Feast of Fools*, his theological essay on festivity and fantasy.

He begins by approaching "Christ the Harlequin" through Paul's words in the First Epistle to the Corinthians: "For the foolishness of God is wiser than men, and the weakness of God is stronger than men." He points out that the symbol of Christ the clown seems eminently right in early Christian history, a judgment which, in the light of satirical Greek drama and the Roman *Fabulae Atellanae*, is quite credible. He sees the clown figure in Christ as a travelling troubadour, a minstrel frequenting dinners and parties, the clown in a circus parade entering Jerusalem, a jester defying custom and scorning priests and kings, and at the end clothed like a mock king and crucified under a sign lampooning his divinity. When Chaplin was making *The Circus*, he once thought of titling it *The Clown* and was speaking at the same time of how he would like to make a film on Christ:

If I could produce a film on the story of Christ, I would show him welcomed with delirious joy by men, women and children; they would throng round him in order to feel his magnetism. Not at all a sad, pious, and stiff person, but a lonely man who has been the most misunderstood of all time.

Instead, Charlie's tramp was a lonely figure amid the overflowing gaiety of circus life: the pathos of his clowning was never more explicitly felt than in *The Circus*. It is one of the most religious films ever made.

Cox uses the tongue-in-cheek, playful *esprit* of Sister Corita Kent's slogan-posters ("He cared enough to send the very best") as an example of "faith as play." He refers to Maurice Béjart's 1967 *Mass for the Present Time* (acclaimed at the Théâtre National Populaire in Paris), in which "liturgy" is described by Béjart himself as "a joke in the middle of a prayer. If you can joke about something very important, you have achieved freedom." Cox summarizes:

Anyone who gives vent to joy, sorrow, or gratitude, or refuses to be bound by the narrow world of facts is really living a prayer. Faith too is more than mindless credulity. Both prayer and faith are really forms of play.

Cox's definition of Christ the harlequin as "the joke in the middle of the prayer" recalls Agee's analysis of Chaplin's genius as "*inflection* — the perfect, changeful shadowing of his physical and emotional attitudes toward the gag." Chaplin was always joking about something very important; indeed, he is the only film comedian in the twentieth century who understood the full scale of emotions well enough to put prayer and faith in the middle of his gags.

Cox's reference to Peter Berger's essay *The Precarious Vision* is relevant:

Berger sees eschatology as the comic element in Christianity. The clown refuses to live inside this present reality. He senses another one. He defies the law of gravity, taunts the policeman, ridicules the other performers. Through him we catch a glimpse of another world impinging on this one, upsetting its rules and practices.

Berger has captured the essence of Mack Sennett's art of slapstick: the cliffside teeterings of automobiles and dangling bodies, the hijinks of the Keystone Cops, the parodies of the false and the pompous. This is also the essence of the best of the animated cartoon today.

Cox's contention that the comic is rooted in faith, that laughter is hope's last weapon, opens the door for theological discussion on the importance of Chaplin. Agee's writings heralded this important dialogue between theologian and clown two decades ago. In an inspired defense of Chaplin's *Monsieur Verdoux*, written for *The Nation* in 1947, the master essayist praised "that anarchic and immortal lily of the field, the tramp, the most humane and most nearly complete among the religious figures our time has evolved; whom for once in his life Chaplin set aside, to give his century its truest portrait of the upright citizen."

V. INSIDE THE MOVIE CATHEDRAL

The Hollywood Dream Cult has its origin in an announcement in 1913 that Mitchell Mark was going to construct a motion picture theatre in the heart of Broadway to accommodate 3,000 people. By 1916, some 21,000 remodelled or new movie theatres were in operation, and a year later the nickelodeon was obsolete. The big movie theatre became the symbol of Main Street, America. The American movie palaces of the 1920s grew to enormous size, acting as the models from which British and European designers drew their inspiration. Within a decade of Mark's announcement, Hollywood's manufactured dreams were known around the world.

By 1914 the feature film was established. The General Film Company, which had pinned its destiny to the short film, was virtually wiped out and succeeded by huge production companies established overnight in Hollywood. In 1916 Charlie Chaplin and Mary Pickford were commanding salaries over $10,000 a week, which in turn made them greater stars and brought greater salaries. Letters poured in daily to movie magazines from love-crazed viewers, indicating a keen emotional involvement with the stars on and off the screen. It was obvious a cult of worship had arisen overnight. Jacobs comments:

By 1918 the movies were dispensing a new philosophy of life, new standards of morals and manners. The reaction against nineteenth-century attitudes mounted steadily during the war years, and the movies supported it. As an escape medium, as a stimulant to daydreaming, as a provider of vicarious experiences, movies had proved unsurpassed.

The change came quickly with the war years, but it was already evident in the public's reaction to a nostalgic past rapidly receding before the age of the machine and the revolution in communication.

Woodrow Wilson's second term in office (1916-1920) merely showed how drastic this change had become. In 1916 he was warmly respected in America for his liberal fairness; two years later, when he went to the Paris Peace Conference with the trust of the people in his pocket, his hopes were dashed. Trying to carry the torch to the people, he found instead an apathetic nation bent on political isolationism. In 1920 he was defeated by a small-town politician in a Republican landslide securing 60 percent of the vote.

The movies told very much the same story. When Thomas Ince made *Civilization* (1916), the country was not yet at war and the film was conceived as a salute to Wilsonian Pacifism. Made right in tune with Wilson's campaign motto of 1915, "He Kept Us Out of the War," it featured a submarine hero refusing to fire a torpedo at a passenger ship. The pacifist is thrown into prison for advocating peace, but Christ enters his body and eventually triumphs: a very ambitious production for Ince and a notable success. On the heels of *Civilization* later in the year came D. W. Griffith's *Intolerance* (1916), conceived in the glow of pacifism but released during the trumpets of war; it was a colossal failure and Griffith was never fully to recover from the loss. A few months later came Cecil B. DeMille's *Joan the Woman* (1917), with its panoramic war scenes and naked thirst for the glories of the battlefield; it was a brilliant anticipation of public taste.

Warren G. Harding's "Return to Normalcy" campaign in 1920 also reflected the concern of the wide rural population, in danger for the first time of becoming a minority. Waves of immigrants populated the large industrial cities, mostly Catholics, Jews and Orthodox from Eastern and Southern Europe: America's traditional Protestant base was suddenly in danger. "We have become strangers in the land of our fathers," complained the Ku Klux Klan, recruiting five million members by 1922. A form of political hysteria reigned until the middle of the 1920s, a time of extremist political movements and a variety of extremist political figures. To a great extent, the United States succumbed to a wave of repressive, nationalist, puritanical and moralist hysteria, growing out of the fear of many groups that radical social and industrial change was destroying the fabric of old America.

The feature film reached out to catch this longing for a nostalgic past in the growing popularity of the Western and such "small-town masterpieces" as Henry King's *Tol'able David* (1921). Themes on the West took hold with the Broncho Billy Anderson series in 1908 for Essanay and Jacobs contends that by 1909 the Western "was a forceful expression of democratic feeling and moral standards — more forceful, perhaps, than the deliberate morality dramas." Ince, one of Hollywood's first creative producers, turned cowboy-actor William S. Hart loose in 1914 to document the frontier's fading past; for a decade his true pictures of the West as it really was succeeded in magnifying the reality into a myth that has endured very nearly to the present. (Hart's career spans the halcyon days of "Inceville," the prototype of the Hollywood movie lot, turning out in fast succession action-packed narratives based on a predetermined movie script and standard production techniques.)

Audiences in big cities also longed for romance and intrigue, the luridness of Theda Bara in *Cleopatra* (1917), the daring exposure of sex in DeMille's *Male and Female* (1919), the picture of an exuberant America on the move in Douglas Fairbanks films, the excitement of underworld, gangster, travel and monster films, and the "sweetheart" every family wanted to call its own, Mary Pickford. Out of these elements grew the movie cathedral and the Hollywood Dream Cult.

The rise of the movie palace in American cities between 1910 and 1920 was nothing short of phenomenal. But as it is best known and remembered today, it was the invention of practically one man: S. L. "Roxy" Rothafel, theatre manager, interior decorator, public relations man and impressario. When one of the first "luxury" theatres, the Regent, went up in New York's Harlem in 1913, it was considered an extravagant folly by a dreaming architect, Thomas W. Lamb. Nobody came — until "Roxy" took over. The Regent was turned into a showplace at prices people could afford, decorations and side attractions for steady customers were added — and the Regent overnight was the talk of the town. When Lamb designed a second luxury theatre in the middle of Manhattan, Mitchell Mark's Strand, the following year, Rothafel was invited in to manage it. Lamb's designs were immediately in demand across the country; by 1921 the architect himself had erected over 300 theatres.

His chief rival, Dennis Sharp writes in *The Picture Palace*, was John Eberson. Lamb was born in Scotland, Eberson was trained in Vienna and Dresden; their styles were distinctly different:

Basically there were two schools of thought about movie buildings in the States: one advocated the use of neo-Classical form and motifs and was known as the "hard-top" school, the other advocated a more experimental type of structure where a completely artificial environment could be created and was known as the "atmospheric" school. Thomas W. Lamb was the doyen of the first group of designers and was firmly rooted in the *Beaux-Arts* tradition. John Eberson inspired the more bizarre designs of the atmospherics. In between there were the designers who would conceive their buildings as the mood took them or the promoter dictated.

In general, Lamb's constructions combined the classical manner on the outside with Empire decorations on the inside (murals, chandeliers, staircases, draperies, panels), while Eberson's meant exotic environments, lighting effects, decorative gimmicks and painted blue ceilings ("a therapeutic value, soothing the nerves and calming perturbing thoughts"). Lamb's hallmark was class and taste; Eberson's was the romantic and the exotic. Throughout the silent era of the 1920s the shift was gradually in Eberson's direction, particularly in crowded, "Catholic" neighborhoods where the architecture had a baroque, churchy effect to contrast with its exotic excesses.

Eberson built his first atmospheric theatre in Houston, Texas, in 1923, which literally took the public's breath away with its sky-blue ceiling. His designs ranged from a sacred shrine in Persia to the garden of the Tuileries, as he cast every exotic motif known into a fitting design. He wrote:

We visualize and dream a magnificent amphitheatre under a glorious moonlit sky in an Italian garden, in a Persian court, in a Spanish patio, or in a mystic Egyptian temple-yard, all canopied by a soft moonlit sky.

Sidney Patrick Grauman, proprietor of the famous Egyptian and Chinese theatres in Hollywood, dictated the construction of his palaces. For his Egyptian theatre erected in 1922, he introduced a huge organ overlooking the stage guarded by two gold sphinx; Egyptian-garbed ladies-in-waiting attended the customers; at premières guards in Egyptian attire walked the lighted parapets outside; the Hollywood Symphony Orchestra performed twice a day; he provided a nursery with attendants and story-tellers. Not satisfied, and perhaps fearing competition, Grauman built the Chinese Theatre in 1927. Beth Day's description in *This Was Hollywood*:

Ever since his San Francisco days Grauman had cherished a fondness for Chinese motif, and his new theatre was decorated with *objets d'art*, draperies, and statues imported from the Orient. The rugs were so thick "you sank to your knees."

Full-scale wax figures in Oriental costume, commissioned from an artist in San Francisco, turned out so lifelike that tourists often pinched them to see if they were real. Handsome Oriental divans framed the proscenium until it was found necessary to remove them in order to discourage the heavy traffic of young lovers who were discovered there when the lights came on after each performance.

Rothafel's "Roxy" opened in New York in 1927: another "in-betweener," its architecture set a precedent comparable to the opulence of Garnier's Paris Opera. With a seating capacity of over 6,000 and a rotunda to rival Penn Station's, it combined the lavishness of a royal palace with the equipment of a luxury liner — all at prices the poor could afford on a night out. Paul Morand's description in *New York*:

As for the Roxy, that surpasses the impossible. Find a way through those dense crowds queued up there all day long; pass the tall goldlaced ushers, at once door-keepers and custodians of order; enter this Temple of Solomon. The overheated air is unbearable, the din of the mechanical orchestra, which one failure in the electricity could bring to a standstill, is merciless — amid palm-trees and gigantic ferns one moves forward into the Mexican palace of some Spanish governor whom the tropics have turned stark mad. The walls are of a reddish rough-cast, treated with a liquid to give a semblance of age, and the brazen doors of the Ark of the Covenant open into a hall with golden cupolas, in old style, and a ceiling with storied panels. Satan has hung this disused sanctuary with scarlet velvet; a nightmare light falls from bowls of imitation alabaster, from yellow glass lanterns, from branching ritual candlesticks; the organ pipes, lit from underneath by greenish lights, make one think of a cathedral under the waves, and in the walls are niches awaiting sinful bishops. I find a seat in a deep, soft fauteuil, from which for two hours I witness giant kisses on mouths like the crevasses of the Grand Canyon, embraces of titans, a whole propaganda of the flesh which maddens, without satisfying, these violent American temperaments. It is more than a Black Mass; it is a profanation of everything — of music, of art, of love, of colours. I vow I had there a complete vision of the end of the world. I saw Broadway suddenly as one vast Roxy, one of those unsubstantial treasures, one of those joy-baited traps, one of those fleeting and illusory gifts woven by the spells of wicked magicians.

Lamb's design for the Fox Theatre in San Francisco, movie tycoon William Fox's "shrine to the world" erected in 1929, was the last of the great " fabulous and foolish" movie cathedrals of the 1920s. Costing $5 million to construct and seating 5,000 people, it was to display America's growth and wealth as well as serve as a symbol of Fox's movie empire. Three years later Fox was bankrupt and the theatre was closed.

Romanticism was the packaged goods of the movie cathedral from the silent era to television. Indirectly, it got a big boost in 1909 when D. W. Griffith prevailed on his cameraman, Billy Bitzer, to create a "profile portrait effect" for *Edgar Allan Poe* (based on "The Raven"). It was referred to in the trade as Biograph's "Rembrandt lighting," which inspired the "soft-focus" style popular in romance stories. Rex Ingram, who started directing in 1916, applied these techniques to the cool, reserved beauty of Alice Terry. Female scriptwriters with rich imaginations were employed as special assistants to directors: Mary Pickford scripted some of Griffith's films; Anita Loos was a writing prodigy at the age of 15; Jeanne Macpherson became the chief scriptwriter of Cecil B. DeMille's films; and June Mathis helped discover Rudolph Valentino.

Mathis had seen Valentino in villain roles and persuaded the Metro Studio to star him as the romantic lead in Ingram's *The Four Horsemen of the Apocalypse* (1921); the Latin Lover immediately caught the imagination of the public. A good deal of Valentino's charm can be traced to Ingram and the "soft-focus" perfected by his cameraman, John F. Seitz. Ingram described the effect this way:

It is the modelling obtained by a judicious arrangement of lighting and shade that enables us to give something of a stereoscopic quality to the soft, mellow-tone closeups that take the place of the human voice on the screen and help to make audiences intimately acquainted with the characters.

Lighting also furthered Greta Garbo's success. Cameraman William Daniels at M-G-M devised the "Garbo look" — arched eyebrows, finely etched bone structure, pale skin, cool complexion, illuminated face. Her favorite director was Clarence Brown, who caught her presence as a sensual, distant goddess, a mixture of wickedness and ethereal beauty, to which she added her rare sensitivity as an actress. Kenneth Tynan measured her image on the screen:

Neither Hepburn nor Dietrich could have played Garbo's scenes with her son in *Anna Karenina*; something predatory in them would have forbidden such selfless maternal raptures. Garbo alone can be intoxicated by innocence. She turns her coevals into her children, taking them under her wing like a great, sailing swan. Her love is thus larger than Hepburn's or Dietrich's, which does not extend beyond the immediately desired object. It was Alistair Cooke who pointed out that in her films she seemed to see life in reverse and, because she was aware of the fate in store for them, offered the shelter of her sympathy to all around her.

Garbo's reign as the screen's chief goddess began with Brown's *The Flesh and the Devil* (1927). Then twenty-two and already a veteran of four films, her passionate love scenes with John Gilbert in some far-off Sudermann landscape struck hidden chords for viewers around the world. The sanctity of a childhood blood-oath between rivals Gilbert and Lars Hanson, the sacred element in the film, and the war raging inside her (her sensuality reached a height in the church scene, in which she sips communion wine from the same spot on the chalice Gilbert's lips touched) results in a sacrificial gesture to protect the innocents about her. It was the first of four films in which Gilbert co-starred, the first of seven directed by Clarence Brown, and the first of nineteen photographed by William Daniels. Garbo maintained her magnetism with movie audiences up to the day she retired in the early 1940s.

The star system was at the center of the Hollywood Dream Cult: so long as it worked, Hollywood maintained its prestige. Carl Laemmle was the first producer to reveal a star's name, when Florence Lawrence, the "Biograph girl," became the "Imp girl" in 1908. He claimed that ninety percent of his customers went to the movies to see a star and the others accompanied them there. By 1925, at the death of Valentino, crazed females accompanied their idol to the grave; it verged on a national tragedy. The tragic death in 1962 of Marilyn Monroe signalled the death of the Dream Cult, she herself being its sacrificial offering. It was a loss from which Hollywood never recovered.

The care and feeding of a star took special pains. Elinor Glyn, a sensational novelist in England's Edwardian period, came to Hollywood in the early 1920s to write scripts and adapt her pre-1914 novels on European aristocracy (as viewed by servant girls); she was soon referred to in the trade as the "madame" of the cult. She invented afternoon teas, discovered IT, lent a hand to the careers of Gloria Swanson and Clara Bow, and supervised every detail of her mythical, aristocratic, romantic "Ruritania" productions. For the star Madame Glyn was second in importance only to the movie "mogul."

Men of minute stature (about five foot four) and mostly of Jewish origin (the orthodox Jewish immigrants worked their way to the top of the movie industry like the Irish in city politics and the Italians in the Mafia), the moguls were driven to excesses of patriotic fervor by the wave of xenophobia sweeping across America after the 1920 census showed the rural Anglo-Saxon Protestant in the minority. The most colorful and richest of the moguls was Louis B. Mayer: Russian immigrant, head of M-G-M, champion of family entertainment, he had a religious commitment to motherhood and meant every word of "I will have no whores in my pictures." In 1942 he commanded one of the highest salaries in America.

The high priest of the day and a key figure in the Hollywood Dream Cult was Cecil B. DeMille.

A latter-day Victorian playwright raised in the tradition of David Belasco, DeMille understood the cinema's commercial potential in blending good and evil in the typical melodrama. Attentive to the paradoxes of the age, he recognized the importance of the New Morality in the 1920s. A nation troubled by the aftermath of a great war, labor unrest, Prohibition and the beginnings of the "Red Scare" was seeking luxury and ease, and was not likely to be scandalized by flaunted laws, religious hypocrisy, or messy politics. DeMille intuitively sensed public taste; beyond this he was an excellent light-comedy director who would sacrifice any illusion for clarity, and from Belasco he had learned continuity and construction. He had no desire to aspire to Griffith's powers of poetry and vision, but contented himself with audience reactions during "sneak" previews of his latest film; if the public reacted differently than expected, he immediately made readjustments. Lastly, he appears to have been a genuinely religious man, but with his own moral code to back up everything on the screen. (His father was a playwright and lay minister, and the Bible played an important role in the DeMille household: he could quote chapter and verse to fit any occasion on the movie set.)

The measure of the man's worth was his ability to rework the same formulas for fifty years with astonishing success. His social comedies, beginning with *Male and Female* (1919), always began with a biblical motif and a bathtub in the first reel. The biblical spectacles had to have an orgy to be righteously condemned, and this usually took up the great middle of his productions. His films on Americana were glamorous adventure stories full of mawkish sentimentality and spicy nuance. His formulas were simple: everything good contains a fatal flaw to be corrected before real happiness is achieved — which of course permitted a small indiscretion, lasting nearly the length of the film, before the flaw could be corrected. His indiscretions, his debauches, his bathtubs were the best in the business: they kept him on top until sound came in and religious censorship bodies prevented the putting of words to images. Undeterred, he rewrote history books, advanced the spectacle in the realm of the wide-screen and drive-in theatre, and topped all his achievements by giving God a "voice"! Scriptwriter Art Arthur recalls:

At the first New York screening of *The Ten Commandments* at the Criterion we were both disturbed by the same thing: strange-clicking noises in the sound during the "voice of God" scene. We both wondered if they were on the film's sound track, but then realized the clicks were coming from the audience, not coming from the screen. As the emotional impact of the "Voice of God" scene took effect many a woman sought her handkerchief, and the clicking sounds were the snaps of opening purses.

DeMille's first *The Ten Commandments* was made in 1923, cost an unheard-of million and a half dollars, but returned a small fortune. He had had a hunch it would work since his success with a scantily covered opera singer, Geraldine Farrar, in *Joan the Woman* (1917), but his backers were hesitant: they recalled the disaster of the last "bathrobe epic," D. W. Griffith's *Intolerance* (1916), costing two million dollars. A contest run in a Los Angeles newspaper, to discover which religious theme the public preferred, convinced DeMille to go ahead. Following a usual custom in the silent era, he set the biblical story inside a modern frame for the proper moral perspective and let his orgy run its natural course. It made enough money to free DeMille to set up his own production company — and, following his example, M-G-M immediately invested six million dollars in *Ben Hur* (1926).

For his "authentic" Life of Christ, DeMille hired Bruce Barton, author of the 1925 best-seller *The Man Nobody Knows* (linking Christianity with Big Business), as one of his religious advisors (along with a minister, a priest and a rabbi). *The King of Kings* (1927) opened in the palace of courtesan Mary Magdalen, angry over the loss of her boyfriend Judas to a passing preacher. DeMille supplied no chapter and verse for this scene and others to follow, and, try as he might, he couldn't find a way to exonerate the Jews, but the film was still a success. The film opened Grauman's new Chinese Theatre in May, 1927, running non-stop to a capacity house for five-and-a-half months.

The excesses of DeMille's debauchery reached a climax at the beginning of the 1930s in one of his best all-round films, *The Sign of the Cross* (1932). Freely adapted from Wilson Barrett's melodrama on Pagans and Christians in Nero's Rome, but with a greater helping of sex and sadism than usual, it aroused the ire of the Catholic Church and conservative religious bodies in America. The Hays Office, formed in 1922 by the Motion Picture Producers and Directors of America (MPPDA) to stop excesses among the member companies, had formally adopted a production code of ethics in 1930 drawn up by Catholic layman Martin Quigley and Jesuit Daniel Lord; only token attention was paid it. Quigley and Lord took their appeal directly to the public through Lord's youth magazine, *The Queen's Work*, and DeMille was singled out:

A letter from Mr. DeMille followed the appearance of his film *The Sign of the Cross*. I had loved that old melodrama when it appeared in my boyhood in Chicago. When Mr. DeMille decided to film it I congratulated him. The film version, with its sadistic cruelty, its playing up of Roman lust and debauchery and crime, seemed to me intolerable. An executive of the company told me that the picture was taking a beating, and mentioned a large financial loss over a brief period. Could I do anything to get the young people to change their attitude? I answered that I was largely responsible for their attitude and hoped it would continue.

DeMille's religious sensibilities were bruised. His next religious spectacle, *The Crusaders* (1935), on a heavy historical theme, was a shadow of his former films. *The Plainsman* (1937), *The Buccaneer* (1938) and *Union Pacific* (1939) were religion of a different sort. Following the weariness of a second great war, DeMille returned to the same formulas that had served him so well for three decades. *Samson and Delilah* (1949), to everyone's amazement, resurrected the bathrobe spectacle and proved it the only sure answer to the threat of television. Among the wide-screen attractions DeMille's *The Ten Commandments*, made in 1956, his seventieth and last film, is still one of the most popular. Pauline Kael commented:

The wide screen and the rediscovery of Christianity have restored films to their second childhood. In the thirties we thought Cecil B. DeMille passé; the American film of 1955 represents his full triumph. In the infancy of films there was promise and fervor; the absurdities were forgivable — we could find them amusing and primitive because we thought we saw the beginnings of a prodigy and we knew there were real obstacles ahead. But this synthetic infancy is monstrous

— a retracing of the steps, not to discover the lost paths of development, but to simulate the charms of infancy — and, for all we know, there may be a return to each previous (and doomed) period of film.

The cinema spectacle, imitated to the point of absurdity in a few short years, broke the back of the Hollywood industry. Not unexpectedly, the two biggest box office winners of the genre, *The Ten Commandments* (1956) and *Ben Hur* (1959) (directed by William Wyler), were repeats of past successes; they both earned in the area of $40 million. DeMille to his credit erected the best papier-maché tabernacles, holy mountains and parting seas in the business. Pretentious he was, but never vulgar. There was something genuinely primitive in his epics, an art fashioned crudely, commercially out of the stuff of the people. If true humanity could only be found in the best of his sex comedies, he at least sensed the meaning of mankind's tarnished dreams.

The secret of Garbo lay not so much in the training she received at the hands of the biggest star studio in Hollywood (she rather meticulously avoided it after the near disaster of her first film there), but rather in the solid foundation provided by the Swedish school of "repressive acting" and the special pains taken by director-mentor Mauritz Stiller. When she arrived at M-G-M in 1925, the style of the leading romantic idol, Rudolph Valentino, was more a grotesque of the emotions than a recognizable state of mind; and the melodramatic flourishes associated with the Griffith method were not that much better. The reigning star at M-G-M was then Lillian Gish (a Griffith discovery), who was to undergo a metamorphosis at the hands of Swedish director Victor Sjöström (his Hollywood name was "Seastrom"). Garbo's meteoric rise to the top, and her ability to remain there for more than a decade, was founded on the credo never to make a move that was not calculated beforehand in its finest detail.

When she arrived in New York, under contract to Louis B. Mayer for $600 a week (high for a beginner), she had one good film behind her (Stiller's *The Saga of Gösta Berling*, 1924) and one minor one (Pabst's *The Joyless Street*, 1925). Ten years later, she was listed as the highest paid woman in America, receiving $250,000 per film. It was Stiller who helped her during these early, troubled Hollywood days. He complained bitterly to Mayer for matching her with a Valentino imitator, Ricardo Cortez, in *The Torrent* (1926) and another Latin Lover, Antonio Moreno, in *The Temptress* (1927), both based on popular Blasco-Ibanez "vamp" novels. Stiller, who started as director of *The Temptress*, was fired on the set (reportedly for asking Moreno to shave off his moustache), and it was with misgivings that Garbo embarked on another vamp role in *The Flesh and the Devil* (1927). Matters were helped considerably by pairing her with the American outdoor type, John Gilbert, and setting the scene in Sudermann's East-Prussian landscape. Both *The Temptress* and *The Flesh and the Devil* were big popular successes, opening the way for tragic roles in *Love* (1927), based on Tolstoy's *Anna Karenina*, and *The Divine Woman* (1928), a tribute to Sarah Bernhardt. The latter was directed by Victor Sjöström and co-starred Swedish actor Lars Hanson: it was a parting nod to Sweden's Golden Age of silent cinema.

Naturalism in literature, theatre and cinema at the turn of the century drew its primary impulses from the French realist novels (above all, Zola), the Moscow Art Theatre (Stanislavsky's productions of Tolstoy, Gorki and Chekhov), and the Ibsen-Hauptmann plays in Scandinavia and Northern Germany. Ibsen's fame owed a great deal to his voluntary exile in Germany, and it was there, after Otto Brahm took over direction of the Deutsches Theater in Berlin in 1894, that the plays of Ibsen, Hauptmann and Schnitzler (the Austrian Ibsen) took deep root during one of the great periods in European theatre. In a manifesto Brahm had announced: "The battle-cry of the new art is the one word — truth; and it is truth, truth in every walk of life, which we, too, are striving for and which we demand." "Nature" (or "Truth") in the reproduction of reality was to take primary emphasis over poetic forms, theatrical conventions, and dramatic climaxes. Set against the rigid doctrinalism of this manifesto of the 1880s, at a time when the realist school of Zola, Flaubert and the Goncourts was at the height of its influence, came another form of realism springing from deeper elemental and emotional sources. Tolstoy's realism was rooted in Russian peasant life and imbued with mysticism; Selma Lagerlöf dug deeper into the folklore of Southern Sweden for her passionate sagas of legendary times, tales which were in fact journeys into the roots of her emotional life. Swedish silents were characterized by Lagerlöf's marked ethical and religious conception of life, whose dominating theme is human guilt and the necessity for penance and atonement.

The Swedish cinema flourished in the decade between 1916 and 1926, a late flowering of realism, especially psychological realism, and a beauty-conscious "naturalism" — sparked by a romantic provincialism, a nostalgic longing for the past, a mythological culture, as Sweden changed from an agricultural to an industrial country. Essentially it was not a naturalistic, Ibsen-influenced movement, but a cinema of lyrical mysticism, the inner struggles of man played against a background of the forces of nature. The masters of this period, Victor Sjöström and Mauritz Stiller, drifted into cinema from the theatre. Sjöström was the more somber of the two, a true Lagerlöf disciple, a romantic realist, whose films faithfully transcribe her message of moral guilt; often he played the leading role himself and his films are characterized by a high degree of fatalism. Stiller, a Russian émigré never at home in Sweden, stressed the melodramatic, spectacular side of Lagerlöf in his adaptations of her novels: hardly adhering to Lagerlöf's puritanism, he leaned in general toward sophisticated comedy. In many ways, the two directors, and friends, complemented each other.

Between 1912 and 1914 the Danish melodrama and thriller were in vogue, influencing both Sjöström and Stiller. Sjöström entered cinema as a matinée idol but he also demonstrated a keen interest in social problems as the director of *Ingeborg Holm* (1913). Stiller's first important film was *Vampyren* (1912), starring Sjöström and directly influenced in style and technique by the powerful Danish film (at this time the Lidingö studios, where Stiller and Sjöström worked, was nicknamed "Little Copenhagen"). In contrast to the Danish film of this period, they both tried to give a true picture of human beings amid their surroundings. They made works of integrity, of a poetic-documentary nature, whose uncompromising artistic ambition matched the best in Sweden's literary and pastoral traditions. Sjöström's artistic journey was from the outer world of landscape and nature to the interior realm of the soul. Stiller sought to reflect the psychological depths of the inner being in the forces of nature. Their contribution later to the American cinema was extensive.

Sjöström, with little taste for comedy or intimate drama, took his camera outdoors for authenticity almost from the beginning. In his film version of Ibsen's epic poem *Terje Vigen* (1916) (he played the title role of Terje), Sjöström discovered natural backgrounds could reflect astonishingly well the poem's dramatic conflict. It is a tale of a fisherman captured while running the Napoleonic blockade for food, and who languishes in prison while his family starves. The hero later meets his captor in a boat during a storm and is delivered from revenge when he encounters his enemy's wife and child. In *The Outlaw and His Wife* (1917), based on an epic play set in the eighteenth century (Sjöström had often played the outlaw on stage), two lovers are forced to flee into the mountains where they spend idyllic years of happiness; but during a severe winter they are frozen to death in a snowstorm. In Lagerlöf's *The Girl From Stormycroft* (1917) (the first of her adaptations), he contrasted realistically and psychologically the hard life of an unwed but genuinely unselfish mother in the mountains with the happiness of dwellers in the valley; Lagerlöf helped on the film as to locations, so that nature was used not only symbolically but to reflect the emotional state of two social classes. In *The Sons of Ingmar* (1918), another Lagerlöf, he has advanced far enough to render her extremely complicated characters in the introductory part of the epic novel *Jerusalem* totally convincing; the high point is the hero's spiritual ascent to heaven to talk over his personal guilt with his ancestors.

From 1918 to 1922 the Swedish film industry sought in vain to find a place in the fast expanding international market. The expiation theme is to be found in the somber world of *The Testament of Your Honor* (1919) and *The Monastery of Sendomir* (1919), remarkable works adapted from Hjalmar Bergman and Franz Grillparzer; then Sjöström turned again to Lagerlöf's *Jerusalem* for a sequel, *Karin, Daughter of Ingmar* (1919), another magnificent, outdoor, pastoral epic with a masterful blending of psychological content. The Sjöström masterpiece, however, is his classic, large-scale studio production of *The Phantom Chariot* (1920), a tale of love, sin, death and expiation, whose religious depth has made it more lasting and influential than any other silent film. A forerunner of Ingmar Bergman's *The Seventh Seal*, it shows the hero atoning for his misdeeds before his time elapses; he repents and saves his family. A great commercial success (even today at church screenings), its exquisite photography and solid acting could not save the Swedish film industry; in 1923 Sjöström left for Hollywood. His friend Stiller and actors Garbo and Lars Hanson joined him there soon after.

Stiller was more suited to Hollywood than Sjöström, considering his skill with the comedy-of-manners long before Ernst Lubitsch made it his Hollywood stock-in-trade. Indeed, a direct line can be drawn from Stiller to Lubitsch to the Hollywood sex comedies of the 1930s — their fluid narrative style, emphasis on innuendo and unspoken thoughts, and the amusing war between the sexes. While Sjöström was echoing man's emotions in the forces of nature, Stiller relished the crackle of comedy and the psychological power of a glance or gesture (often frustrating the duties of Sweden's puritan censors). He was known as a tyrant on the set, subduing stage mannerisms, controlling movements, ranting and raving until he got the exact results he wanted. The results in *Love and Journalism* (1916), *Thomas Graal's Best Film* (1917), and *Thomas Graal's First Child* (1918) (in which the Graals, played by Sjöström and Karin Molander, were the prototypes of the eternally battling couple on the screen) were always good. For *Erotikon* (1920) he repeated the sophisticated ploys of his earlier films (his protégé is Karin Molander during this period), but he did so in a calculated attempt to reach the international audience; it became his true calling card at the Hollywood studios.

Turning to the epic, guilt-possessed world of Selma Lagerlöf, he turned her legendary story, *Sir Arne's Treasure* (1919), into a sensational melodrama rivalling Hollywood's spectaculars. Originally intended to be directed by Sjöström (who was working on Lagerlöf's *Karin, Daughter of Ingmar* at the time), the epic tale was molded by Stiller into a superficial, pictorially beautiful, dynamic film, insensitive to its inner reality. He followed with *The Fishing Village* (1919), written for Stiller by the Swedish poet Bertil Malmberg, which contrasts the honest joy of life with a parson's oppressive intolerance on the puritan-dominated west coast of Sweden. For *Johan* (1920), an adaptation of a Finnish novel, he imbued the romantic, outdoor theme, fitted to a melodramatic substructure of the eternal triangle, with a professional sense of irony. Returning to Lagerlöf, he stressed again his own world of superficial, pictorial beauty in *The Saga of Gunnar Hedes* (1922) over the epic's titanic struggle of the individual with his soul and the forces of nature. The film brought an official denunciation from the Nobel Prize winning author, who saw little of the original in the script and condemned the film as a forgery of her writings. It was not to end there: he next adapted her great classic, *The Saga of Gösta Berling* (1923), the story of a defrocked pastor (Hanson) whose amorous adventures against a changing pastoral background end in redemptive love with a young Italian countess (Garbo). The spectacular epic was a great success in a two-part exhibition, but with the coming of sound it later was cut down to one at the sacrifice of Stiller's narrative skills. It so impressed Louis B. Mayer at a Berlin screening that he invited the Swedish trio to come to M-G-M.

The six Lagerlöf productions, divided equally between Sjöström and Stiller, make up the heart of Swedish silent cinema. Her moral conflicts between dark, destructive forces and the power of kindness, understanding and expiation in the human condition grew partially out of the historical conflicts between Christianity and Paganism in the Middle Ages. Christianity had barely won this battle of the spirit when another took place in the Reformation revolt, followed by the rise of Sweden to a world power. These upheavals left their marks in the marriage of church and state, in puritanism and the conflicts between flesh and spirit, nature and soul, light and darkness. The mountains and valleys, rocks and rivers in the Sjöström-Stiller-Lagerlöf world were thus imbued with a moral inner expression of man struggling with his soul as well as the forces of nature: man is the master of his own soul and destiny only if God (and Nature) allows it. With the departure of Sjöström and Stiller for America, Swedish cinema suffered a momentary eclipse, although Sjöström's pupil, Gustaf Molander, finished Lagerlöf's epic novel *Jerusalem* in *The Inheritance of Ingmar* (1925) and *To the Orient* (1926). Alf Sjöberg's adaptation of Rune Lindström's folk-play, *The Road to Heaven* (1942), in which the hero strides off to seek justice from the hands of God for his fiancée condemned as a witch, is another fantasy-allegory in the mold of Sjöström's *The Sons of Ingmar*. The motifs of light-darkness, summer-winter, life-death are to be found today in Ingmar Bergman's and Bo Widerberg's films.

Fitting the Swedish style to Hollywood was something else. Stiller's uncompromising nature made him the first tragic figure, although his sophisticated sex comedies were further advanced than both DeMille's and Lubitsch's in the 1920s. He quarrelled with Mayer at M-G-M (fired on the set of Garbo's second Hollywood film), drifted to Paramount to make the atmospheric and commendable *Hotel Imperial* (1927), and returned to Sweden to die in 1928. Sjöström fared somewhat better on the back-lots of M-G-M, starring a new Lillian Gish (she stepped down with the coming of Garbo) in Hawthorne's *The Scarlet Letter* (1926) and *The Wind* (1927). Hawthorne's classic of an adulterous priest and unwed mother in puritan

New England has the guilt overtones of Lagerlöf's *Gösta Berling*, and because of its American flavor it was to succeed beyond his own adaptation of a Lagerlöf novel, *The Tower of Lies* (1925) (based on *The Emperor of Portugallia*). His lyrical treatment of the story and sense for the landscape, as well as the superbly restrained acting performances of Gish and Lars Hanson as the principals, vanquished Mayer's anxious fears that the motherhood of the nation might be slurred. They were together again in *The Wind*, one of the classics of silent cinema and the height of the Swedish influence in Hollywood, in which a sensitive girl from the East arrives in the wilderness on the frontier and her mental disintegration parallels the symbolic force of an unrelenting wind. Garbo requested Sjöström and Hanson for *The Divine Woman* (1928), but the film did little to further the careers of any of them. Garbo returned to her Hollywood mentors, Hanson left with the coming of sound (to attain success as Sweden's foremost actor), and Sjöström departed for Stockholm to be at the deathbed of his friend Stiller.

John Eberson's taste for the baroque, the romantic and the exotic in the architecture of his "atmospheric" movie theatres in the 1920s has its roots in the neo-romantic dramas of Hugo von Hofmannsthal and the productions of Max Reinhardt, all three natives of Vienna. Hofmannsthal's cosmopolitan mind and creative genius were equally at home in lyrical poetry and poetic drama at the turn of the century, setting his scenes in ancient Greece, the Italian Renaissance, the court of the Sun King, the Spanish Baroque and the romantic history of his own Austria. H. F. Garten recounts how Reinhardt, the pupil and successor of Otto Brahm at Berlin's Deutsches Theater in 1905, pushed Naturalism aside for the neo-romantic Hofmannsthal and symbolist playwrights:

Reinhardt brought to the sophisticated German capital a southern breeze, a dazzling display of colour, light, music, fantasy. For him the stage was not merely a faithful mirror of reality but a magic world radiating its own light. "The world is merely reality, but its reflection (in the theatre) has infinite potentialities," Hofmannsthal wrote in an essay, *The Stage as a Dream-Image*, evidently with the theatre of Reinhardt in mind. It was quite consistent that these two, Hofmannsthal and Reinhardt, jointly called into being the Salzburg Festival: in it they saw the realization of their conception of the theatre as a festivity, uniting all the arts in a single whole.

Reinhardt directed the Deutsches Theater for twenty-eight years (1905-1933), giving Berlin its richest period in modern theatre history.

He was open to experiments and new trends of every sort, paving the way for intimate theatre in his smaller adjoining house (the *Kammerspiel* was founded in 1906) and the conversion of a former circus with a seating capacity of over three thousand into the Grosses Schauspielhaus designed for mass spectacles (opened in 1920). He gave the first real impetus to German filmmaking (advising young actors to enter the field) and responded with enthusiasm to the forms of Expressionism creeping into the art world. But his main love was the neo-romantic and Salzburg; he opened the festival in 1920 with the première of Hofmannsthal's *The Salzburg Great Theatre of the World* (written as a counterpart to his religious drama and recreation of the old morality play, *Everyman*). The drama, with its prominent dance-of-death theme, was based on Calderon's *El gran teatro del mundo* written at the height of seventeenth-century Spanish Baroque, and it reigned as the official symbol of the festival until Reinhardt's departure after the 1937 season. Reinhardt in an interview explained his and Hofmannsthal's religious philosophy:

The *memento mori* springs from a deep Austrian feeling: death is not a destroyer but an organizer of the soul, without which there can be no life. Death transforms life into a spiritual festival.

The transitoriness of life and its constant closeness to death was the dominant theme in most of Hofmannsthal's mature works. It is also the motif that underlines Reinhardt's famous production of Shakespeare's *A Midsummer Night's Dream*, first performed at the Deutsches Theater in 1905 (the breakthrough of neo-romanticism) and produced twelve times during his lifetime.

When Reinhardt gave his blessing to cinema in 1911 to accommodate an overabundance of students, movies had already become a "legitimate" art with the appearance of Sarah Bernhardt in a Film d'Art production of Sardou's *La Tosca* (1908). Paul Wegener and Ernst Lubitsch were the first to heed the call, reflecting in their own way Reinhardt's dramatic principles in expressionism and social comedy. In the pre-war period of German cinema they were the primary figures. After the war, in the Golden Age of German Expressionism (1917-1927), the hothouse atmosphere in German filmmaking continued to be encouraged by the solid success of the German Theatre dominated by Reinhardt. Nearly all of the great films of the silent period were shot in an artificial, indoor studio, dealt with fantasies or romantic themes of one kind or another, and relied on lighting or studio effects common to theatre. A great many of these studio effects and controlled mass scenes were adapted to the propaganda film of the following decade.

German cinema marks its artistic beginning from *The Student of Prague* (1913), directed by Stellan Rye and starring Paul Wegener. It may have been inspired by the Edison production of *Frankenstein* (1910) or the Jekyll-and-Hyde theme in Max Mack's *Der Andere* (*The Other*) (1913), produced in Germany just before the Rye-Wegener production; in any case, all three have their antecedents in the legend of the Golem in Prague, the Faust story, the tales of E. T. A. Hoffmann and Edgar Allan Poe, as well as the projected phantasmagoria shows of the nineteenth century. Ulrich Gregor commented on *The Student of Prague*:

This film anticipated several themes and traits that were to characterize the German cinema in its most important phase — the Twenties: the inclination towards the ghostly and sinister, the preoccupation with morbidity, with demoniac power, and with the will of Fate, which, personified in a mighty tyrant or satanic adversary, overcomes the hero and drags him into the abyss.

Director-actor Wegener and scriptwriter Henrik Galeen collaborated on the first *The Golem* in 1915 (since lost); Galeen (like Rilke, Kafka and Franz Werfel in the expressionist movement) knew Prague and its strange and peculiar mystical tradition. It was one of the first of the popular monster pictures that have endured down to the present: the formula was so successful the pair were soon competing against other demoniac powers in the six-part thriller *Homunculus* (1916) (billed as "the man without a soul"), Joe May's *Hilde Warren and the Death* (1917), and Lubitsch's *The Eyes of the Mummy* (1918). Galeen was to contribute as scriptwriter to a long string of horror films, still known today for their rich morbidity and fantasy: a second *The Golem* (1920) with Wegener, Paul Leni's *Waxworks* (1924), a self-directed repeat of *The Student of Prague* (1926), and Wegener again in *Unholy Love* (1928). An interesting aspect of the early Wegener films, particularly *The Student of Prague* (1913) and *The Pied Piper of Hamelin* (1918), is that they were shot on location on the banks of the Rhine, a far cry from the well-equipped studios of the 1920s; there's not much concern for romantic anguish and darkness when working in the open air and sunshine.

Ernst Lubitsch tired of small roles in the Reinhardt productions and began making his celebrated short comedies in 1915. Shot during the war with little knowledge of Griffith's editing techniques, they were extremely popular with the public and pushed Lubitsch quickly to the forefront when UFA was established in 1917 with government money. He learned a great deal from Reinhardt's crowd scenes in his large-scale theatrical productions, applying them to a series of film "spectacles" starring Pola Negri: *Carmen* (1918), *Madame Dubarry* (1919), and *One Arabian Night* (1920). These films achieved world recognition, apparently influencing Griffith's *The Orphans of the Storm* (1921) on the French Revolution theme. Mary Pickford felt he was the answer to her own problem of a good director, and offered him $5,000 a week to come to Hollywood. He sailed for America in 1923, the same year Sjöström left Sweden.

As Wegener and Lubitsch consciously imitated Reinhardt flairs for mystic fantasy and crowd scenes, the "purists" of the new school of Expressionism began to fashion an avant-garde cinema of abstract design and extreme subjectivism reflecting "the anguished cry of the soul." A violent reaction in German art and literature against the domineering patterns of life and culture established in the late nineteenth century was taking place principally among those artists born in the 1880s and 1890s. In art, *Die Brücke* and *Der Blaue Reiter* schools (formed in 1905 and 1910) rejected impressionism and realism in painting; in music, Arnold Schoenberg's *Die glückliche Hand* (1913) and Alban Berg's *Wozzeck* (1921) marked the change; painter Oskar Kokoschka, sculptor Ernst Barlach, and lyric poet Franz Werfel produced dramatic pieces of deep religious fervor and mysticism after the First World War; playwrights Ernst Toller and Georg Kaiser transformed the political outcry against the war and the Wilhelmine state into a movement for the moral reawakening of man and society; and in the cinema, critics began to note that Otto Rippert's *Homunculus* series in the middle of the war was also directed at man's deep concern for the spiritual self. One of the richest impulses in modern art and literature, German Expressionism lasted between 1910 and 1925 in its purest form and drew its energy primarily from the social and spiritual upheaval resulting from the war and revolution (1917-1920). It emphasized the supremacy of the spirit over matter, often reaching into extreme subjectivism and anarchy to prove that man was his own driving force free from the restraints of his environment. Fundamentally it was a religious movement concerned with the timeless issues of human existence.

Advocates of the movement attacked the insanity of authority, delving into the writings of Kleist and Büchner in the *Sturm und Drang* period to compare their findings with the modern world of Freud and Kafka. Playwrights Frank Wedekind and Carl Sternheim, whose antagonism to hypocritical conventions and whose reduction of characters to social types set them apart in the Wilhelmine period of corrupt materialism, were revived and hailed as forerunners of Expressionism. Another was the Swedish playwright August Strindberg: his evolvement from the naturalistic *The Father* (1887) to the religious, expressionistic *A Dream Play* (1902) was a journey into the self, by which he viewed other characters and the material world only in his own reflection. H. F. Garten cites his principles of expressionist drama:

The pre-eminent example is his trilogy *The Road to Damascus* (1898-1901). In this work, the chief formal principles of expressionist drama are for the first time clearly applied: firstly, the reduction of the characters to mere types, named by general terms such as the Stranger, the Beggar, the Doctor; secondly, the unfolding of the action in a succession of scenes, denoting stages of the central character's development towards a spiritual goal; thirdly, the identification of the author with his central figure, the Stranger, who on his road of martyrdom passes through every form of mental agony until he attains redemption in the Christian faith. There is no antagonist equivalent to the hero: all the other characters are merely projections or embodiments of his inner struggle. Thus *The Road to Damascus* stands as the prototype of expressionist drama long before this actually came into being.

The rich period of German Expressionism in the cinema is mostly a result of these dramatic influences, the combined efforts of an art world exploring the self through a movie camera (in which the art director and scriptwriter were as important as the director, cameraman and actor), a fortunate state of economic inflation (in 1922 this "economic miracle" made possible the production of 474 features), and a genius who left his stamp on the most vital films of the period — Carl Mayer.

Mayer was twenty-five when he co-scripted *The Cabinet of Dr. Caligari* (1919), the film which set the tone for the movement: indoor sets, lighting, costumes, visual decorations, a rejection of reality for a religious or abstract theme of the self (although social and political motives are imputed). He was an Austrian who had spent his youth as a wandering orphan, studied acting and painting, and apparently wrote his first script, *Caligari*, with pacifist army officer Hans

Janowitz after seeing a Wegener film. Janowitz was a native
of Prague, the city where shadows on the walls seem to breathe
dark, foreboding, haunting terrors, an apt reflection of the war's
spiritual upheaval. Somehow the pair convinced Erich Pommer, a
key producer in German film history (who began his career with
Gaumont in Paris in 1907), that a parable on the madness of the age
was worth doing: the story was turned over to Robert Wiene after
Fritz Lang proved unavailable. Wiene, to the distress of Mayer and
Janowitz, changed the script and the ending, but the story was to
receive sound echoes in the expressionistic shadows and drawings
painted directly onto the sets by artists-designers Hermann Warm,
Walter Röhrig and Walter Reimann (some claim it was as much for
lack of electrical power in the studios as anything else). The figure
of Caligari came out of Mayer's reading of Stendhal's *Unknown
Letters* and Janowitz's anti-militaristic bouts with an army psychia-
trist. The film was an instant success, particularly abroad; it was one
of the most influential silent films made.

Out of this film grew the term "caligarism", which not only
defined a subjective attitude to environment but took in the major
expressions of the movement and its off-shoots. Among pure expres-
sionist films were Karl Heinz Martin's *From Morning to Midnight*
(1920) (based on a play by expressionist dramatist Georg Kaiser),
Wiene's *Genuine* (1920) (script by Mayer), *Raskolnikov* (*Crime and
Punishment*) (1923) and *The Hands of Orlac* (1924), and Paul Leni's
Waxworks (1924). Others very much in the same style include
Wegener's *The Golem* (1920), F. W. Murnau's *Nosferatu* (1921) and
The Last Laugh (1924), Fritz Lang's *Dr. Mabuse the Gambler* (1922),
Leopold Jessner's *Backstairs* (1921), Arthur von Gerlac's *Vanina*
(1922), and Karl Grune's *The Street* (1923). Lang's "monumental"
films and the *Kammerspiele* (particularly those scripted by Mayer for
Lupu Pick) grew out of Expressionism, while a group of cameramen,
set designers, scriptwriters and directors were directly influenced by
Mayer. It is said that Upton Sinclair's novel *They Call Me Carpenter*,
the story of Christ returning to earth in the form of a dream, was
inspired by a screening of *Caligari*. In his first attempt at script-
writing Mayer had turned cinema into a sort of "celluloid couch."

He got better as he went along. His next script for Wiene,
Genuine (or *The Tale of a Vampire*) (1920), was a failure in trying to
wed anti-war feelings with runaway passions of lust, jealousy and

greed; but Jessner's *Kammerspiel* approach to *Backstairs* (1921) (at his own Staatliches Schauspielhaus in Berlin his style of non-realistic production was constructed around a flight of stairs, the famous "Jessner Treppe") isolated the study of passions and instincts in a setting involving three characters. He then began a fruitful relationship with Lupu Pick, who directed the masterfully written scripts for *Shattered* (1921) and *New Year's Eve* (1923) employing scarcely no titles in a fully integrated symbolic and psychological environment; in between, he wrote for Jessner an analytical script based on Wedekind's *Erdgeist* (1922), and adapted Stendhal's *Vanina* (1922) for Gerlach, among others. *Genuine, Erdgeist* and *Vanina* are extensions of the tyrant or satanic adversary theme begun in *Caligari*, while historian Siegfried Kracauer feels the series beginning with *Backstairs* and carrying through *Shattered* and *New Year's Eve* is constructed on an "instinct" theme with one feature in common:

They are laid in a lower middle-class world which is the meaningless remnant of a disintegrated society. The lower middle class appears in Mayer's films as a breeding ground for stunned, oppressed creatures who, reminiscent of Büchner's Wozzeck figure, are unable to sublimate their instincts. This was undoubtedly the plight of the German petty bourgeoisie during those years.

Jessner's *Backstairs* is the bridge between the tyrant and instinct phase of Mayer's career; it makes a sardonic reference to the latter in the closing scene as the murder and suicide merely cause another unnecessary disturbance. In the Pick films he points to the same tragedies, but it is now as a consequence of deep psychological and social complexes, which the misery of the times (the same inflation that made the film industry a source of revenue abroad) did little to dispel. Since these films dealt with the substrata of existence, titles or explanations of the action were superfluous and the driving force of the narrative was fate or destiny expressed through objects the camera selected for observation. These unique methods paved the way for another artistic milestone in German expressionist cinema, *The Last Laugh* (1924) (also known as *The Last Man*), the culmination of the instinct series.

It was slated to be directed by Lupu Pick, but F. W. Murnau stepped in at this time to direct four Mayer scripts in a row (two in America) and thus link their names inseparably. Murnau's contribution to *The Last Laugh*, in which the downfall of a hotel porter is intensified and magnified, was to lift the role of fate or destiny to something close to tragedy. The hey-dey of Expressionism in theatre and cinema was passing, and as Berlin struggled to compete with Hollywood for the "art" market and hopefully stem the flood of talent to America, Mayer's script-writing abilities were not to be wasted on the *Kammerspiel*. All the new techniques proven sound in the Pick films were tested again by Mayer, Murnau, cameraman Karl Freund, and actor Emil Jannings. Freund, who lived in the same hotel as Mayer, recalls:

In the two and a half months of preparation on *The Last Laugh*, Mayer conferred every day with at least one of us — with Murnau, with the designers Herlth and Röhrig, with Pommer, with Jannings, or with me. It was out of this team-work that all the innovations in *The Last Laugh* evolved.

The most striking of these techniques was the moving camera, which in the hands of Murnau was creatively utilized for its field of vision and perspective, a mingling of realism with fantasy. Kracauer emphasizes that it was Mayer who sensed the possibilities of a new aesthetic:

Carl Mayer himself was quite conscious of what he achieved in unchaining the camera. In his preface to *New Year's Eve*, he first defines the spheres of the merry crowds and the natural scenery as the "surroundings" of the café-owner's rooms, and then states that certain movements of the camera are calculated to express the idea of a world including the "surroundings" as well as the scene of action proper. "As the events progress, these movements are... to encompass depths and heights, so as to picture the frenzy shaking the whole human world amidst nature."

The main difference between Pick's *New Year's Eve* and Murnau's *The Last Laugh* is the possibilities a newly devised, portable camera provided, permitting fluidity in narrative techniques and pictorial style. Andrew Sarris places Murnau's moving camera ahead of Eisenstein's montage:

Murnau's influence on the cinema has proved to be more lasting than Eisenstein's. Murnau's moving camera seems a more suitable style for exploring the world than does Eisenstein's dialectical montage, and the trend in modern movies has been toward escaping studio sets so as to discover the real world.

The moving camera coincided with the realism of New Objectivity (*Neue Sachlichkeit*), the return to the concrete plot and characters of flesh and blood in search of more constructive and enduring values. The movement was signalled by the blazing sunshine in Arthur von Gerlach's adaptation of Theodor Storm's *The Chronicle of Grieshuus* (1924), a film which in other respects followed the principles of

Expressionism; it also featured set designers Robert Herlth and Walter Röhrig, who worked on *The Last Laugh* in the same year. In 1925 Eisenstein's *Potemkin* appeared with its revolutionary editing techniques. Mayer noted the change and shortly set out with Freund to photograph Berlin in "a melody of pictures." Walter Ruttmann edited *Berlin, Symphony of a Great City* (1927) instead into a *montage* of dialectical argument, much to Mayer's displeasure.

With the end of inflation in 1923, the German film industry turned to the classics to compete with Hollywood on the level of the art film. After some success with a Mayer adaptation of Molière's *Tartuffe* (1925) and Hans Kyser's script for Goethe's *Faust* (1926), Murnau and Jannings joined the growing crowd of German artists in Hollywood. Murnau's first film for Fox was another Mayer script from a Hermann Sudermann story, re-titled *Sunrise* (1927), one of the classics of the silent screen which set a standard for the written script in Hollywood. Another Mayer script for Murnau's *Four Devils* (1928), adapted from a pungent Herman Bang short story on circus life, and *Our Daily Bread* (1929) (released as *City Girl* in 1930), a "woodcut of life" set in the Dakota grain fields, proved unsuccessful. The last film of Murnau, *Tabu* (1931), echoed the force of destiny in a South Seas tale (begun with Robert Flaherty); he died in an automobile accident in 1931. With the rise of Nazism in Germany Mayer went to Paris and London, working as a scriptwriter and film advisor. He died in 1944.

In speaking of Carl Mayer, Paul Rotha contends that "almost every German film of the Golden Period leads back to his imagination," a very high tribute to a scriptwriter. Between 1918 and 1932 approximately two thousand films were turned out by the German studios, the best of these in the decade of Expressionism (1914-1923) in art, theatre and cinema. Some other examples stemming from Mayer are Arthur Robison's *Warning Shadows* (1922), drawn from the same psychological theory of hypnotism introduced in *Caligari*; Karl Grune's *The Street* (1923), exploring the twisted mind of a philistine in the expressionist style of Mayer's *Kammerspiel*; Ernst Lubitsch's *The Flame* (1923) (his last film before leaving for Hollywood), a variation on Mayer's exposure of the bourgeois mentality; E. A. Dupont's *Variety* (1925), an object lesson in film expression, using all available means of the film medium in an instinct-leading-to-murder motif; and G. W. Pabst's *The Secrets of a Soul* (1926), an attempt to apply psychotherapy to the murder instinct (based on an actual case recorded by Freud and made with the collaboration of two of his assistants). Mayer's influence also reached beyond Germany, mostly through the stream of talent following to Hollywood in the early 1920s. Chaplin's *A Woman of Paris* (1923), a *Kammerspiel* film subtitled "a drama of fate," might have originated from his 1921 visit to Berlin, at least germinally, although the direct influence is Griffith. It seems unlikely, however, that he influenced Fritz Lang's monumental "fate" films. Kracauer observed:

> From 1920 through 1924 — years in which the German screen never championed or even visualized the cause of liberty — films depicting the sway of unchecked instincts were as current as those devoted to tyrants. The Germans obviously held that they had no choice other than the cataclysm of anarchy or a tyrannical regime. Either possibility appeared pregnant with doom. In this plight contemporaneous imagination resorted to the ancient concept of Fate.

Lang's path never crossed Mayer's, but runs parallel to his in theme: while Mayer was pitying the individual trapped by his own obsessions, Lang was releasing this anguish on huge canvasses depicting the Teutonic soul wrestling with its own destiny. He was inspired by the broad stage of Reinhardt's Deutsches Theater, while Mayer satisfied himself with the intimate atmosphere of the *Kammerspiele*. The romanticized purgatory and expiation theme in Lang-Harbou's *Destiny* (*The Tired Death*) (1921) contrasts with Pick-Mayer's religious purgatory leading to suicide and murder in *Shattered* (1921). Mayer's struggle to tear the individual away from the "womb instinct" in *New Year's Eve* is matched by Lang's shrine to past ritual in the two-part *Nibelungen* saga (1923-1924). Nowhere perhaps is the force of destiny stronger felt than in the heavy pessimism pervading Mayer's script for Murnau's *The Last Laugh* (1924) and the elaborate architectural density of Lang's *Metropolis* (1926), the two most representative films of the entire German silent period. Lastly, the *Kammerspiel* world of Mayer is echoed in Lang's preference for the motif of claustrophobia found in the best films of his German and American period. Both, in short, are tragedians of the closed universe, where man desolately wrestles with his destiny — and loses.

The Golden Age of German cinema between the two revolutions (1918-1933) has three distinct phases: the period immediately following the revolution (1918-1923) (the height of Expressionism in art), the period of stabilization (1923-1929) (the turn to New Objectivism), and the final relapse into social and political anarchy (1929-1933) (the rise of heroic tragedy and nationalism). In a single decade the positive aspects of Expressionism — that "man is good," that he will awake to a sense of moral responsibility to overthrow society's rigid laws exploiting the individual, that the full realization of the ideal is just around the corner — had sunk into depression and despair in the upheaval of revolution and inflation. Whatever contribution Mayer's studies of the instincts and tyranny offered to free the individual of the past was centered in the dignity of man: he was more aware of the problem than he was sure of a possible solution. Expressionism as a purely abstract concept was to have no regenerative force, although its overall idealism was to continue having far-reaching effects long after nationalism and propaganda pushed it completely aside. It is ironic that with the rise of Nazism the motif of destiny was converted into an heroic virtue and a visual motif of emotional power. Lang was offered the post of artistic superintendent in the Third Reich, but refused; Leni Riefenstahl, utilizing the architectural form of Lang's *Nibelungen* and *Metropolis*, turned *The Triumph of the Will* (1934) into a glorious testament on the destiny of National Socialism.

Hollywood witnessed the twilight of Expressionism. Reinhardt who gave a strong impetus to Expressionist cinema in shadow lighting devised for a stage production of Reinhard Johannes Sorge's *The Beggar* (1912), the first genuine Expressionist drama, was to leave behind a Hollywood production of *A Midsummer Night's Dream* (1935), a legacy of former elegance. It was co-directed by William Dieterle, a former pupil; Reinhardt's flair for fantasy and imagery was evident once again in many brilliant, magnificent touches. It was a kind of High Mass for the movies as "spiritual festival."

The star system was at the center of the Hollywood Dream Cult, responsible for stripping movies of much that was genuinely religious and human. In the artificial atmosphere of the movie palace contact with the real world and real problems was effectively precluded. Technical innovation was replaced by the formula; directors gave way to "creative" producers; there was no place for a Griffith or a Stroheim. At a time when some of the fun and pure enjoyment of making a film for its own sake was being continued briefly in the *avant-garde*, Hollywood was consolidating its position of power around the star system. Between 1925 and 1955 the American movie stagnated. Toward the end of this period André Bazin noted:

We have only to go back 10 or 15 years to observe evidence of the aging of what was the patrimony of the art of cinema. We have noted the speedy death of certain types of film, even major ones like the slapstick comedy, but the most characteristic disappearance is undoubtedly that of the star. Certain actors have always been a commercial success with the public, but this devotion has nothing in common with the socioreligious phenomenon of which Rudolph Valentino and Greta Garbo were the golden calves. It all seemed as if the area of cinematic themes had exhausted whatever it could have hoped for from technique. It was no longer enough to invent quick cutting, or a new style of photography, in order to stir people's emotions. Unaware, the cinema has passed into the age of the scenario. By this we mean a reversal of the relationship between matter and form.

Again:

As Rosenkrantz wrote in 1937, in *Esprit*, in an article profoundly original for its period, "The characters on the screen are quite naturally objects of identification, while those on the stage are, rather, objects of mental opposition because their real presence gives them an objective reality and to transpose them into beings in an imaginary world the will of the spectator has to intervene actively, that is to say, to will to transform their physical reality into an abstraction. The abstraction being the result of a process of the intelligence that we can only ask of a person who is fully conscious." A member of a film audience tends to identify himself with the film's hero by a psychological process, the result of which is to turn the audience into a "mass" and to render emotion uniform. Just as in algebra if two numbers equal a third, then they are equal to one another, so here we can say, if two individuals identify themselves with a third, they identify themselves with one another. Let us compare chorus girls on the stage and on the screen. On the screen they satisfy an unconscious sexual desire and when the hero joins them he satisfies the desire of the spectator in the proportion to which the latter has identified himself with the hero. On the stage the girls excite the onlooker as they would in real life. The result is that there is no identification with the hero. He becomes instead an object of jealousy and envy. In other words, Tarzan is only possible on the screen. The cinema calms the spectator, the theatre excites him.

He concluded:

The reasoning of Rosenkrantz concerning opposition and identification requires in effect an important correction. It carries with it, still, a measure of equivocation. Rosenkrantz seems to equate identification with passivity and escape — an accepted fact in his time because of the condition of the cinema but less and less so in its present state of evolution. Actually the cinema of myth and dream is now only one variety of production and one that is less and less frequent. One must not confuse an accidental and historical social condition with an unalterable psychological one — two activities, that is to say, of the spectator's consciousness that converge but are not part of one another. I do not identify equally with Tarzan and Bresson's curé.

The religious implication of the Hollywood Dream Cult is inseparable from the social conditions that made these dreams both possible and necessary. The same dreams that motivated the baroque-style churches in city ghettos erected the movie cathedrals that went up beside them, or prominently on Main Street, America. As Daniel Lord, S.J., the author of the Production Code, noted in his reminiscences:

Summer after summer I returned to find my mother and father more and more addicted to the movies. Two places claimed their pilgrimage: the parish church of a morning, the neighborhood theatre of an evening. Many a fellow parishioner was inclined to genuflect on entering the local movie house and noticing my parents ahead of him.

As for the dreams themselves, Bazin's "identification theory" overlooks the positive aspects of daydreaming and fantasy. Pauline Kael observed:

People go to the movies for the various ways in which movies express the experience of their lives, and as a means of avoiding and postponing the pressures they feel. The latter function of art, generally referred to disparagingly as escapism, may also be considered refreshment, and it may be a major factor in keeping the world sane.

And again:

Movies are going to pieces; they are disintegrating, and the something called cinema is not movies raised to an art but rather movies diminished, movies that look "artistic." Movies are being stripped of all the "nonessentials" — that is to say, faces, actions, details, stories, places, everything that makes them entertaining and joyful.

Harvey Cox feels that the age of science and technology has been hard on fantasy: "Our fact-obsessed era has taught us to be cautious: always check impulsive visions against the hard data. Secularism erodes the religious metaphors within which fantasy can roam." The Hollywood Dream Cult may have supplied our only accessible haven for festivity and fantasy in modern life. For this reason the films of John Ford, Josef von Sternberg and Max Ophuls, those films of heroic legend, erotic dreams and romantic myths, continue to be as popular today as when they were made. Ophuls once expressed a desire to know and work for "the Laskys, the Samuels, the Mayers, the Loews," the merchants and adventurers who founded the movie industry:

Experience — one only learns this late — means losing the ignorance and dreams of childhood. One changes illusion for reality; one passes from things divined, desired, inaccessible, to the world of limitations. A man of experience is a broken child.... Unfortunately, in my *métier*, it appears that the time of the adults has begun, the time of broken children.

The director who knew the Hollywood Dream Cult best is Howard Hawks. Hawks began his career in 1926, and worked in every genre (westerns, comedies, detective stories, war films, musical comedies, gangster films, science fiction, the biblical epic) over a span of forty years. William Faulkner, one of his scriptwriters, said of *The Land of the Pharaohs* (1955): "It's the same movie Howard has been making for 35 years. It's *Red River* (1948) all over again. The Pharaoh is the cattle baron, his jewels are the cattle, and the Nile is the Red River. But the thing about Howard is, he knows it's the same movie, and he knows how to make it."

Hawks had a compassion for the dreamer. His adventure stories and comedies form the positive and negative poles of the Hawksian vision. The heroic adventure tales are concerned with the foolish deeds that lead men astray, the individualism that sets them apart from the social fabric. The comedies expose the childhood fantasies that make this foolishness possible. Such is the strength and the limitation of a dreamer.

VI.   THE POLITICAL USE OF RELIGION

Propaganda is as integral to the motion picture as sex and religion: it was there in the very first year of filmmaking, continuing a tradition already established in magic lantern shows, Dioramas and early Giant Peep Shows. The tradition goes back as far as the French Revolution. W. K. L. Dickson made propaganda films at Biograph for the election of President McKinley in 1896, and Méliès made one on Dreyfus in the same year. The instant popularity of C. B. DeMille's *Joan the Woman* (1917), glorifying American participation in the war, overshadowed D. W. Griffith's *Intolerance* (1916), preaching pacifism and understanding. The period between the wars in Europe, in which film industries became ultimately the responsibility of the State, is characterized by the reign of the propaganda film. Paul Rotha noted the change in the 1930s:

The First World War undoubtedly began this era of mass-persuasion, but the rapid development of the radio and the cinema, as well as the increasing influence exerted by the press, has subsequently trebled the importance of this new factor in the social structure. There can be little question that the immense persuasive properties of the two electric mediums — cinema and radio — have played an incalculable part in the shaping of mass-thought in post-war Europe. It is being generally recognized, moreover, that propaganda may become, as indeed in some countries it already is, one of the most important instruments for the building of the State. It is surely only a matter of time before the State will make full and acknowledged use of education, radio, cinema, pulpit and press to ensure public reception of its policies. Russia, Italy and Germany have already taken this course by their adoption of their particular system of government.

The national film industries in the Soviet Union, Italy and Germany rapidly fell into government hands; in France a doctrine of "cinema as instrument of the apostolate" was fostered under recommendations listed in Pope Pius XI's *Vigilanti Cura*; and the Hollywood product was supervised by the Production Code Administration (PCA) and its watchdog, the Legion of Decency. Movie entertainment was reduced to a formula (Bazin lists comedy, burlesque, dance, crime and gangster films, psychological and social dramas, horror and fantasy films, and the western as the basic genres), with the hope that a set of rules could dictate the tastes of the worldwide entertainment public.

The word "propaganda" in film history is inseparable from the impact made by Sergei Eisenstein's *Battleship Potemkin* (1925), its political message instantly felt on the international scene. Raymond Spottiswoode noted the alarm this film caused in England in 1935:

This film was perhaps the first Soviet work of art to achieve wide recognition outside Russia; everywhere its remarkable force was the subject of discussion and praise; but in England its public exhibition was forbidden by the censor. For many years the Americans had swamped this country with propaganda for their own domestic standards and morals, set forward in films devoid of any vestige of aesthetic value. Yet because they represented a stable and democratic, even if degraded, society, they were considered innocuous; while the Russian films, springing from a renaissance of life which, even if it was misguided or futile, was the historical development of a great people and thus entitled to respect, were denounced as pernicious and banned. The strong presentation of opinion, if acceptable, was called publicity; but if alien, propaganda.

Potemkin proved that *montage*, or editing, of the simplest material could evoke powerful emotions, and that the motion picture could wed a people to the State as nothing before.

Russian propaganda films originated in Lenin's remark in February 1922: "For us the cinema is the most important of the arts." Russian audiences had already seen the popular French comedies, Russian silent melodramas and historical themes, the Vertov newsreels on the war and the revolution (his cinema-eye use of the hand camera was far ahead of the times), and the pioneer experiments of Meyerhold and Kuleshov (the teacher of Eisenstein). Screenings of the American films, particularly Griffith, demonstrated the importance of editing psychological content into a story, but Eisenstein's theories of *montage* owed as much to Freud, Pavlov and the agitprop experiments of Meyerhold and Mayakovsky. In the golden period of Russian silents between 1924 and 1929, the films of Eisenstein, Pudovkin and Dovzhenko got their messages over in a formalistic manner that stressed editing as a dialectical principle. The approach had certain inherent weaknesses, as when Eisenstein attempted to adapt his theories to the realistic environs of collectivization in *The Old and the New* (1929); but these were relatively minor in comparison with the overall results.

Often the formalistic side of Soviet propaganda films had a rare, self-contained, esthetic beauty. Such were the epic poems of Alexander Dovzhenko. The son of Ukranian peasants, Dovzhenko knew little about filmmaking when he set out for Odessa in 1926 to seek employment at the new cinema studio: the lyrical passion and patriotic fervor of his films stem from the vision of a great primitive poet. Of his two classics, *Arsenal* (1929) and *Earth* (1930), the first is a hymn to the revolutionary spirit and the second a pastoral epic of major proportions rooted in the Ukranian soil, the cycles of nature and the rhythms of life and death. Paul Rotha on *Earth*:

> The age-old theme of the supremacy of the new over the old, the Soviet methods overthrowing the ancient privileges of the Kulaki (the rich farmers) and the superiority of the machine over the animal, these are all present, but they are subservient to Dovzhenko's beautiful rendering of nature and the ingenuousness of the peasant mind. A crude form of propaganda is overcome by a visionary outlook — an outlook that seeks to express the richness and materialism of life. There is nothing glorifying in the coming of the tractor in *Earth*: rather does Dovzhenko evoke our sympathy and love for the graceful horses and milk-white oxen whose tasks are now at an end. *Earth* gives us something new in cinema, something which — although slightly similar in technical methods of approach — is a thousand removes distant from the revolutions of an Eisenstein and a Pudovkin or the shuttlecock activities of a Dziga Vertov.

Dovzhenko's approach to cinema was through comedy. His first script, *Vasya the Reformer* (1926), and first film, *The Fruits of Love* (1926), were comedies, as well as many of his unrealized projects (among them *Chaplin Lost*, about Charlie on a desert island). The main character in *Vasya the Reformer*, directed by F. Lopatinski (no print has survived), is a young Soviet pioneer who gets himself into trouble trying to right wrongs, but manages in the process to expose a drunkard, a slacker, a priest and a thief as social parasites. The priest is working a fraudulent miracle, which Vasya reveals, whereupon the congregation converts the church into a cinema with the priest as the projectionist. The same playfulness runs through the fantasy *Zvenigora* (1928), an important forerunner to *Arsenal* and *Earth*.

Lev Kuleshov's *The Extraordinary Adventures of Mr. West in the Land of the Bolsheviks* (1923) and Alexander Medvedkin's *The*

Fortune (1935) were important satires on the young revolutionary state. The fresh, experimental, fun-loving nature of these films, relatively free of ideology, rivalled the polemics of Eisenstein and Pudovkin in the 1920s and the rigid Socialist Realist films of the 1930s. Satire died on the Russian stage in 1928, when Gorki's last-minute intercession with Stalin before the première of Meyerhold's production of Nikolai Erdmann's *The Suicide* failed. In the play unemployment drives a beaten-down citizen to threaten suicide, leading to a lottery among intellectuals, clerics, artists, workers and aging Cleopatras for the "prize" suicide note — the hero should die for a real cause! In the end he is too weak to go through with it, but another commits suicide in his place; Mayakovsky did so in 1930.

Upon Eisenstein's return from abroad in 1932 after the aborted *Que Viva Mexico!*, an epic on Mexican culture, he had difficulties from the start with *Bezhin Meadow* (1936), ostensively a film on the struggle for farm collectivization. Because of illness and other interferences it was only half completed and then destroyed, but a piecing-together of 1,200 cuts from the film in 1963 (saved by Eisenstein's widow) reveals an extolling of humanism over propaganda. In the sequence on the desecration of the church by peasants, he contrasts human faces with the artifacts of Christianity; it's the most religious film Eisenstein has made. An examination of *Alexander Nevsky* (1938), the glorification of a military genius who also is a saint venerated in the Russian Orthodox Church, reveals the same tensions at the root of the drama. A comparison between the first and second parts of *Ivan the Terrible* indicates again a preference for humanism over ideology: its portrait of a maddened leader is powerful and unforgettable; the second part was released in 1958 after Stalin's death. He never finished the third part before his death in 1948, but his sketches of the project point to a spiritual character in keeping with the best tradition of Soviet cinema.

Catholic propaganda films were officially approved at a religious congress sponsored in Paris by Cardinal Dubois in 1929. Julien Duvivier, one of the leading figures in French cinema of the 1930s, presented a model propaganda feature on *The Wonderful Life of Thérèse Martin* (1929). There was material enough in the silent era to build on; the best known religious epic since the Passion Plays was Jacques de Baroncelli's *The Legend of Sister Beatrix* (1923), based on the pious legend about the Virgin impersonating a novice who temporarily deserted the convent (the basis of Max Reinhardt's *The Miracle*). Religiosity permeates Abel Gance's *La Roue* (1923), the love story of a railway engineer impressive for the grandeur of its conception. The roots of Catholic propaganda films are to be found in these legendary, romantic tales of valor and piety, although the official movement inaugurated by Cardinal Dubois began immediately after the impact of Eisenstein's *Potemkin*.

To support the cause of Cardinal Dubois, Pope Pius XI introduced the motto "cinema in the service of faith" in encyclicals *Divini illius Magistri* (1929) and *Casti Connubii* (1930). Duvivier produced his picture-book Passion, *Golgotha* (1934), with Jean Gabin taking honors in the role of Pilate. Duvivier then moved over to the commercial arena for *The Golem* (1936) and *The Phantom Carriage* (1939), while his biggest success was *Pépé le Moko* (1937). Charles Ford credits Léon Poirier as the leading French director espousing clerical and military fervor in cinema:

On the whole all of Léon Poirier's films were impregnated with belief: in *La Brière* (1924) the peasants trust in God while plagued with misfortunes; in *Verdun* (1928) it is the death of the atheist intellectual, arms crossed in a blessing by the chaplain; in *Caïn* (1930) a poverty-striken victim of the machine finds God again in uncovering the vestments of a missionary; in *Sœurs d'armes* (1937) Louise de Bettignies and Léonie Vanhoutte unite their faith and their patriotism under the same fervor.

Poirier's favorite saint was Charles de Foucauld in *L'Appel du Silence* (1936) and *La Route inconnue* (1947), an army officer turned priest who died as a missionary in the African desert.

Such fervor brought predictable reactions from French intellectuals. Jean Vigo's *Zéro de Conduite* (1933) and *L'Atalante* (1934) ridiculed moral convention; they both fell under the heavy hand of the censor. The best of the surrealist films, Luis Bunuel's *Un Chien Andalou* (1928) (script by Dali), Germaine Dulac's *The Seashell and the Clergyman* (1928) (script by Antonin Artaud), and Jean Cocteau's *The Blood of the Poet* (1930), were directed against the horror for sexual love in the propaganda film. Bunuel's *L'Age d'Or* (1930), the most famous *avant-garde* film made, was an open attack on the church. Jeff Musso's *The Puritan* (1939) portrayed a religious fanatic driven by sexual obsessions to murder. Renoir made two parables on the conditions of the times, *The Grand Illusion* (1937) and *The Rules of the Game* (1939), which met with censorship difficulties at home and abroad. With the Occupation surrealist poets Benjamin Péret and André Breton sailed for Mexico, Cocteau was under house arrest, and only Marcel Carné and poet-scriptwriter Jacques Prévert kept the once-thriving French industry alive with the fatalistic, sensitive *The Children of Paradise* (1945).

After the war some accounts had to be settled. A new wave of religious films responded to the horrors of the war. The best of these, Maurice Cloche's *Monsieur Vincent* (1947) from a script by Jean Anouilh, set a standard. Photographed by Claude Renoir and starring Pierre Fresnay, the film was awarded the Grand Prize at the Venice Film Festival and selected in America as the Best Foreign Film of 1948. Pauline Kael wrote on this controversial film:

Pierre Fresnay's performance as the desperately compassionate Vincent de Paul gives extraordinary feeling and depth to Jean Anouilh's sensitive, lucid scenario. Though de Paul's very considerable intellectual gifts are minimized, this diminution is preferable to the usual dreadful solution of having an actor mutter platitudes while the other actors gasp, how brilliant! Although the character is simplified, it is quite possibly the best biographical film ever made: the emotions — the revulsion and horror at poverty, misery, cruelty — come through without mawkishness.

Monsieur Vincent was a parable of the times, a reflection on the inhumanity of the war, which accounts for the contribution of recognized talent to the project. The saint biographies to follow — Marcel Blistene's *Heaven and Earth* (1949) on Jean Baptiste Vianney, Marcel Garand's *Athlete With Bare Hands* (1952) on Michel Garricoits, and André Haguet's *Trial at the Vatican* (1952) — returned to the old format. An ebullient Fernandel in Julien Duvivier's French-Italian coproduction, *The Little World of Don Camillo*, raised it to an above-average comedy.

An indirect condemnation of church complacency during the war years lay below the surface of Jean Delannoy's adaptation of André Gide's *Symphonie Pastorale* (1946), in which the pastor's misplaced attention for his blind charge carried wider implications; the film won a prize at the Cannes festival. Delannoy followed with the ambiguous *God Needs Men* (1950), the story of a simple man on a primitive isle (Pierre Fresnay) assuming the office of priesthood for the sake of humanity. In *Destinies* (1953), a three-part film, Delannoy has Michèle Morgan as Joan of Arc performing meaningless miracles. Claude Autant-Lara's *The Red Inn* (1951) featured Fernandel as a

Rabelaisian monk clumsily trying to prevent the murder of his companions and still keep the seal of confession at the same time; reference to the war was obvious. René Clément's *Forbidden Games* (1952), the story of children playing morbid games in wartime, reflected provincial Catholic thinking in bitter, satirical terms; it was another controversial prize winner at the Venice festival.

A new humanity crept into religious films in the 1950s. The films of Léo Joannon, seldom seen outside of France, are representative of the broadening of "cinema in the service of faith" doctrine. *The Renegade Priest* (1953) is the story of a defrocked priest who sinks to the depths but cannot live down his past, Pierre Fresnay again in the lead role. Philippe Agostini, the photographer on Robert Bresson's *Les Anges du Péché* (1943), made the acclaimed *Dialogue des Carmélites* (1960), based on a true incident in the French Revolution: a group of nuns are martyred for their faith.

A love-hate relationship with the church characterizes the best of modern French cinema. The barbs directed at the church on the side in Clément's *Purple Noon* (1959) and Louis Malle's *Viva Maria* (1965) are matched by moments of understanding in Georges Rouquier's *Lourdes et ses Miracles* (1954) and Chris Marker's interview with the priest-worker in *Le Joli Mai* (1962). Jacques Rivette's *La Religieuse* (1966) and Jean-Pierre Melville's *Léon Morin, Priest* (1961) are ambiguous films that stir the imagination. For a profound view of religion in French cinema, the films of Robert Bresson are unparalleled.

Religious propaganda in Italian films was strengthened by Mussolini's rise to power in 1922; he immediately imposed controls on the press, radio and film for the betterment of the State. His rapid rise to power was undoubtedly aided by the "Roman Question," whereby the Vatican in effect forbade Catholics to enter government until the Papal States were returned. Mussolini settled the question through a concordat with Pope Pius XI in 1929. Immediately afterwards, the church approved cinema as an "instrument of the apostolate" in the encyclical *Vigilanti Cura* (1936); it went so far as to support government film censorship. Mussolini opened the first international film festival at Venice in 1933 as a showcase for cinema propaganda. Three years later he timed the release of Goffredo Alessandrini's *The Apostle of the Desert* (1936), the story of a missionary saint in North Africa, with the invasion of Ethiopia.

Matters took a swift change in wartime. Scriptwriter Cesare Zavattini and director Vittorio De Sica were hidden away in 1943 with actors, technicians and extras on a film about miraculous cures at the shrine at Loreto. Pauline Kael on *The Gates of Heaven*:

He managed to keep this project going for two years — at times with as many as three thousand people taking refuge with him in the Basilica of St. Paul's, where he had built a replica of Loreto. As soon as the Allies took over, he completed the film in a week. The Church, indignant at the way his thousands had carried on within the holy precincts, was not mollified by the movie — *The Gates of Heaven* (1945) — in which, as De Sica put it, "The miracle which had been invoked did not take place, but the resignation which the sick people learned seemed to me to be a real miracle." *The Gates of Heaven* was suppressed.

The chief architect of neo-realism was Cesare Zavattini, but the best films of the movement are those made in equal partnership with De Sica. Their collaboration on *Shoeshine* (1946), *Bicycle Thief* (1948), *Miracle in Milan* (1950) and *Umberto D* (1952) forms a unique chapter in the history of cinema. The human dimension of neo-realism colors De Sica's description of *Miracle in Milan*:

Here is no hymn in praise of poverty — as I read somewhere to my horror — nor any condemnation of riches. (I do not think either Zavattini or I can be accused of such bad taste in making use of an antithesis that would leave little room in the work for any art!) This is a fable, slightly wistful perhaps, but quietly optimistic within poetic framework, if I may be allowed to give it such a name. Men and angels are to be found here, living on good terms together. Toto works miracles for all comers and works them, obviously, for the benefit of those who need them — that is to say, the poor. But these people, with their dreamy, ingenuous looks, do not ask only for things that will satisfy their material needs and alleviate their distress. They ask also for superfluous, even ridiculous things, to appease some secret longing for them. A wardrobe, yes, but a phonograph too.

Neo-realism was defined by Zavattini as a "hunger for reality," the thirst after the moment in which we live in as immediate a way as possible. But it was also a reaction against the limitations of making innocuous films, the movement beginning in the early 1940s with Visconti's *Ossessione* (1942) and De Sica's *The Children Are Watching Us* (1943) to last for a decade until approximately 1952. Rossellini's *Open City* (1945) gave the movement acclaim, using non-professional actors and actual locations in occupied Rome for the story of a priest and a communist working together in the Resistance. *Paisan* (1946), a hymn to the Resistance, followed in the same mold and is remarkable for its subtle evocation of humanity. In the monastery sequence a Jewish army chaplain accompanying his Catholic and Protestant colleagues causes an irregularity in the lives of the monks. The last film of the war trilogy, *Germany, Year Zero* (1947), dealt with the reality of a divided Europe. After the scandalous *The Miracle* episode in *Love* (1948), the story of an idiot shepherd girl (Anna Magnani) seduced by a wandering tramp (Federico Fellini) she believes is St. Joseph, he made *The Flowers of St. Francis* (1949), the cast composed of monks from the *Paisan* episode. Federico Fellini assisted as scriptwriter.

With the close victory of the Vatican over the Communists at the polls in 1946, the concordat with Mussolini held firm. The situation was reflected in the most curious of postwar Italian films, Curzio Malaparte's *Il Cristo Proibito* (1950), in which a primitive Passion Play provides the background for a strange, somber exploration of guilt and moral responsibility. Alessandro Blasetti's *Fabiola* (1948), a tired rehashing of Christians in ancient Rome, was the first film produced by Universalia, a Vatican-sponsored film company.

As in France during the 1950s, a new humanity crept into religious themes: Blasetti's *First Communion* (1950), a Zavattini-scripted story, deals with a father's dilemma when his daughter's communion dress doesn't arrive on time; Augusto Genina's *Maddalena* (1954) is a fascinating story of revenge, in which a prostitute from a rival town passes herself off as a virgin to play the madonna in a religious procession; and Mario Camerini, another old-time propaganda director, made the delightful *The Awakening* (1956) from a Zavattini script, in which a nun's womanly instincts betray her when she takes charge of an unwanted boy. Neo-realism influenced the cinema of Fellini, Michelangelo Antonioni, Ermanno Olmi, Pier Paolo Pasolini, Francesco Rosi and Pietro Germi, as well as Socialist cinema in the 1950s.

Goebbels's broad definition of propaganda was simply to win the heart of the people and keep it; it meant plenty of entertainment and little haranguing. A propaganda ideal was fashioned out of the architecturally sound Fritz Lang spectacles and the mountain films of Arnold Fanck. Motifs from these two sources are clearly visible in Leni Riefenstahl's *The Triumph of the Will* (1934), required viewing for every German after the rise of Hitler. It was considered a dream film of the country's future glory.

The political use of religion in Nazi films demonstrates a complete understanding of the importance of ritual and symbol. Hans Stein-

hoff's *Hitler Youth Quex* (1933) blends scout uniforms, campfire ceremonies, songs, flag-waving, marching and mother-love into a martyr
theme of powerful proportions. Folke Isaksson and Leif Furhammar
describe the religious psychology of this film:

> The religious overtones become increasingly noticeable as the film nears its end,
> but they are well established from the outset. Martyrdom can be predicted from
> the start for poor, frail little Heini, the film's saintly hero. He grows up in a
> poor Berlin family, and although his mother is a good woman, his unemployed
> father has been led astray by socialist ideas. Little blond Heini is drawn into
> communist youth activities, and "the commune" will obviously be seen later on
> in the film as the negative pole in opposition to the wonderful Hitler Youth, but
> it is indicative of the film's psychological tactics that the communists are portrayed
> at first with some sensitivity and the gradual transition into caricature is so subtle
> as to be almost imperceptible. With elaborately disarming tactics, Stoppel, the
> leader of the commune, is introduced as a sympathetic, authoritative element of
> security in Heini's impoverished existence, only to be gradually revealed as a
> seductive force, destructive and evil.

Both *The Triumph of the Will* and *Hitler Youth Quex* are masterful
displays of the psychological power of film as propaganda: they
astonish audiences even today, who have little understanding as to
why they were made. The formulas were so minutely worked out as
to be applicable in other films without fear of detection. *Hitler Youth
Quex* provides the sacrificial motif for Peter Hagen's *Village in a Red
Storm* (1935), a story set in a German community on the Volga in
which a pacifist pastor is gradually driven to rebel against drunken
Russian soldiers violating his church; he dies a martyr defending the
honor of God and his people. Mercy-killing was sold to the public
through Wolfgang Liebeneiner's *I Accuse* (1941), the story of a fun-
loving, vivacious housewife reduced to a helpless cripple by an accidental fall leading to a doctor's "act of love" to put her to sleep
permanently. These difficult-to-refute private arguments, wedded to
the motif of sacrificial martyrdom, closed the public's eyes to the
truth.

The case of Leni Riefenstahl is different. In Kael's estimate, her
propaganda films, *The Triumph of the Will* and *Olympiad* (1936),
transcended political purposes to reach a level of art:

> Ironically, this beautiful young woman proved herself one of the dozen or so
> creative geniuses who have ever worked in the film medium. Out of the Nuremberg
> Rally of 1934, she made the most outrageous political epic of all time, the hypnotic
> *Triumph of the Will* (the outrage is that she could make a great film of it); out of

the Berlin Olympics she made a great lyric spectacle. *Olympiad* is only inciden-
tally a record of the actual games: she selected shots for their beauty rather than
for a documentary record. After eighteen months of editing she emerged with
over three hours of dazzling quality — a film that moves one kinesthetically in
response to physical tension, and psychologically in response to the anguish and
strain of men and women desperately competing for a place in history. And
despite Hitler's Aryan myth, she knew beauty when she saw it: in the throbbing
veins in Jesse Owens's forehead (in her book on *Olympiad*, Leni Riefenstahl has a
simple caption for his picture — "*Jesse Owens, der schnellste Mann der Welt*");
in the lean Japanese swimmers; in the divers soaring in flight so continuous that
they have no nationality. Now, *Olympiad* is an elegy on the youth of 1936: here
they are in their flower, dedicated to the highest ideals of sportsmanship — these
young men who were so soon to kill each other.

Athletic heroism is very much alive in Viktor de Kowa's *Head
High, Johannes* (1941), a junior version of the youth festivities in
Triumph and *Olympiad* and similar in tone to Norman Taurog's *Boys'
Town* (1938) for M-G-M. Eduard von Borsody's *Wish Concert* (1941)
(after a well-known radio program of the day) opens with the Olympics and a tale of romance to end with heroism on the Polish front,
as a young soldier sacrifices himself to save his companions by playing
on an organ in a burning church. One of the most popular of Nazi
films, *Wish Concert* is excellent entertainment: the radio program
was a contact between families at home and husbands and sons on the
front, providing songs and comedy routines by leading show people.

At the height of the war the church became a symbol of comfort
and protection. In Veit Harlan's *The Great King* (1942), a film about
Frederick the Great in battle (easily transferred to the personality of
Hitler), the film ends with the king seated in a light-splattered cathedral weeping for his fallen soldiers. In Harlan's *Kolberg* (1944), the
last war epic, the church provides comfort and inspiration to carry on
the struggle.

The Jewish vilification films often contradicted themselves. In
Hans Heinz Zerlott's *Robert and Bertram* (1939), released after
Hitler's speech against the Jews in the Reichstag in January 1939,
two comical characters wander into a Jewish masquerade ball; it is
evidently meant to be parody, but humor dominates and the losers
turn out to be winners. Fritz Hippler's *The Eternal Jew* (1940), the
most notorious of racist films, argued through "documentation" that
Jews were a lower form of humanity, but the arguments reach such
levels of absurdity ("Jews decided what could be called art and culture;
Max Reinhardt was the Jewish dictator of the stage; Jewry is a con-

spiracy against all the peoples of the world") they offend the intelligence. Veit Harlan's *Jud Süss* (1940) stars the gifted Ferdinand Marian as a Stuttgart Shylock of the 1730s. Werner Krauss also plays a rabbi, but Marian in particular, as an attractive, sympathetic character, is far more interesting than Heinrich George's dull-witted German prince. (George at this time was known for his fatherly, typical-German-citizen roles; his portrait of a stupid, incontinent monarch was thus all the more unbelievable.) The film is said to have upset Goebbels because the audience's sympathy should have been the other way around!

The *Jud Süss* experience necessitated a new approach to acting. Fritz Hippler, second only to Goebbels in the film department of the Ministry of Propaganda between 1939 and 1943, offered this solution, according to Isaksson and Furhammer:

In a pamphlet entitled "Betrachtungen zum Filmschaffen" ("Some Thoughts on Filmmaking") published in 1942, Hippler develops his new conception of films as both art and propaganda. A film must be the clear expression of a message. "In the cinema the audience must know with greater certainty than in the theatre whom to love and whom to hate." In an anti-semitic film the Jews must appear unsympathetic and all other characters must inspire at least some degree of sympathy.

The frightening factor in Hippler's bid to teach people "whom to love and whom to hate" is that he could make such a statement with the certainty of acceptance. The illusion that civilized man is in complete control of his thoughts and emotions has been erased by the bloody conflicts of this century, the extermination camps and the ominous spectre of the bomb. James Agee commented on the Nazi atrocity films exhibited in America at the same time as a harsh peace was delivered to the people of Germany:

I think (revenge) has taken such strong hold on so many of us most essentially because we suspect the passion itself, and know that even if the passion were a valid one to honor there would be no finding a victim, or forms of vengeance, remotely sufficient to satisfy it. We cannot bear to face our knowledge that the satisfaction of our desire for justice, which we confuse with our desire for vengeance, is impossible. And so we invent as a victim the most comprehensive image which our reason, however deranged, will permit us: the whole of a people and the descendants of that people: and count ourselves incomparably their superiors if we stop short of the idea of annihilation. And we refuse to grant that this war has proved itself lost — if indeed it ever could have been won — as surely in our own raging vengefulness as in that of the mob in the Milan square. Indeed, we are worse than they and worse, in some respects, than the Nazis.

There can be no bestiality so discouraging to contemplate as that of the man of good-will when he is misusing his heart and his mind; and there can be no trusting him merely because, in the long run, he customarily comes part way to, and resumes his campaign for, what he likes to call human dignity.

In America pressure groups grew after the First World War. Sensing trouble, the Hollywood moguls enlisted Will H. Hays, the Postmaster General of President Harding's cabinet, to reign as czar over the hastily formed Motion Picture Producers and Distributors of America (MPPDA) in 1922 (at a salary of $100,000 a year). Hays kept the job until 1945 and the office (changed to MPAA in 1945, the Motion Picture Association of America) took his name, while the Production Code he helped install became known as the Hays Office Code.

With the advent of radio, Catholics in city ghettos banned together into the National Union for Social Justice under the voice of Father Charles Coughlin. Coughlin in the mid-1930s had a million registered members, with reliable polls indicating that he could command a fourth of the voting population. (His ruination was attempting to start a third party in the 1936 elections challenging Roosevelt.) The Protestants formed the Christian Defenders under Gerald Winrod. Both political pressure groups were anti-semitic and pro-Nazi, in addition to being diametrically opposed to one another. They were able to mend their fences on one primary issue: the morality of the movies in the hands of Jews and bankers. Winrod's champion was Hays; Catholics backed the quasi-religious organization known as the Legion of Decency.

The Legion of Decency owed its existence to the Depression years, as the only entertainment and escape for the poor then was going to the movies. With the birth of the talkies, and the wedding of word to image, the industry realized that a production code was necessary to set some standards for the presence of bedrooms and bathrooms on the screen. The belief that sex sold the most tickets paralleled the sensationalized findings of Henry James Forman's *Our Movie Made Children*, thirteen studies on movies and children conducted by the Motion Picture Research Council between 1929 and 1933. In the midst of this research the first Code was written in 1929 by two Catholics in the Midwest, the Jesuit Daniel A. Lord (religious advisor on Cecil B. DeMille's *The King of Kings*) and Martin Quigley, the publisher of a motion picture journal; it was adopted by the industry in

1930. Studio heads were held to their "word of honor", which meant violations were common. By 1933 the Vatican's Apostolic Delegate in the United States announced: "Catholics are called by God, the Pope, the bishops and the priests to a united and vigorous campaign for the purification of the cinema, which has become a deadly menace to morals." In 1934 the Episcopal Committee for Motion Pictures was formed; Cardinal Dougherty of Philadelphia then requested a pledge from his congregation to "volunteer" to stay away from the movies for a designated length of time. Business fell off forty percent; Catholic bishops pulled the strings on ten million viewers, plus many favorably minded Protestants and Jews. The national Legion of Decency was born.

Hollywood, frightened by the church's ability to command so large a share of the mass population, immediately made the code mandatory and placed Joseph I. Breen, a member of Hays's Hollywood branch, in charge of a newly established Production Code Administration. The power of the Legion and the PCA lasted into the mid-1960s, choking off much of what was original and creative in the industry through a rigid censorship of scripts and the former's system of rating films for the general public. Fritz Lang on how he handled the role of the prostitute in *Man Hunt* (1941):

(Joan Bennett) cries like a child because the man whom she wants so very much doesn't sleep with her. There is so much in it: shame — "maybe I'm not good enough for him?" Desire — "why can't it be fulfilled?" And I think it was beautifully written. But, naturally, the Hays Office insisted that we couldn't show or glamourize a prostitute — that's impossible. (They said she should not swing her purse back and forth.) You know how we overcame it? We had to prominently show a sewing machine in her apartment: thus she was not a whore, she was a "seamstress"! Talk about authenticity.

The puritanism of the system gave some directors the boost they needed. Just as Stiller was able to fashion a distinct style and approach to visual eroticism under the eyes of puritan censors in Sweden, so Ernst Lubitsch developed a "touch" for the psychology of closed doors, shadows across beds and stolen glances. The humor of W. C. Fields and director Gregory La Cava only makes sense in a captive Hollywood. In Fields's *The Dentist* (1932), directed by Leslie Pierce for Mack Sennett, he is busy pulling a tooth when his patient conveniently wraps her legs about him: who could yell foul in such circumstances? Described by Agee as "the toughest and the most warmly human of all screen comedians," Fields got better as the system grew worse: *The Bank Dick* (1940) is a satirical portrait of stiff-necked Hollywood prudery. Andrew Sarris, who bases much of his *auteur* theory on the in-fighting at the Hays Office, places La Cava on "the far side of paradise":

Gregory La Cava's best films — *She Married Her Boss* (1935), *My Man Godfrey* (1936), *Stage Door* (1937), and *Unfinished Business* (1941) — reveal a flair for improvisation and a delicate touch with such expert comediennes as Claudette Colbert, Carole Lombard, Katherine Hepburn, Ginger Rogers, and Irene Dunne. The seduction scene of Irene Dunne and Preston Foster in *Unfinished Business*, like that of Jean Arthur and Joel McCrea in Stevens's *The More the Merrier* (1943), demonstrates the conflict between Hollywood's erotic images and its laundered scripts. Significantly, La Cava was most effective when he could work between the lines of his scenarios and against the conventions of his plots. W. C. Fields credited La Cava with the best comedy mind in Hollywood next to Fields's own, and *Life* magazine once reproduced La Cava's on-the-set sketches for the Billy Rose takeoff in *Unfinished Business*. Of such trifles was the legend of La Cava fashioned.

As Hollywood grew more protective, and the Red Scare added more gloom to the industry's hothouse atmosphere, many comic directors who helped create the Golden Age of Comedy lost contact with reality and the public. The downfall of Frank Capra can be measured by matching the carefree gaiety of his Harry Langdon silents (*The Strong Man*, 1926, *Long Pants*, 1927) with the political populism of *Meet John Doe* (1941) and the cracker-barrel philosophy of *It's a Wonderful Life* (1946). Leo McCarey, who worked with nearly every major comedian in Hollywood in the 1930s, descended to oath-taking in *My Son John* (1952) to cite his allegiance to the McCarthy Hearings. George Stevens, who began his career in Laurel and Hardy two-reelers, finished with one of the box office duds of all time, *The Greatest Story Ever Told* (1965), the apogee of the Passion Play.

The heyday of the Code and the Legion also witnessed the "screwball" comedies of the 1930s and the Preston Sturges productions of the 1940s. About Sturges's *The Miracle of Morgan's Creek* (1944) Agee wrote: "The Hays Office has either been hypnotized into a liberality for which it should be thanked, or has been raped in its sleep." The Warner Brothers "protest films" (Mervyn LeRoy's *I Am a Fugitive From a Chain Gang*, 1932), as well as the wacky comedies of the Marx Brothers, Fields and Mae West, indirectly owe their existence to the Hollywood straight-jacket; they challenged the moral conventions of the time with a lust for life.

Worst of all were the "priest films" of the 1930s: Spencer Tracy in W. S. Van Dyke's *San Francisco* (1936) and Norman Taurog's *Boys' Town* (1938) are just two soppy, unrealistic examples. The genre gave way to the "nun pictures" of the 1940s: Leo McCarey's *The Bells of St. Mary's* (1945) and John Stahl's *The Keys of the Kingdom* (1944). The Hollywood saint biographies, as Henry King's *The Song of Bernadette* (1944), were designed to move into the foreign market at the close of the war, while "religioso" films (*Variety*'s name for the biblical, religious epic) from DeMille's *Samson and Delilah* (1949) to Robert Wise's *The Sound of Music* (1965) were a throwback to the Victorian melodrama. The Supreme Court "Miracle" case in 1952, permitting exhibition of Rossellini's *The Miracle* (now an episode in a three-part film titled *Ways of Love*, opening in New York in 1950), ended the reign of the Legion of Decency as the country's strongest pressure group.

The Legion and the Production Code Administration sowed the seeds of future discontent by their rigid approach to moral, theological and political issues beyond the pale of entertainment. Richard Corliss documents how the Legion, while approving ninety percent of the Hollywood product up to 1942, nevertheless took a stand on the Spanish Civil War in deciding against the Loyalist view in Walter Wanger's production of *Blockade* (1938), directed by William Dieterle; the action was severely criticized in the trade magazines. And Agee strongly objected to the moral reasoning in Robert Florey's *God Is My Co-Pilot* (1945):

In *God Is My Co-Pilot* the Flying Tiger hero, Dennis Morgan, tells a priest, Alan Hale, that he has killed a hundred men that day; he obviously feels deeply troubled by the fact, and is asking for spiritual advice. Since the priest does not answer him in any way about that, but pretends to by commenting comfortably on a quite different and much easier perplexity — *every* death makes a difference to God — it is regrettable, not to say nauseating, that they bothered to bring up the problem at all. Aside from these religious conversations, any of which would serve to unite atheists and religious men in intense distaste for the lodgers in the abyss which separates them, there is a good deal of air combat on process screens, obstructed by the customary close-ups of pilots smiling grimly as they give and take death in a studio, for considerably more than soldiers' pay, a yard above the ground. The picture is not as bad, I must admit, as I'm making it sound; but it is not good enough to make me feel particularly sorry about that. God is my best pal and severest critic, but when He asked for this touching March afternoon off, I didn't have it in my heart to refuse Him.

The ritualistic side of religion lends itself naturally to symbols and parables in the movies. The rebirth of Christ as clown, presently so popular in music, painting and theatre, has its modern film expression in the clown figures appearing in Bergman's *Sawdust and Tinsel* (or *The Naked Night*) (1953) and Fellini's *La Strada* (1954), both drawing their inspiration from Chaplin's *The Circus* (1928) (his own Christ film). The same figure appeared in the popular, symbol-laden *The Parable*, a short film produced for the Protestant pavilion at the 1966 New York World's Fair. The following year Stuart Rosenberg's *Cool Hand Luke* (1967) paraphrased the Life and Passion of Christ in a southern chain gang. The Virgin Birth was fodder for Roman Polanski's *Rosemary's Baby* (1968); the Parable of the Good Samaritan motivated John Schlesinger's *Midnight Cowboy* (1969); and everything from the Wedding Feast of Cana to the Transfiguration (the pot trip) was thrown into Dennis Hopper's *Easy Rider* (1969). The Last Supper made one of many appearances in Robert Altman's *M.A.S.H.* (1970), and the movement was capped with the Norman Jewison production of *Jesus Christ Superstar* (1973). They all made big money for backers. *Variety* commented:

The Sunset Strip's reconstructed junkies first spawned the "Jesus freaks" a couple of years back, but the gospel handclapping and religioso cycle has accelerated into a number of vivid show biz milestones this year. *Jesus Christ Superstar* may be the unquestioned all-media show biz parlay in show business history. From a 3,000,000 album bestseller (retail gross $35,000,000), the (Robert) Stigwood Organization with MCA (which owns Decca Records, producer of the two-platter package) the stage property rights have kept a host of their legal correspondents around the country almost as busy as vet copyright attorneys... pursuing and suing cassette pirates.

The fervor of Hollywood in postwar years to milk every penny out of biblical epics, symbol-laden parables and Jesus cult films has left little room for a cinema of genuine religious dialogue. This has been almost entirely the domain of European cinema.

VII.   CINEMA AS REFLECTION OF MAN

Jean Renoir discovered in 1938:

Naively and painstakingly I tried to imitate my American teachers: I had not realized that a Frenchman living in France drinking his red wine and eating his brie cheese and looking out on the grey Parisian skyline can only produce a work of excellence by relying on the traditions of people who have lived as he has lived.

The one exception is the universal character of Robert Flaherty's documentaries. But he practised the wisdom of Renoir without tying himself to any particular land or culture; he took the time to know intimately the people he was filming: ten years with the Eskimo for *Nanook of the North* (1911-1921), two years in Polynesia for *Moana* (1923-1925), three years on the coast of Ireland for *Man of Aran* (1932-1934), and three years with a Cajun boy in the bayous for *Lousiana Story* (1946-1948).   John Grierson wrote about him:

His idea of production is to reconnoiter for months without turning a foot, and then, in months more perhaps, slowly to shape the film on the screen; using his camera first to sketch his material and find his people, then using the screen, as Chaplin uses it, to tell him at every turn where the path of drama lies.

Flaherty shaped his film into the thinking of an already existing social structure. He approached the secrets of life and living with an open mind. He was in communion with man's universal aspirations, with the ties binding him to nature, to his social environment, to his fellow human being. He accepted the universe as mysterious and secretive: man was its privileged chalice. All his films radiate this "sense of the holy."

Only a few directors have rendered in a personal style authentic portraits of the life they know best.   Renoir and Rossellini are in the first rank; others like Ford, Eisenstein, Sjöström and Bunuel strike familiar chords; the documentaries of Georges Rouquier, Bert Haanstra and Arne Sucksdorff have Flaherty's way of using the camera. None of these, however, approaches the world with the same sense of the holy — or with Flaherty's second gift, his "sense of anticipation," which allowed him to penetrate man's thinking process. Only on occasion do these directors, as significant as their contribution to cinema is, manifest a listening to the heart and soul of a people.

Flaherty's habit was to search into the lives of people to find what was to them of vital significance; by beginning with the simple, everyday things this led him to the feelings and thoughts which lay at the heart of the lives of every people. Renoir's films are anchored in a deep personal humanism; his best films are created in communion with the public.

According to my notion, at any rate in the great arts — the important arts — the work of art is also created by the public. In fact a picture, shall we say one by Picasso, is great because the public that loves that picture can put into it as much of itself as did Picasso. And to my thinking that is an essential condition of a work of art. I was speaking about this recently to my friend Pierre Gaut, the producer of *Toni*, a film I made at least twenty years ago. Together we had decided that it would be interesting to make a film entirely out of doors, with a few professional actors, but many amateurs, without a studio, with people talking as people talk, with their accent, without make-up. In brief, we did, not a few years before, something of what the Italians (whom we call "neo-realists") and my friend Rossellini were to do after the war, after the liberation of Italy.

Rossellini's main interest was man: he tried to express man's innermost self, his essence, the soul; at the same time this individuality was intimately tied to a sense for man's surroundings, which took their meaning from someone looking at them. His *The Flowers of St. Francis* (1949), viewing the universe through the eyes of Franciscan monks, is the key expression of this philosophy.

Through Flaherty an evaluation of cinema as reflection of man becomes easier. His "sense of the holy" separates the humanistic and the sublime in cinema from the didactic, the dialectic and the ethnographic. There is a major difference, for example, between Flaherty, Renoir and Rossellini and the school of Joris Ivens, Chris Marker and Jean Rouch. Ivens has been to every corner of the globe too, but his observations are tied to the central theme of man's universal struggle against social and natural oppression. The Ivens argument in *Song of the Rivers* (1953), utilizes footage shot in thirty-two countries to join the largest rivers of the world together as an expression of the united struggle of trade unions. Chris Marker is another social critic and essayist with a predetermined point of view to sell. Ethnographer Jean Rouch uses his camera for educational purposes, often selecting details for communication at the expense of the whole. These views of man's universe are not so much observations as rational arguments.

Cinema as reflection of man works at the level of everyday reality. If we place Georges Rouquier's *Farrébique* (1946), Bert Haanstra's *Alleman* (1964), Kaneto Shindo's *The Island* (1960), Satyajit Ray's *Aparajito* (1956), and Arne Sucksdorff's *The Great Adventure* (1953) side by side, we discover they say as much about the family of man as about France, Netherlands, Japan, India and Sweden. Sucksdorff speaks for the whole when he says:

I try to create life — at least, that is my aim and purpose. I think there is something uplifting in human endeavor that is praiseworthy, even ennobling. That is an eagerness for life, which I see as an embryo growing to life itself.

Today, with film distribution and exchange more accessible through festivals and forums, it is gradually becoming possible to compare the religious and social character of one people with another. An increasing trend in modern cinema everywhere is the recording of everyday life, of people in their own environment. On occasion, documents of lofty spirituality are created. As Michel Guntz pointed out, "the Western standpoint is humanist, individualistic, each personal drama calling the world in question; the Eastern vision is cosmic, spiritual, the trials of the individual having their roots in the immensity of creation and being resolved by acceptance." On this basis we can postulate a humanistic culture of world cinema.

In the Orient the Japanese cinema came into being during the reign of Emperor Meiji (1867-1912), a period of commercial expansion and trade with the West. Kenji Mizoguchi, the most spiritual of Japan's directors, viewed the social conditions of his times through the nostalgia, romance and myths of the Meiji period (apparently because of the severe censorship on contemporary subjects). He was a painter, actor and scriptwriter who began directing around 1923, earning a reputation equivalent to the popularity of Griffith and Ford (who reached back into the same historical period for their Civil War epics and Western sagas). Anderson and Richie affirm that Mizo-guchi's favorite myth, "the one seen at the core of most of his films, is that man's soul is saved by a woman's love." The films known best to Western audiences are *The Life of O-Haru* (1952) and *Ugetsu Monogatari* (1953). Close behind Mizoguchi come Yasujiro Ozu, considered the most Japanese by his colleagues, and Akira Kurosawa, whose humanism is in the vein of Renoir. Ozu views the universe through the microcosm of the family, and shoots his scenes from the eye level of a viewer seated on his *tatami*. The plotless story but rich character portraits in *Late Spring* (1949), about a father's relation-ship to his daughter before marriage, is typical of Ozu's profoundly religious world. Kurosawa's *Ikiru* or *Living* (1952), on the last days of a minor bureaucrat dying of cancer but seeking to leave behind something meaningful, is the best of his human documents. Kaneto Shindo's *The Island* (1961), the life of a peasant family deprived of water on the island where they live, is representative of the mysticism pervading the trials of the individual, whose roots are in the immen-sity of creation.

China became a major film-producing country in the 1930s. Yen Mou Che made *Street Angels* (1937), depicting the life pulse of the city of Shanghai. Tsai Tsou Sen's *The River Flows Eastward* (1948) follows the turmoil in a Chinese family during the war years and civil disturbances. Not much is known about humanist cinema in Hong Kong, which supplies films for much of Asia.

Vietnam under Ho Chi Minh developed a national cinema in 1948 with China's help. *Vietnam Fighting* (1951) and *The Girl From Hanoi* (1974) concentrate more on the life of the people than the war.

India was introduced to its own national cinema in 1913 by D. G. Phalke, a primitive artist who specialized in the mythologies. International recognition came with K. A. Abbas's *Munna* (1954), a socially critical film on conditions in the crowded cities. Its counter-part was Bimal Roy's *Two Acres of Land* (1953), a neo-realist story of a peasant leaving his land for the degrading work of a rickshaw man. The high point of Indian cinema is the Satyajit Ray *Apu* trilogy: *Pather Panchali* (1955), *Aparajito* (1957) and *The World of Apu* (1959). In the tradition of Robert Flaherty and the neo-realist school, Ray used natural backgrounds and non-professional actors for his tale of the miseries and hopes of a poor Bengali family. The success at home of *The World of Apu*, a free extension of the Bibhutibhusan Bandopaddhay novel forming the first two parts, paved the way for other personal documents on Indian life. His controversial *Devi (The Goddess)* (1960), *Two Daughters* (1962) and *Charulata* (1964) had some success at home as well as abroad. The spiritual realities of everyday life permeate Ray's films in the fullest sense: nowhere in Eastern cinema is "the sense of the holy" more felt than in the Apu trilogy, comparable in breath and depth to Flaherty's masterpieces.

Cinema in the Middle East has recently found itself; the industries are young after being held back by a strong Western influence. In the late 1950s a movement began in Morocco, Lebanon and Tunisia to seek a film style close to the people, and in 1966 a film conference was sponsored among the Arab nations to improve the overall condition. Among these nations Algeria is making the most progress, allowing young directors to wrestle with national problems to find their way. Mohammed Lakhdar-Hamina's *The Wind From Aurés* (1965), about a mother searching for her son during the Algerian war of independence, is this country's first authentic document, while his *Chronicle of the Years of Ashes* (1974) (Grand Prix at 1975 Cannes festival) is an impressive epic on Algeria's agonizing struggle for independence. Mohammed Bouamari's *The Inheritance* (1974) touches on village life immediately after the colonial period.

A new director, Sohrab Shahid Saless, has given young Iranian cinema its finest hour. In the style of Chekhov's short stories, his *A Simple Event* (1973), about a young boy in a fishing village, *Still Life* (1974), on the retirement of a gatekeeper at an isolated railway crossing, and *Far From Home*, on Turkish workers living in Berlin-Kreuzberg, are remarkable, quiet meditations on the human condition.

A group of African directors has emerged, among them Senegal's gifted Ousmane Sembene. A former dock worker in Marseilles and writer, he duplicated Ray's feat of finding a distinct style in his first film, *Borom Sarret* (1963), about a dock worker and class differences. His *The Mandabi* (1968) and *The Black Girl* (1965) are the first authentic Black African features treating the after-effects of colonialism in Senegal, while *Emitai* (1972) and *Xala (Impotence)* (1975) criticize Neo-colonialism. His films are characterized by the use of his native language, Wolof, and he has achieved in a short time a wide international reputation. Other African directors are still finding their way, too often crippled by their formation as émigrés (Désiré Ecaré's *Concerto for an Exile*, 1969) to make genuine documents at home. Sembene is the exception that should be the rule.

In Central and South America a cinema of social importance has developed with limited resources. This cinema in general is characterized by a revolutionary face. It began with Mexican cinema in its most productive national period (1935-1955); other countries conscious of a cinematic identity are Brazil and Cuba.

In the aftermath of the country's revolution, Mexico produced a large number of socially engaged features and documentaries. Among them was Emilio Fernandez's striking trilogy on the suppression and poverty of the Indians: *Maria Candelaria* (1944), *Enamorado* (1946), and *Rio Escondido* (1948). To these should be added Luis Bunuel's *Los Olvidados* (1950), on the slums and juvenile delinquents of Mexico City, and his *Ascent to Heaven* (1951), on the lives and morals of village people. Benito Alazraki's *Roots* (1955), a collection of Indian tales, marks the end of a truly native cinema without outside influence.

Cuba after a good beginning declined with the rise of Hollywood, but striking progress has been made again since 1959. Castro's first cultural decree was on cinema, and the fruits of a ten-year program are now evident. Tomas Gutierrez Alea's *Death of a Bureaucrat* (1967) and *Memories of Underdevelopment* (1968) view the revolution with self-criticism and introspection; they are relatively free of propaganda. As a gifted editor Santiago Alvarez has achieved world acclaim with a number of "message" documentaries, in which form outweighs content in the manner of early Russian propaganda films. Of special interest is Octavio Cortazar's *For the First Time* (1968), about a mobile projection unit venturing into the mountains to bring cinema for the first time to isolated villagers.

South American cinema has developed rapidly in the past decade. Jorge Sanjines in Bolivia attracted attention with his social document on Indian life in *Ukamau* (1966). Argentina has a more consistent film history, although held back by a predominant middle-class approach to social problems. Film pioneer Jose Ferreyra documented his country's progress in the silent era, as Salvador Toscano Barragan did during Mexico's revolutionary period. Like Mexico's, Argentina's film industry flowered briefly in the postwar years. Leopoldo Torre-Nilsson won international acclaim for *The House of the Angel* (1957) and *Hand in the Trap* (1961), about middle-class suffocation and drifting. Recently Fernando Solanas's *The Hour of the Furnaces* (1968) astounded audiences with its dynamic editing techniques to support a protracted political thesis on conditions in South America.

Brazil rose to a leading position in world cinema during the 1960s, only to see it erode in the past few years. Cinema Novo, or "Brazilian Cinema for Brazilians," grew out of the documentary influence of Alberto Cavalcanti and Italian neo-realism. Cavalcanti made *Song of the Sea* (1953), a human document on life in shanty towns around Recife, and initiated Vitor de Lima Barreto's *O Cangaceiro* (1953), a salute to the epoque of honorable bandits; it was the country's first acclaimed feature. Social themes characterized these films, but nothing really took hold until Nelson Pereira dos Santos's semi-documentary on slums, *Rio 40 Degrees* (1955), and his powerful testament to the famine-stricken poor of his country, *Barren Lives* (1963). The stark reality and authenticity of *Barren Lives* opened the way for the violent, lyrical and exotic wave of Cinema Novo films in the late 1960s, particularly the poetic, political films of Ruy Guerra and the religious, mystical epics of Glauber Rocha. These films are set in the huge wilderness of the Northeast, a land of myth and reality, bandits and prophets, violence and superstition — in Rocha's terms, gods and devils.

Guerra and Rocha complement each other. Guerra, the more Western of the two, molded his *The Guns* (1963) into a condemnation of violence and superstition, a dynamic political thesis that preaches rebellion at every turn. Rocha, moving away from the realism of Dos Santos's *Barren Lives* and the political analysis inherent in *The Guns*, made in the same year *Black God and White Devil* (1963) (its actual, poetic title is *God and Devil in the Land of the Sun*), a ballad on the myths, violence and revolution that compose this waste land; it is a visionary film of epic proportions. He next abandoned the Northeast for a romantic parable on the political forces active in contemporary Brazil, *Land in Trance* (1966), a story about an Eldorado placed somewhere in South America.

Needing a stronger political base, he returned to the land of gods and devils for his most important film to date, *Antonio das Mortes* (1969), a spectacle abandoning realism for the symbolism of a primitive morality play. Taking up where the last line in *Black God and*

White Devil left off — "the land belongs to Man and is neither God's nor the Devil's" — Rocha presents a bandit-killer who performs his duty and then renounces his mission to champion the rights of the people. The visual style of this film ballad is very close to the mythical American western, but is concretized by the harsh reality of a wilderness breeding hunger and violence. The last film in this cycle, Guerra's *The Gods and the Dead* (1971), shows a strong Rocha influence in its stylization of myth as a bizarre, expressionistic festival of death, violence, blood, pain, obsession, revolution — the whole of Brazilian reality in a sweeping epic of rich floral colors, cult worship and dispassionate cruelty.

The documentary traditions of England and the United States in the 1930s, as well as the finest work done at the National Film Board of Canada in the postwar years, can be traced to the magnetic personality of John Grierson. Born in Scotland in 1898, he joined the Empire Marketing Board in 1927. It had been founded "to promote all the major researches across the world which affect the production or preservation or transport of the British Empire's food supplies." At the bottom of its forty-five departments (below surveys, research programs and sales drives) was a film unit, eventually England's most important contribution to world cinema. Grierson was appointed joint officer of this unit, and he immediately began an exhaustive study of film technique. He ended by making *Drifters* (1929) with little experience and money, an impressionistic portrait of herring fishermen in the North Sea. On the basis of this first attempt Grierson was offered the position of film producer for E.M.B.; he immediately founded a school of documentary.

We believe that the cinema's capacity for getting around, for observing and selecting from life itself, can be exploited in a new and vital art form. The studio films largely ignore this possibility of opening up the screen on the real world. They photograph acted stories against artificial backgrounds. Documentary would photograph the living scene and the living story.... We believe that the original (or native) actor, and the original (or native) scene, are better guides to a screen interpretation of the modern world.... We believe that the materials and stories thus taken from the raw can be finer (more real in the philosophical sense) than the acted article.

Grierson noted that the power of the documentary lay in its emphasis on the dignity of man and its vigorous approach to social problems. It serves mankind on the simple, direct level of ordinary human existence, without sentimentality or pretense. It studies man's relationship to society, whether social, political, economic or scientific. Man, in a real world with real problems, is the only important issue.

Grierson's socially-conscious movement received a lift with the arrival on the scene of individualist Robert Flaherty, who worked with him on *Industrial Britain* (1932) and indirectly influenced the entire film unit. When E.M.B. was abolished in 1933, Grierson transferred his film unit to the General Post Office (G.P.O.). Here documentary film was given even greater support; among the name filmmakers working in the unit were Alberto Cavalcanti, Harry Watt, Basil Wright, Humphrey Jennings and Paul Rotha. Some outstanding documentaries made during this period were Grierson's *Granton Trawler* (1934), Wright's *Song of Ceylon* (1934-1935), and Watt and Wright's *Night Train* (1936). Just prior to the war in 1938 the G.P.O. disbanded its film unit, although the documentary film continued to play an important role in the war effort; the spirit of a beleaguered nation responded enthusiastically to Jennings's *Listen to Britain* (1941) during the London bombings.

Grierson meanwhile went to Canada in 1939 to supervise the newly founded National Film Board, today one of the most influential and important producers of short films and documentaries in the world. It was originally housed in an old saw mill near Ottawa, but in the mid-1950s moved to a modern plant on the outskirts of Montreal. Grierson returned to England in 1945, leaving behind a trained staff of over 700 employees and a distribution system that is considered the best in the world. But its high standards of creativity had other rewards: *cinéma-vérité* got its impetus in the camera work of Michel Brault and Gilles Groulx (*Les Raquetteurs*, 1958). The NFB has been able to attract and retain film artists of the highest quality and integrity, fostering such widely divergent and individualistic talents as those of Colin Low (*Corral*, 1954), the "candid eye" techniques of Wolf Koenig and Roman Kroiter (*Lonely Boy*, 1962), the animation discoveries of Norman McLaren, and the montage films of Arthur Lipsett. All of these films reflect the Board's major interest: to make and distribute "films designed to interpret Canada to Canadians and to other nations."

These words of the Film Act of the Canadian Parliament are similar in tone to a statement by a group of young British filmmakers, the "Committee for Free Cinema," in 1956:

Our aim is first to look at Britain, with honesty and affection. To relish its eccentricities; attack its abuses; love its people. To use the cinema to express our allegiances, our rejections and our aspirations. This is our commitment.

"Free cinema" was begun by the editors of the film review *Sequence*, Lindsay Anderson and Karel Reisz. The movement had been influenced by the documentaries of John Grierson and Humphrey Jennings and included, in addition to Anderson and Reisz, Tony Richardson, Walter Lassally, Gavin Lambert and Lorenza Mazzetti. They had in common a belief in the freedom and importance of the individual, in the significance of everyday.

During the decade (1950-1960) in which "free cinema" flourished, a series of excellent documentaries on contemporary British life was made with 16 mm cameras, little money and plenty of volunteer help. Among them: Lindsay Anderson's *O Dreamland* (1953) and *Every Day Except Christmas* (1957), Reisz and Richardson's *Momma Don't Allow* (1955), Reisz's *We Are the Lambeth Boys* (1958), Lambert's *Another Sky* (1954), and Mazzetti's *Together* (1955). The freshness of the movement prompted a quick absorption into the established film industry: directors Anderson, Richardson and Reisz and photographer Lassally are now recognized names in the cinema world, and Gavin Lambert for a time edited *Sight and Sound* at the British Film Institute.

The American documentary film flowered briefly between 1936 and 1943, a period of domestic unrest in the face of the Depression and war years. Pare Lorentz, a film critic, brought to life a national problem in the uneven but timely *The Plow That Broke the Plains* (1936), photographed with the help of still-photographer Paul Strand for the government's Resettlement Administration. Lorentz plunged into a study of the British documentary school, and for government film agencies he secured the help of photographers Willard Van Dyke, Stacey Woodard and Floyd Crosby, and composer Virgil Thomson. He wrote, directed and edited *The River* (1937) for the Farm Security Administration, a milestone in American documentary. Paul Rotha wrote:

Widely discussed in England and America, *The River* was a far more important film than *The Plow That Broke the Plains*. It had some of the same faults: lack of human beings, "difficult" music, and again a tacked-on end with the propaganda message. (It is worth noting that both Lorentz's films carry their message in an epilogue, almost as if he was embarrassed by the propaganda; whereas, in most British documentary films, the propaganda is inherent from start to finish.) But *The River* had a bigness about it that was truly American, and a sentimentality that caused the commentary to dwell over and repeat fascinating place-names. It had moments of romantic quality which *The Plow* lacked, and sequences of visuals — such as the rain-sodden tree stumps — for which the cameramen deserve their credit. It did more to secure the popular recognition of the documentary film in America than any other picture. And, above all, it played its part in the expression of the awakening need for social reconstruction in the United States.

Both *The Plow That Broke the Plains* and *The River* spoke to the land reforms that were needed to stop erosion and to better living conditions, opening the way for government sponsorship of the United States Film Service in 1938 with Pare Lorentz at its head. A year later with the publication of John Steinbeck's *The Grapes of Wrath* on the plight of the "Okies," the shanty-towns and Hoovervilles — an indictment of the existence of dispossessed and starving in a land of plenty and "over-production" — Congress put a halt to the new agency because of its favoritism to President Roosevelt's New Deal. But the American documentary had already won wide recognition and that made possible (under different auspices) such milestones as Van Dyke's *The City* (1939) and *Valley Town* (1940), Joris Ivens's *The Power and the Land* (1940) and Robert Flaherty's *The Land* (1939-1942), high points in documenting America's willingness to wrestle with its industrial and agricultural problems. Rotha cites the difficulties of these "forgotten years":

The documentary makers were suddenly thrown back upon non-Governmental sources of sponsorship. But industry and advertising circles were suspicious of a film form which had come into prominence under New Deal auspices. The academic world, except for a few gestures, was cautious. Most important, the documentary makers themselves instinctively drew back from the job of selling the propagandist potential of documentary to the alien worlds of politics and business.

The war years saw the British and American documentary film movement in disarray. Between 1938 and 1940 the British documentary was kept alive by a grant from the Rockefeller Foundation. Throughout the war a body of factual information was produced and distributed by the American Armed Forces (the Army's *Why We Fight* series, supervised by Frank Capra), but this was hardly in the best traditions of the American documentary. Veterans of the movement took refuge for a while in the Office of War Information, until in June 1943 Congress cut appropriations for its domestic branch from $1,222,904 to $50,000 and labelled this money specifically to "carry on liaison activities between the Government and the Hollywood film industry." The heart went out of one of the most promising movements in film history, although its humanistic spirit was eventually to carry over to the feature film.

Certain American feature directors created a body of work running parallel to and growing out of the documentary movement. One of them, King Vidor, actually anticipated it. The best moments in *The Big Parade* (1925), *The Crowd* (1928) and *Hallelujah!* (1929) (an all-Negro production) were very close to pure documentary footage. His independently produced *Our Daily Bread* (1934), a complete flop at the box office, had the human faces and feelings of the Depression years that Lorentz's *The Plow That Broke the Plains* lacked two years later. John Ford's *The Grapes of Wrath* (1940) owes a debt to both Vidor and Lorentz: the best film made on the plight of the Okies, it was too romanticized and lacks the authenticity of Vidor's low-budget portrait. Vidor's *The Citadel* (1938) also anticipated Ford's *How Green Was My Valley* (1941); on the working conditions of Welsh coal miners, it spoke indirectly about similar conditions at home. Vidor spent three years and three million dollars on *An American Romance* (1944), criss-crossing industrial America from the iron-ore pits of Minnesota to the steel mills of Gary and the automobile factories of Detroit. M-G-M cut out the human elements of the story (Vidor's trademark) to speed up the action; it failed at the box office. Vidor's early period was one of the few examples in Hollywood of the use of cinema as an expression of hope and faith in trying times.

A different John Ford than expected emerges in the films he personally liked:

The Sun Shines Bright (1953) is my favorite picture — I love it. And it's true to life, it happened. Irvin Cobb got everything he wrote from real life, and that's the best of his Judge Priest stories.

It came out the way I wanted it to — that's why (*The Fugitive*, 1947) is one of my favorite pictures — to me, it was perfect. It wasn't popular. The critics got at it, and evidently it had no appeal to the public, but I was very proud of my work.

I wrote the original story. Along with *The Fugitive* and *The Sun Shines Bright*, I think *Wagon Master* (1950) came closest to being what I had wanted to achieve.

All these films have the character of real-life documentaries set on the rugged frontiers of civilization. They deal with a moral issue (in *The Sun Shines Bright*, Judge Priest defends a Negro accused of rape just before election time), a priest fugitive on the run, and the wagon-train adventures of simple people.

To these fiction features should be added the Academy Award winning documentary, *The Battle of Midway* (1942), and the fiction documentary, *They Were Expendable* (1945), both prompted by Ford's naval experiences during the war. *The Battle of Midway* was photographed with a single camera at the scene of action and it has a key scene that "really happened": the raising of a flag in the midst of bombing. About *They Were Expendable* ("what was in my mind was doing it exactly as it happened"), Agee commented:

For what seems at least half of the dogged, devoted length of *They Were Expendable* all you have to watch is men getting on or off PT boats, and other men watching them do so. But this is made so beautiful and so real that I could not feel one foot of the film was wasted. The rest of the time the picture is showing nothing much newer, with no particular depth of feeling, much less idea; but again, the whole thing is so beautifully directed and photographed, in such an abundance of vigorous open air and good raw sunlight, that I thoroughly enjoyed and admired it. Visually, and in detail, and in nearly everything he does with people, I think it is John Ford's finest movie.

John Huston's best films starred Humphrey Bogart: *The Maltese Falcon* (1941), *The Treasure of Sierra Madre* (1948), *Key Largo* (1948), *The African Queen* (1952) and *Beat the Devil* (1954), a recognizable Dashiell Hammett tough guy who is demythologized for a changing, maturing Hollywood public. Clark Gable and Marilyn Monroe received similar treatment in *The Misfits* (1961), stars out of tune with the times, human, vulnerable. And Stacy Keach as the battered, boxing anti-hero in *Fat City* (1972) is a Bogart-type who briefly recaptures his dignity on the edge of nowhere, U.S.A. His portrait of Moses in *The Bible* (1966) seems to reflect his own vulnerability; this is also one of the few religious epics in which a communion between man and nature shines through.

Fred Zinnemann's credo, "the most interesting landmark is still the human face," charges his best films with a self-contained integrity. At a time when other "modern" directors were overpowering audiences with technical tricks and devices, Zinnemann anchored his style to a straightforward, convincing simplicity. After the war, as M-G-M was committed to a project on children in refugee camps, he was chosen from the studio's lower ranks to film *The Search* (1948) on a modest budget. It was successful enough to allow him to work independently thereafter. He spent weeks of solid preparation on *The Men* (1950), a story of paraplegics in war veteran hospitals, which also formed the basis of his Academy Award winning short, *Benjy* (1951). His last significant film of this period, *Teresa* (1951), centered on the problems of GI war brides. The Zinnemann films, *A Hatful of Rain* (1957), *The Nun's Story* (1959), and *The Sundowners* (1960) are remarkable for their moments of authenticity and reverence for detail.

Italy's Ermanno Olmi is the most prominent of many West European directors whose interest in the everyday broadens the realist tradition in modern cinema. He learned his craft between 1953 and 1959, making a series of industrial shorts with a group of young Milan filmmakers critical of the commercial Italian studios. Under trying conditions he completed a feature from an original script, *Time Stood Still* (1959), a fiction documentary about a growing friendship between a watchman and a student during an Alpine winter. It was a financial failure; but it did make possible support for his second and best feature, *The Job* (*Il Posto*, or *The Sound of Trumpets*) (1961), a brilliant treatise on a young man's nonexistent chances for self-realization in an impersonal industrial firm. Money was easier to obtain for his next film, *The Fiancés* (1962), but this intimate study of a couple's relationship in the working man's world failed to bring a return for his backers. His *A Man Called John* (1964) was an off-beat portrait of Pope John. His latest successes are *One Fine Day* (1969) and *The Scavengers* (1970), finely-woven, human, psychological views of the soulless, industrial world.

The realist tradition gradually gains ground in the efforts of East European filmmakers to project a human face in Socialist cinema, as well as in attempts of young American, Canadian and West European directors to adapt *cinéma-vérité* and "direct cinema" techniques to the human problems of everyday. The recent, short-lived Czech New Wave had a realist exponent in Milos Forman, who was greatly influenced by *cinéma-vérité* techniques. The Renoir tradition in French cinema has been carried on by François Truffaut, whose humanistic themes (*Jules and Jim*, 1961) far outweigh the journalistic, Godard side of New Wave cinema. Eric Rohmer's *My*

Night at Maud's (1969) and *Claire's Knee* (1970), two of six "moral tales," are already considered classics of the modern realist tradition, while Jean Eustache's *Mes petites amoureuses* (1974) is a meditative reflection on the tender age between innocence and maturity. Other directors and films with timeless messages: John Cassavetes's *Faces* (U.S.A., 1968), Bo Widerberg's *Joe Hill* (Sweden, 1971), Kenneth Loach's *Family Life* (England, 1972), Pantelis Voulgaris's *Anna's Engagement* (Greece, 1973), Michel Brault's *The Orders* (Canada, 1974) and Werner Herzog's *Everyone For Himself and God Against All* (West Germany, 1974). To these should be added Theodor Angelopoulos's epic masterpiece on modern Greek history, *The Journey of the Actors* (1974), and the general trend in Third World Cinema towards the epic.

Cinema as Reflection of Man means a vigorous approach to social problems and the inherent dignity of man.

The "sense of the holy" as the central attribute of the Flaherty tradition is not an alien concept to the world's higher religions. E. E. Kellett summarized the "humanist" position in modern theology:

We cannot, with our utmost endeavors, avoid anthropomorphism. "We cannot step out of our shadow"; and the man who strives, with all the metaphysical thought at his disposal, to fashion a god unlike himself, yet retains the likeness. That God created man in his own image is only another way of saying that man creates God in *his*. Deny as we please that God is human, we must yet think of him with human thoughts, and define him with human phrases. And man is ever changing, sometimes moving upward and sometimes tending downward. As he thus changes, his God inevitably changes with him.

Flaherty was one of the most perceptive observers of mankind in this century, inspiring a score of filmmakers to study man for his own sake. Religious scholars, in search of points of contact between the world religions, need only turn to the "sense of the holy" in world cinema. The approach might resolve a common dilemma in inter-religious dialogue, as pinpointed by theologian Wilfred Cantwell Smith:

There is the developing area of intercommunication among religious communities. "Dialogue" between members of differing traditions is nowadays replacing polemics, debate, and monologue preaching of traditional missionary policy. Terms in which it can be conducted have not yet, however, been widely found.

Theologians could also learn a great deal about the world's religions by screening in succession the best films of Flaherty, Renoir,

Rossellini, Ray, Mizoguchi, Ozu, Rocha and Sembene in an ecumenical climate. Smith contends:

As with all other elements of a religious tradition, theological propositions are to be understood in relation to the personal life, a life of personal faith, of the men and women who use them. As we have seen also with all those other elements, these expressions have a form that is mundane, and that is historically related to the particularities of the time and place where they are fashioned — as it is the business of the observing historian to descry — and once launched they develop a certain momentum and independence of their own, and play their role in the historical vicissitudes of specific situations. Yet religiously they, like the others, I would contend, can be understood only as they serve each generation anew, and concretely in each town, each hamlet, ultimately in each human heart, as an expression of a faith by which those particular persons are oriented, within their mundane situations, to transcendence.

Thus the realist film, addressing itself to the question of personal faith in a particular locality, deserves the theologian's attention.

The theologian today has some difficulties with such terms as "religious," "mystical" and "sublime." The film scholar also finds himself stumbling over the same words in trying to describe the essential qualities of the cinema of Flaherty, Ray, Renoir, Mizoguchi, Rossellini, among others. A. C. Bouquet points out that "mysticism" is a term which came into common use at the beginning of this century; since then, it has been terribly overworked. Nevertheless, the mystics themselves — Christian, Moslem, Hindu — agree on the fundamentals:

(1) that all division and separateness is unreal, and that the universe is a single indivisible unity; (2) that evil is illusory, and that the illusion arises through regarding a part of the universe as self-subsistent; (3) that time is unreal, and that reality is eternal, not in the sense of being everlasting, but in the sense of being out of time.

There is no essential difference between Western and Eastern mysticism. The Christian form of mysticism has its meaning in St. Paul's "I live, yet not I, but Christ lives in me," a Hebraeo-Christian position. The accent is on the individual; it is personal, humanistic. The Non-Christian or Indian form of mysticism (introduced into medieval mysticism through the pseudo-Dionysius tract) is pantheistic, as found in Hindu and Buddhist literature. The accent here is on the universe, of which man is only a part; he must learn to accept his fate in the immensity of creation. Rossellini's *The Flowers of St. Francis* (1949) and *India* (1957) demonstrate, although imperfectly, how and where the two traditions overlap.

In the case of Flaherty's *Nanook of the North* (1922), the universe here seems to be a single indivisible unity; evil is illusory, time unreal, and reality eternal. His approach to life was open-minded.

I grew up among primitive peoples, Indians and Eskimo; I was thirty years of age before I knew much about what you call civilization. Perhaps even now I don't know very much more.

The only word that adequately describes Flaherty's cinema is "mystical."

VIII.   CINEMA AS RELIGIOUS DIALOGUE

There was a time when the audience approached movies fresh and unspoiled. In the nickelodeon, the storefront, the tent and the mobile wagon on the fairgrounds, it responded to a flickering image freely and arbitrarily. If the filmmaker had any power over the audience at all, it was in the art of suggestion and fantasy. Soon, the nickelodeon became a palace and the film director gave way to the star. By the time the young art had reached its fiftieth birthday it was a great social and political force. The audience no longer responded freely but on impulse. As cinema passed into the hands of the State in Europe, Hollywood became the vassal of New York bankers; only a few pockets of freedom remained in the avant-garde and the underground. Occasionally, contact was maintained with the audience through the documentary and the realist tradition.

After the Second World War matters changed again radically. European cinema put the director and the scriptwriter back in charge. Hollywood quarrelled over the best star at the biggest price, until the star became the producer and molded the script to fit his own image. The gimmick of the wide screen countered the threat of television, but ultimately the stars and the super-spectacles lost money and Hollywood was dead. Meanwhile, the director struggled for his independence over the producer and the star, the State and the script. It was not just the tyranny of the studio that stifled creativity, Jean Renoir complained, but the demands of specialization in an age of communication:

One of the things communication has led to has been specialization. We have reached a point where the gentleman who writes a story is not the gentleman who writes the scenario; the gentleman who writes the scenario is not the gentleman who will direct the film, who will control the actual scenes. And this gentleman who will shoot scenes is not the gentleman who will do the cutting. To my mind it's heartbreaking. It is essential that we should combat these modern evils and, even in an organization as modern as ours, successfully maintain unity of conception, the union of creation.

The modern cinema is presently witnessing a struggle to use the medium as an avenue of dialogue between the filmmaker and the audience. In the world of computers robbing the individual of his identity, in a contemporary civilization geared to alienation and non-communication, the film artist feels called upon to supply the dialogue, to deliver the faith that is missing. In Renoir's terms it is a dialogue rooted in the nature of daily existence, a dialogue of relevance and understanding which the artist and the audience share in equally. In terms of modern theology it is a dialogue founded on traditional wisdom, a religious dialogue to help people decide what to do, to permit hope. Despite its many imperfections, but primarily because it maintains its contacts with a young, fresh, alive audience, the modern cinema is more suited to dialogue and inspiration than any other modern art form.

Dialogue begins in the national character of the movies. John Grierson devoted his life to rebuilding a British film industry:

If we are concerned with our great medium as an instrument of national persuasion and national inspiration, we are in fact concerned with the dreams and beliefs, illusions and faiths, purposes and convictions: indeed all the loyalties explicit and implicit, known and unknown, which hold men to their courses, or drive them to new ones, or give them especial delight or, as they say, inspire, or put spirit into them.

Cinema as an instrument of national persuasion and inspiration differs greatly from political propaganda for its own sake. The British documentary of the 1930s wore its national traits openly on its sleeve, but spoke to mankind as well as to England. Vernon Young observed that "all art is a game played with ethnic rules."

Religious dialogue in the cinema hinges on the question of belief in God. Here the problem becomes muddled. Many critics of Luis Bunuel cite his atheistic approach to religion; yet he himself stated:

I have no attitude toward the Catholic religion. I was brought up in it. I could say this: I am still, thank God, an atheist. I believe that one must search for God in man. That is a very simple attitude.

He thus has his feet in both camps. Although a transcendental God is out of the question, an immanent approach to God through man is hardly the credo of an atheist. Some theologians would embrace him wholeheartedly as a man of faith. Certainly his films prepare the way for dialogue between theologian and humanist, theist and atheist. In a similar way the Marxist-Christian poles in Pasolini's early cinema open the way to dialogue.

The dialogue between atheists and theists through the medium of cinema is not a new phenomenon. In Europe it began with the postwar film festival and film retrospectives in cinémathèques. Catholic and Protestant juries serve at the major feature and short film festivals. The writings of Amédée Ayfre, French Catholic critic and theorist, are well known. The popularity of Ingmar Bergman on American university campuses has prompted dialogue between Newman clubs and film societies. Arthur Gibson, theology professor at St. Michael's College in Toronto, analyzed "the faith of an atheist" in his book, *The Silence of God*, on the films of Ingmar Bergman:

Bergman certainly did not intend his films to be received passively; the sensitized utterly passive film-strip is a mere storage and communication device. On either side of it stand human beings, calling to one another as deep to deep. This book is the answer of one such human being, preoccupied with the problem and the phenomenon of modern atheism, to that other human being who exposed on film his own inner vision.

The main stream of religious-dialogue cinema is found in postwar European films. The richest vein, Marxist-Christian dialogue, is Socialist cinema buried in a religious past and traditions of the people. Another is the uncompromising career of Carl Theodor Dreyer, dedicated to tolerance and compassion for the individual; his films are a plea for renewed faith. The "absence" of God in the films of Ingmar Bergman, particularly in the trilogy, has been interpreted as modern man's plea for rescue from the abyss of unbelief. The anticlerical, Catholic cinema of Luis Bunuel, Federico Fellini, Pier Paolo Pasolini and others treats religious problems in a distinctly Latin manner, inseparable from the tradition of art and literature in Spain, France and Italy. An understanding of the themes of grace, love and salvation in Robert Bresson's cinema requires a knowledge of Pascal and Bernanos. André Bazin wrote in *Cahiers du Cinéma* in 1951 at the release of *The Diary of a Country Priest*:

So, probably for the first time, the cinema gives us a film in which the only genuine incidents, the only perceptible movements are those of the life of the spirit. Not only that, it also offers us a new dramatic form that is specifically religious — or better still, specifically theological: a phenomenology of salvation and grace.

Socialist cinema is generally characterized by the pre-eminence of script over director. Eisenstein and Dovzhenko became victims of hack writers in later years. The only director to escape the scourge of heavy didacticism during the Stalin years was Mark Donskoi, whose filmed versions of the Gorki novels (they were friends) stand as individual accomplishments. Stalin's personal psalm-singer was the Georgian, Mikhail Chiaureli, whose *The Vow* (1952) was made at the height of Social Realism. By 1951 film production in Russia was down from a hundred to ten on the grounds that quality was better than quantity: Stalin was depicted as an all-seeing, all-wise, ubiquitous and gracious god. By 1957 the Russian cinema was multi-national with studios situated throughout the country, but V. Sourine in the Ministry of Culture was complaining: "The careless attitude of the director towards the script is the cause of many obstacles to filmmaking.... Unhappily the writer has not yet taken the place due to him at the side of the director."

With the decline of Socialist Realism in the late 1950s came a growing acceptance of a variety of genres. During the Khrushchev years (1955-1965) Grigori Chukhrai, Mikhail Kalatozov and Marlen Khutsiev restored command to the film director. Chukhrai's *The Forty-First* (1956) and Kalatozov's *The Cranes Are Flying* (1957) won prizes in Cannes, while Chukhrai's *Ballad of a Soldier* (1960) and Kalatozov's *The Letter That Wasn't Sent* (1960) are remarkable for their emphasis on both form and content. A temporary setback occurred in 1964, when Khutsiev's *Ilyitch Square* (finished in 1963, released in 1965 as *I Am Twenty*) was singled out by Khrushchev for condemnation, together with abstract painting and Yevtushenko's poetry. Khutsiev, the one director deeply committed to contemporary problems, was able to complete his study of nonconformity in the younger generation, *July Rain* (1967), only with difficulty.

A knottier problem than the contemporary theme is the use of religion in the Russian cinema. An old Russia with spiritual ties to the Orthodox Church (before the 1917 Revolution there was no difference between religious and civil spheres in a theocratic state) still exists inside the new Soviet Union. Church holidays converted into national anniversaries have lost little of their former character, and new holidays (the 1964 plan to introduce pseudo-religious rites into a new set of twenty-two national holidays) have met with indifference. State authorities tried to deal with the situation by reformulating the traditional definition of rite:

A rite is the symbolic and aesthetic expression (and manifestation) of collective social relations, of the collective essence of man, and the bonds linking him not only with his contemporaries but also with his ancestors. A rite is the thread of time by holding on to which people form a nation. A rite is created as the expression of the spirit, traditions and way of life of a society.

The definition was officially turned down.

Religious rites in Sergei Paradjanov's *Shadows of Our Forgotten Ancestors* (1964) illustrate the aforementioned dilemma. The film appeared in the midst of discussions on cultural (and religious) traditions, was reportedly laughed off the screen by audiences in Moscow, but found acceptance and approval among Georgian audiences. Paradjanov made a number of run-of-the-mill features until his documents on folk culture in the Ukraine provided the inspiration for *Shadows of Our Forgotten Ancestors*. In his research into the traditions of the Romanian-speaking Moldavia province (adjacent to Poland, Czechoslovakia, Hungary, and Romania, it was annexed to the Soviet Union after the war), Paradjanov settled on a thematic style:

I already knew some material. Museums, books, drawings. There had been a film, *Oleksa Dovbush* (1959), about the hutzul national hero. The creators of it tried to reveal the Carpathians, but once again in the framework of the old writing, the old visual culture. They dressed Dovbush in red, which designated, as was obvious, the hero's revolutionary spirit. They came to the Carpathians filmically educated. Most of all they were attracted by the exotic, decorative motif, and we could not recognize the hutzuls in their film — we didn't see their walk, we didn't catch the charm of their speech, the course of their thought. When a hutzul on meeting someone says "hello" instead of "glory to Jesus," that is an untruth of life and an untruth of art.... I became convinced, when I was working on *Shadows*, that a perfect knowledge justifies any fiction. I can turn song material into action, and action into song — which I wasn't able to do when I was shooting *The Ballad* (a short film on Ukranian folk culture, 1964). I could translate ethnographic material, or religious, into the most ordinary and everyday. For ultimately they have one and the same source.

Paradjanov's next feature, *Sayat Novar* (1969), a co-production of the Armenian, Georgian and Azerbaijan studios on the life of the eighteenth century monk and poet, has never been released. His recent imprisonment has never been adequately explained.

As Paradjanov follows in the tradition of Dovzhenko, so Andrei Tarkovsky is hailed as the true successor to Eisenstein. Soon after graduating from the film academy he made the internationally acclaimed *My Name Is Ivan* (1962), a poetic work about a child's experiences in wartime. During the period of discussion on cultural traditions his monumental epic, *Andrei Rublev* (1966, released in 1969), caused a stir; it's the biography of Russia's leading medieval iconologist and caused a walk-out by the Soviet delegation at the Cannes festival in 1970. His latest films are the science-fiction *Solaris* (1972) and the autobiographical *The Mirror* (1975), both spiritual in character.

Writer-filmmaker Vasily Shukshin is the latest Soviet filmmaker to fully capture the public's imagination. The originality of his four films, his poetic vigor as a writer, actor and filmmaker, and the frankness of his themes place him outside the mainstream of Soviet cinema. Shortly after completing *The Red Snowball Tree* (1974), the story of an inveterate criminal (played by Shukshin) returning to society, he died suddenly at 45.

Hungarian cinema has a reputation second to none in Europe. Its high craftsmanship between the wars (forty films a year for its own ten million and Hungarian colonies along the Danube) resulted in a steady flow of talent to Hollywood. French critic Louis Marcorelles noted after the war: "Naturally gifted for the cinema, famous for their directors and writers, Hungarians no longer quit their country but make on-the-spot films with a standard of technical excellence and formal refinement, which in my view place Hungary, with its modest means, in the first rank of European filmmakers East and West." Even during the Rakosi regime the Hungarian equivalent of Socialist Realism in its formal perfection outdistanced the drab Russian model. Afterwards, Imre Nagy's "intellectual" government (1953-1955) brought fresh air back into the film industry, and up to the October Revolution of 1956 a sense of the poetic and tragic imbued the country's cinema.

The best of these films are still impressive today. Zoltan Fabri's *Merry-Go-Round* (1955), a Romeo-and-Juliet theme against the background of farm collectivization, and *Professor Hannibal* (1956), his tragi-comedy condemning national extremism during the 1920 white terror, restored humanism to a rigid Socialist society. Felix Mariassy's *A Glass of Beer* (1955) was influenced by the neo-realist movement, and Zoltan Varkonyi's *The Bitter Truth* (1956) took the Rakosi dictatorship to task in its exposé of a careerist reaching his position over the bodies of political prisoners. It was released after Rakosi's fall from power, first shown at the height of the 1956 Revolution. During this time Imre Feher made the nostalgic, tender *Sunday Romance* (1957), remarkable for its honest treatment of bourgeois society in the last days of the Habsburg Empire; while Gyorgy Revesz's *At Midnight* (1957) struck another sensitive chord in the story of an actor's agonizing decision to remain in his country during the Soviet intervention, because he prefers to play Hamlet only in his own tongue. The latter film is an indication why even difficult film experiments are often commercial successes at home: the Hungarian "feel" for a language rich in cultural tradition.

Andreas Kovacs and Miklos Jancso, among others, developed distinct personal styles to bring Hungarian cinema to the forefront in Europe. Kovacs was impressed by *cinéma-vérité* methods during a period of study in Paris; he caused a stir with his interview-style, clinical observation of the lack of responsibility in bureaucracy in *Difficult People* (1964). He then documented a woman's mental crisis in revolt against Fascism in the powerful *Cold Days* (1966), followed by a clinical observation of intellectual hardening in his own generation in *Walls* (1967); both films were public successes despite lengthy verbal duels.

Miklos Jancso combines intellectual argument with dynamic technical prowess and poetic symbols. His primary theme is mutual trust giving way to fear and isolation but ending in a new self-determination. His camera moves in ever-widening unbroken circles, which propel man's restless spirit toward a final cry of liberty over oppression.

In *This Was My Path* (1964) he added to an already established anti-war and anti-violence theme in depicting a growing friendship between an Hungarian youth and a young Russian soldier on the front. The theme was expanded in *The Round-Up* (1965), about the remnants of Kossuth's patriots psychologically undermined through new interrogation methods by Habsburg police in the 1860s; it's Hungarian title means *The Hopeless*. In *The Red and the White* (1967), a co-production with Russia, the plight of Russian and Hungarian revolutionaries during the Civil War of 1918 surrounded by the White Army is suddenly reversed when the rebels turn on their oppressors to die in formation singing. *Silence and Cry* (1967) is a synthesis of this same struggle in which a refugee from the Red Army refuses an opportunity to commit suicide "honorably" and instead turns the weapon on his benefactor. These four films stand as a humanist's definitive statement on war and violence. His later films echo the same theme.

Among younger directors of the late 1960s and early 1970s, an emphasis on moral, social and religious problems is evident. Peter Bacso's films, *The Fatal Shot* (1968), on adolescent suicides, and *Outbreak* (1970), on the problems of young workers, center on delicate issues seldom attempted in other Socialist countries. Istvan Gaal's *Current* (1964) and *The Falcons* (1969) are psychological studies of disillusionment under an authoritarian system. Istvan Szabo's *Father* (1966) and *Love* (1970) are autobiographical, gentle, lyrical poems of nostalgia and pain. Judit Elek's *How Long Does Man Matter* (1968) and *The Lady From Constantinople* (1969) reverence old age in an unforgettable, quiet manner. Ferenc Kosa's historical chronicle of Hungarian peasant life, *Ten Thousand Days* (1967); Imre Gyongyossy's religious parable on peasant life, *Palm Sunday* (1969); and Sandor Sara's recollections of farm collectivization, *The Thrown-Up Stone* (1969) — all are extremely close to the life-blood of the people. To these should be added Karoly Makk's *Love* (1971), which recounts the release of a prisoner in 1953 through the eyes of an elderly woman (played by Ferenc Molnar's widow). These films, taken together, form a spiritual testament to the Hungarian nation.

Poland's cinema is characterized by a romantic passion. The country's biggest box office successes are Aleksander Ford's *Knights of the Teutonic Order* (1960), glorifying victory over the West (the Battle of Grünwald, 1410), and Jerzy Hoffman's *Colonel Wolodyjowski* (1969), saluting Sobieski's defeat of an Ottoman army invading from the East (1673); both superspectacles are national monuments. The Poles also love their stars: Zbigniew Cybulski (whose accidental death in 1967 amounted to a small national tragedy) was quickly replaced by Daniel Olbrychski (who played Cybulski in an Andrzej Wajda memorial film).

Modern Polish cinema marks its beginnings with Wanda Jakubowska's fiction-documentary on Auschwitz, *The Last Stage* (1948), made soon after the liberation of the extermination camp. The foundations of a nationalized film industry were laid by Aleksander Ford, an eminent prewar director and head of the Polish Army Film Command; his *Border Street* (1948), *The Youth of Chopin* (1952), and *Five Boys From Barska Street* (1953) were romantic, nationalistic, socially-conscious documents on the problems of the "lost" postwar generation, extraordinary for the Stalinist era. He also did much to further the career of Andrzej Wajda, perhaps the best known of East European directors. Following the death of Stalin and the release of Gomulka from prison during the crisis of 1956, relative freedom was granted to the film industry. Immediately Wajda, Andrzej Munk and Jerzy Kawalerowicz stepped to the fore of world cinema: between 1954 and 1963 Poland's film renaissance signalled the importance of national film schools.

Wajda's themes in those years were tragedy and romance, love and heroism, in the lost generation. His first film, *Generation* (1954), about youth in the depressive postwar years, was exhibited only at Ford's insistence. *Kanal* (1957), in the same vein of poetic realism, related the frustrations of the Warsaw Uprising in 1944. The trilogy ended with *Ashes and Diamonds* (1958), the film that, in its personification of the lost generation, made a legend out of Cybulski. A fourth film in this period, *Samson* (1961), treated unsuccessfully the fate of a Jewish outsider searching for his identity after escaping from the Warsaw Ghetto. At the beginning of the 1960s Wajda and the Polish film industry were burdened with an heroic myth they could not easily push aside. Wajda's ambiguous projects early in this decade were shadows of his former work. (Ford also supported another *enfant terrible*, Marek Hlasko, dubbed by Marcorelles as "the James Dean of Polish literature," who wrote the script for Ford's commendable *The Eighth Day of the Week*, 1958, about the bitterness of a young couple's life amid Socialism.)

The Polish anti-hero had a satirical counterpart in the cinema of Andrzej Munk, based on the scripts of Jerzy Stawinski. Munk's second film, *The Man on the Track* (1956), was a detective thriller exposing a multitude of sins in railway working conditions under Stalinism. While Wajda invested Stawinski's script for *Kanal* (1957) with his own passionate energy, Munk turned his *Eroica* (1957) into a spoof of Polish military bravado ("Ostinato Lugubre") and the cult of heroism in the story of a confidence man caught in the middle of a secret mission ("Scherzo alla Polacca"); it's a bitter two-part condemnation of the code-of-honor myth. Stawinski's argument that legend-building leads to more harm than good is a moral thesis fully exploited by Munk in his classic portrait of a comic anti-hero in *Bad Luck* (1960) (starring Bogumil Kobiela, who established with Cybulski the satirical theatre in Gdansk in 1954). Munk was working on *Passenger* (1962), a personal view of Auschwitz, when he died in an automobile accident (the film was edited by Witold Lesiewicz in the spirit of Munk's conception). The loss of his sense for irony and tragedy was irreparable.

Jerzy Kawalerowicz, the most eclectic of Polish directors, shifts his style according to the demands of theme and mood. His best films parallel the Munk period: *It's Not Over Yet* (1957), the tragedy of a married couple who can't make it through the husband's wartime disability; *Night Train* (1959), a psychological examination of the closed worlds among a group of passengers on their way to a Baltic resort; and *Mother Joan of the Angels* (1960), a gloomy tale of possession and exorcism that probes in microcosm the Polish psyche. During this same period Wojciech Has directed a series of sad, poignant literary classics; they recounted, like Polish poetry, the prewar era of decadence and daydreams.

By 1963 it was evident much of the heady freedom of 1956 was being compromised out of existence. Roman Polanski's first feature, *Knife in the Water* (1962), after a series of brilliant shorts, was the last of the exceptionally strong contemporary themes. Kazimierz Kutz's *The Silence* (1963) used metaphors to comment on betrayed trust in church and state affairs of the day. Tadeusz Konwicki's *Salto* (1964), Jerzy Skolimowski's *Walkover* (1965) and *Barrier* (1966), and many animated films at this time (Daniel Szczechura's *The Chair*, 1963, and Jan Lenica's *Labyrinth*, 1962) reflected growing problems in a suffocating bureaucracy. Polanski and Skolimowski, Borowczyk and Lenica, among others, soon left the country to work abroad.

Wajda's return to form in the late 1960s in a series of humanistic parables bettered Poland's position in world cinema. Wajda buried the Cybulski myth for good in *Everything For Sale* (1968); he criticized the spread of materialism among the younger generation in *Hunting Flies* (1969); and he courageously faced the sensitive Jewish question in *Landscape After the Battle* (1970). Among his latest films his adaptation of Reymont's *The Promised Land* (1975) is an epic on the apocalyptic industrial revolution in Lodz, a time of splendor and folly. In these documentary-style treatises on the Polish "identity," he has reached new heights of poetic realism, often more challenging in theme than the earlier period.

Krzysztof Zanussi's films are striking for their understanding of human nature. He began his career with *Death of a Provincial* (1966), a prize-winning short that appeared in the midst of Poland's millenium celebrations. Particularly at home in television plays (the best is *Behind the Wall* in 1974), his taste for the psychological theme developed out of a maturity in working with actors. Zanussi attracted attention with his first feature film, *The Structure of Crystals* (1969), in which he contrasted the states of mind of two scientists, one going on his way toward the fulfillment of his ambitions, the other on the road to retirement. *Family Life* (1971) matches the promise of a young engineer from the old upper-middle class with the crumbling world of his ex-industrialist father. *Illumination* (1973) is another probing portrait of the intellectual in the Socialist state.

Marek Piwowski's satirical shorts, *Fire, Fire, Something's Happening At Last* (1967) and *Sixteen Years Old* (1969), marked him as a talent to watch; but his satire on Socialist life, *Picnic on the River* (shot in 1970), never was released and ended a promising career. On the religious issue, poet Tadeusz Rosewicz's script for brother Stanislaw Rosewicz's *Loneliness For Two* (1968) resulted in a quiet, persuasive film on a Lutheran pastor's troubles in the 1930s. Witold Leszczynski's *The Days of Matthew* (1967), a small-scale humanistic parable about the visions of a country simpleton, is in the best tradition of East European allegorical cinema; its sensitivity for life and nature pleaded for humanity in difficult times. The 1972 decision by Gierek to allow more freedom to the Writers Union has bettered conditions at home: a hopeful sign was the return of Walerian Borowczyk from France to adapt Stefan Zeromski's turn-of-the-century novel, *The Story of Sin* (1975).

Like Poland and Hungary Czechoslovakia had a film industry that was thriving before nationalization of production after the last war, but unlike the others there was no cultural thaw under Novotny in the de-Stalinization period. The only filmmaker to reach any stature was Jiri Trnka, whose gifts extended to animated cartoons, puppet films, book illustrations and the founding of his own puppet theatre (puppet-making is a national tradition). In his shadow stood the equally gifted puppet filmmaker, Bretislav Pojar (*The Little Umbrella*, 1958). Karel Zeman also created fantasy films for children, mixing live action with puppets and animation. Trnka's *Song of the Prairie* (1949) spoofing the American western and *A Midsummer Night's Dream* (1959), together with Zeman's *Baron Munchausen* (1961), upheld the country's film reputation until the arrival of the New Wave.

The most important of Trnka's internationally acclaimed films was his *The Czech Year*. "A work of philosophy and poetry," remarked Czech critic Jaroslav Bocek, "steeped in national tradition yet at the same time thoroughly modern, *The Czech Year* (1947) spanned the great expanse of Trnka's emotional and ideological scope and staked out the boundaries of the artist's entire subsequent work." The humanity of Trnka's art, his compassion for the suffering human being, kept Czech audiences in touch with their historical, cultural, religious and social history. It only seemed natural therefore that in 1955, as a cultural thaw was noticeably felt in the Czech film industry, the young feature director who stepped prominently forward, Vojtech Jasny, followed in the tradition and philosophy of Trnka.

A poetic lyricism imbues Jasny's early films. *September Nights* (1957), an adaptation of Pavel Kohout's play, is about a young soldier who resists the dogmatism of army life in the period of the Personality Cult; *Desire* (1958) draws on the four seasons to depict childhood, youth, maturity and old age in human life (Jasny's bridge to Trnka's *The Czech Year*); *Pilgrimage to the Virgin Mary* (1961), a humorous view of village life and farm cooperatives, exposes hypocrisy and prejudice; and *That Cat* (1963), the first of a string of powerful Czech allegories, uses satire as a force for decency against the misuses of authoritarianism and dogmatism. But nowhere is the relationship between Trnka and Jasny more clearly felt than in *All My Countrymen* (1968), in which his poetic powers are set against the colors of a pastoral landscape to document the mistakes of the postwar years. Jasny is now working in the FRG.

On a broad, poetic scale, the films of Frantisek Vlacil, particularly his adaptation of Vladislav Vancura's epic novel *Marketa Lazarova* (1967) and his panoramic vision of religion and paganism in *Valley of the Bees* (1968), are restless films buried in the cultural traditions of the past. Zbynek Brynych and the directing team of Jan Kadar and Elmar Klos, on the other hand, concern themselves with the lives of simple people and the moral issues of the day. The most important were Kadar and Klos's *The Accused* (1964), about the psychological pressure experienced in living under the Personality Cult, and the internationally acclaimed *The Shop on Main Street* (1965), the tragi-comedy of a little man forced to take over ownership of a shop from an elderly Jewish lady in wartime.

The Czech New Wave was signalled by Stefan Uher's *Sunshine in the Net* (1962), a Slovak film on young people searching for meaning and responsibility in life; imbued with a marked formalism, it nevertheless spoke directly to young people and was released only after heated discussion. Uher then made *The Organ* (1964), exposing religious and political mistakes on the Polish-Slovak border in the war, and *Three Daughters* (1967), dealing with the subsequent anti-clerical, postwar atmosphere.

Another Slovak director, Jurai Jakubisko, depicted a world of cruelty, decadence and sex in a series of striking, personal films. His application of poetic symbols and visual compositions evokes a strong national tradition; even the titles of his films are symbolic: *The Crucial Years* (1967), *Deserters and Pilgrims* (1968), and *Birds, Orphans and Fools* (1969). Two other Slovaks made similar, lyric films on contemporary themes: Elo Havetta's *Festival in a Botanical Garden* (1969), a fairy tale on the necessity of miracles in human life; and Dusan Hanak's *322* (1969), a story about the elusive search for love and meaning in life. And two Slovak television productions on literary works are equally unforgettable: Stanislav Barabas's adaptation of Dostoievsky's *The Gentle One* (1968) and Juroi Herz's production of Maupassant's *The Sweet Games of Last Summer* (1970).

The Czech directors in the New Wave are distinguished either by their humanity or their sense of humor. In the first category are Evald Schorm, Jaromil Jires, Vera Chytilova, Jan Nemec, Pavel Juracek and Hynec Bocan. In the second are Milos Forman, Ivan Passer, Jiri Menzel, Jan Svankmaier (an animator) and Pavel Hobl (a director of children's films). The two groups overlap and complement each other. Critic-historian Jaroslav Bocek outlined the unifying factor in the New Wave:

Even the generation of directors Jasny and Helge still sees man primarily through social associations, whereas the young creators see social associations through man. They penetrate surprisingly deep into the human mind and soul. And they find that not only does man make history but that history forms and often deforms man. They romantically protest against this deformation, guided by their dream of unfulfilled activity, their yearning for a fullness of life that cannot be attained.

The "conscience of the New Wave," Evald Schorm entered features after an apprenticeship in documentaries; his films are in a sense documents on the inner struggles of man to attain the unattainable. He feels that the search for the meaning of things usually meets with failure, but man must search just to keep the endeavor alive for as long as he can. This is the theme of *Courage For Every Day* (1964), his first feature about the tarnished dreams of a young party functionary; it also described the mixed feelings of young Czech directors still trying to find their way. *The Return of the Prodigal Son* (1966) is a religious parable on the unhappiness of living in a society that has lost sight of its responsibility. *The Death of the Priest* (1968), a comic fable about a sexton passing himself off as a priest in a small town, highlights humanism over dogmatism. His *The Seventh Day, the Eighth Night* (1969) has never been released.

Vera Chytilova is the moralist of the group, whose *The Ceiling* (1962), *Another Way of Life* (1963), *Daisies* (1966) and *The Fruit of Paradise* (1969) deal with the world of women and the frustrating emptiness of a wasted life. Her condemnation of parasites for their inability to give and create life, as well as her bitter reflection on lost possibilities for self-realization, set her apart as the most ruthlessly honest director of the New Wave. Jaromil Jires is a romanticist who builds his cinema on accepting the human condition as it is. This is a lesson hard won in *The Cry* (1963), in which an expectant father in a maternity ward dwells on his relationship to his wife, and in *The Joke* (1969), a re-living of a bad joke during the era of the Personality Cult that resulted in imprisonment, while the hero's betrayers merely changed with the times.

Jan Nemec takes a philosophical approach. He formed his experiences out of the Occupation and the Socialist Realism period;

because of their uncompromising nature his films are most controversial. *Report on the Party and Its Guests* (1965) was only allowed exhibition after the Writers Union approved it in 1967, then set the standard for freedom in the arts in the Dubcek era. *Martyrs of Love* (1966), a bitter-sweet trio of stories about the frustrated dreams of shy people longing for happiness in love, is an abstraction of an earlier plea for freedom and dignity in *Diamonds in the Night* (1964), the story of two young fugitives fleeing transport to an extermination camp in wartime.

Scriptwriter Pavel Juracek co-directed with Jan Schmidt *Josef Kilian* (1964), a controversial medium-length film on the Kafka-esque absurdities of bureaucracy during the Personality Cult. His refined sense of irony permeates the script for Hynec Bocan's *Nobody Gets the Last Laugh* (1965), based on a book by Milan Kundera about a small lie that escalates into tragic misunderstandings. Kundera's novels (along with Jires's *The Joke*), first allowed to be published in the early 1960s, supplied an important literary foundation for the "humanity" school of the New Wave.

Bogumil Hrabal supplied the literary source for the distinctly Czech world of absurd humor in the omnibus film, *Pearls in the Depth* (1964), a compilation of five of his stories (a sixth, Ivan Passer's *A Boring Afternoon*, appeared separately) directed by Chytilova, Jires and Nemec in a serious vein, and Schorm, Menzel and Passer in a comic one. Hrabal's book of short stories appeared in 1963, when the ban on Kafka was lifted and Albee plays appeared on Czech stages. His leading film interpreter is Jiri Menzel. Menzel's *Closely Watched Trains* (1966) accurately reflects Hrabal's scorn for gratuitous heroism and bravery; a comedy of a young man's struggle to reach sexual maturity, it reduced the pretentious heroism of the war films to ultimate absurdity. Menzel was ill at ease in adapting Vancura's comedy, *Capricious Summer* (1968), a nostalgic look at yesteryear with no political or contemporary relevance, and *Crime at the Night Club* (1969), in which he tried to wed the detective story to Kafka. Returning to Bogumil Hrabal he made *Larks on a String* (1970); the film has not been released.

Comedy formed the heart of the seven years of the Czech New Wave. Milos Forman, who graduated from the drama department of FAMU, was greatly influenced by *cinéma-vérité* techniques in its use of non-professionals and spontaneous methods of filming. *Talent*

Competition (1963) revealed an observant eye and a taste for the foibles and tricks of human existence without exploiting the weaknesses he finds. *Black Peter* (1963) and *A Blonde in Love* (1965) concentrate on the young generation's dreams, but match these with tarnished reality. *The Fireman's Ball* (1967) operates on a more universal plane in exposing with sardonic humor the petty interests of a small-town fire brigade. *Taking Off* (1971) shows he is equally at home in American culture: it deals with runaway teenagers and the suburbia they are running away from. And *One Flew Over the Cuckoo's Nest* (1975) established him as one of America's leading directors.

Ivan Passer and Jaroslav Papousek helped Forman develop his comical approach to the foibles of the *petit bourgeois*. Passer's *Intimate Lighting* (1965), on a family of musicians in a small Czech village, is, for all its whackiness, a sensitive portrait of family life. Papousek, a scriptwriter of the older generation, continued the tradition of Forman and Passer, using Forman's stock nonprofessional actors for *The Most Beautiful Age* (1968) and *Ecce Homo Homulka* (1969), light comedies to take the public's mind off the real events at hand. Pavel Hobl's children's film *Have You a Lion at Home?* (1964) and Jan Svankmaier's absurd shorts (*The Apartment*, 1969) are remarkable for their comic invention, but also for their universal application to a larger, Kafka-esque world.

Yugoslav cinema came of age through the short film. International audiences appreciated the work coming out of the cartoon studios of Yugoslavia long before the film industry could stand firmly on its own feet. Some old Fleischer cartoons from America of the 1930s found in the archives, plus a recognition of the technical importance of Trnka's animated cartoons (*Perak and the SS*, 1946), convinced a young group of Zagreb newspaper cartoonists headed by Dusan Vukotic to try something different from the reigning Disney method of anthropomorphism. The Zagreb studio under Vukotic, Nikola Kostelac, Vatroslav Mimica and Vlado Kristl was rivalling the Western market by the end of the 1950s. Its modern generation of cartoonists — Aleksandar Marks, Vladimir Jutrisa, Boris Kolar, Zlatko Bourek, Zlatko Grgic, Nedeljko Dragic, Dragutin Vunak, Pavao Stalter, Borivoj Dovnikovic, Ante Zaninovic, Zvonimir Loncaric and Milan Blazekovic — have propelled the studio to the top of the animation world with their unique brand of humanism and social content. Vukotic's *Ersatz* (1961) won the first Academy Award for animation outside the United States.

The Yugoslav movie industry is not state-controlled, unlike those in other Socialist countries, although the power of censorship is not to be minimized, as recent events have shown. The industry as a whole provides a national meeting ground for a country divided into six republics, five nations, four religions, three languages, and two alphabets. After the five-year nationalization plan of 1945 had passed, the film companies at the beginning of the 1950s began to function as private enterprises within a Socialist system (having all the advantages and disadvantages of both).

The first signs of a humanly alive cinema appeared in Slovenia in the cinema of France Stiglic in the mid-1950s. *The Valley of Peace* (1956) and *The Ninth Circle* (1960) had war themes in the neo-realist tradition, but the problems of a Negro and a Jewess were treated with liberality and feeling. The French New Wave directors influenced Bostjan Hladnik's experimental short *Fantastic Ballad* (1957) and his first feature, *Dance in the Rain* (1961), a film on the troubles of youth; but his too formalistic approach in the anti-war film, *The Sand Castle* (1963), proved unsuccessful. Another Slovenian director, Matjaz Klopcic, manifested a sensibility for moral dilemmas and the elusiveness of dreams in *A Non-Existent Story* (1966), *On Wings of Paper* (1967) and *Fear* (1974). His best film, *On Wings of Paper*, deals with a ballet dancer who must decide between love and a career.

The Croatian cinema took a step forward in Veljko Bulajic's *Train Without a Schedule* (1959), about a group migration from the rocky wastes of Dalmatia to the expropriated farms of rich landowners in Slavonia; it recalls the poetic realism of John Ford's *The Grapes of Wrath*. Bulajic turned from this good beginning to war films for the commercial market (he made the monumental epic on Tito's march, *The Battle on the River Neretva*, 1969), but his ability as a first-class documentary filmmaker surfaced in *Skopje 63*, an interpretive account of the earthquake disaster.

Vatroslav Mimica left the Zagreb animation studio in the early 1960s to join Branko Bauer and Fadil Hadzic in making a series of socially engaged films. Bauer's *Face to Face* (1963) dealt with the economic mismanagement of a high official; Hadzic's *Privileged Position* (1964) exposed government abuses; and Mimica's *Prometheus From the Island of Visevica* (1965) explored the thoughts and memories of a partisan fighter turned bureaucrat. The cycle ended with Hadzic's *Protest* (1967), in which social reportage is used to get at the roots of a young worker's suicide. Mimica then drifted into a personal style, exploring primarily man's psychological compulsion to cruelty and violence in *Monday or Tuesday* (1966), *Kaja, I'll Kill You* (1967), *An Event* (1969), *The Well-fed Man* (1970), and *Anno Domini 1573* (1976).

Croatian directors with a taste for psychological themes are Zvonimir Berkovic (*Rondo*, 1966), Ante Babaja (*The Birch Tree*, 1967), and *Gold, Frankincense and Myrrh*, (1971), Branko Ivanda (*Gravitation*, 1968), and Ante Peterlic (*An Accidental Life*, 1969), who deal for the most part with problems of identity and moral indifference. Krsto Papic has made a number of fine documentaries and two critical features on village life: *Handcuffs* (1970) and *A Village Performance of Hamlet* (1972).

Serbian directors wholeheartedly tackle problems of deep social and political import. Whereas Croatia can only boast of Mimica and Papic in the status of *auteur* director, Serbia has four worthy of recognition: Aleksandar Petrovic, Zika Pavlovic, Purisa Djordjevic, and Dusan Makavejev.

Aleksandar Petrovic won international recognition for *Three* (1965), on a trio of real-life incidents, tied together through the experiences of the central character, to condemn war as a tragic, senseless dilemma. *I Even Met Happy Gypsies* (1967) combined cruelty with beauty, poetry with realism, to fashion a bittersweet, tragicomic document on Yugoslav life; while *It Rains in My Village* (1969) and *Master and Marguerita* (1972), based on Bulgakov, are predominantly religious parables on good and evil.

Russian literature is also at the core of Zika Pavlovic's cinema: his first film, *Enemy* (1965), is a Dostoievsky tale on the co-existence of good and evil in man; rejected by Serbian studios, it was made in Slovenia. His view of the anti-hero buried in an emotionally impoverished world of political brutality and contradictions, the same world mirrored in his novels and poetry, has earned him a reputation as "the poet of the ugly." *The Rats Wake Up* (1967), *When I Am Dead and White* (1968), and *Ambush* (1969) moved him to the forefront of Yugoslav film as a political humanist to reckon with. Then, as the political atmosphere worsened, he returned to Slovenia to make *The Red Wheat* (1971) and *Dead Bird's Flight* (1973) on the mistakes of collectivization.

Purisa Djordjevic worked in documentaries before establishing a reputation as a lyric poet on partisan fighting during the war (mostly about the Serbian village in which he lived). *Girl* (1965), *Dream* (1966), *Morning* (1967), and *Noon* (1968) treat this experience in the form of a collage mixing dream with reality. *Cross Country* (1969) satirizes authoritarianism in a spoof on the Orthodox Church; *The Cyclists* (1971) is another nostalgic view of village life at the beginning of the war; and *Pavle Pavlovic* (1974) criticizes corruption in political life.

Dusan Makavejev, a master of the cinema of free associations, made a series of skilfully edited films, a mixture of humor and irony, scientific reflections and eroticism, love and crime, sex and puritanism, and other contrasting themes. In *A Man Is Not a Bird* (1965), similar in tone to his highly critical, controversial shorts (*The Parade*, 1962, satirizing May Day ceremonies), he emphasizes the collective hypnotizing of workers. *A Love Dossier* (or *Tragedy of a Switchboard Operator*) (1967) subjects a flesh-and-blood creature, whose affair-of-the-heart is dissected with care and feeling, to the cold analysis of a sexologist and a police inspection. *Innocence Without Defense* (1968) matches a primitive film by an acrobat made illegally during the Occupation with modern documentary footage to memorialize Yugoslavia's eternal national spirit. *Mysteries of the Organism* (1971), never exhibited in Yugoslavia, investigates the erotic in a witty, outrageous collage on Marxism, politics, Wilhelm Reich, sex, and Socialist puritanism (featuring a clip from Chiaureli's ode to Stalin, *The Vow*, 1952). *Sweet Movie* (1973) less successfully pursues a similar line of investigation into today's moral code.

Political frankness charges the best films of lesser known Serbian directors: Vladan Slijepcevic's *The Protégé* (1966) and *Where To Go After the Rain* (1967) (made in Macedonia) were bitter attacks on corruption in politics; Djordje Kadijevic presented a two-part examination of wartime violence in *Holiday* (1967) and *Expedition* (1968); Mica Popovic treated pathological killing following partisan fighting in *The Tough Ones* (1968); Zelimir Zelnik perfected a style of political theatre in *Early Works* (1969) and the unreleased *Das Kapital* (1970); and Miroslav Antic's poetic study of human passions, *Breakfast with the Devil* (1971), is set against a natural catastrophe (the flooding of Vojvodina in 1947).

Bosnian directors Bato Cengic and Boro Draskovic have managed to fashion a personal style in inexpensive, formalistic features. Cengic's *Playing at Soldiers* (1968) is a rich parable on social, political and religious forces at work in his country after the war, while *The Role of My Family in the World Revolution* (1971) and *Shock Workers* (1972) are vivid, human portraits of the Stalinist period. Draskovic's *Horoscope* (1969) is the best of many good Yugoslav films examining the problems of the younger generation.

Bulgarian cinema rose to prominence with Rangel Vulchanov's *On a Small Isle* (1958), depicting a struggle for dignity among jailed anti-fascists during the war. His *First Lesson* (1960), a Romeo and Juliet conflict between social classes before the war, and *Sun and Shadow* (1962), an abstract meditation on the menace of the atomic age, were not as successful. Binka Jeliaskova spoke frankly to her generation in *We Were Young* (1962), an autobiographical observation on the difficulties of living through the Resistance; her *The Balloon* (1967) is a philosophical allegory on the Bulgarian people. Vulo Radev achieved some recognition for his human, romantic treatment of the war theme in *The Peach Thief* (1964). The directing duo of Grisha Ostrovsky and Todor Stoyanov made the charming light comedy *Detour* (1967). Tudor Dinov (a well-known animator) collaborated with Hristo Hristov on *Iconostasis* (1968), a testament to the country's religious heritage under the suppression of the Turks. A new wave of directors is on the horizon.

Romania won international recognition at the Cannes festival with Liviu Ciulei's *The Forest of the Hanged* (1965), a conscience film about an officer in conflict with his superiors during the First World War. Mircea Dragan's *Golgotha* (1966) treated the psychological crucifixion of a group of wives during a workers' uprising in the previous capitalist society. Lucian Pintilie's *Sunday at Six O'Clock* (1965) and *Reconstruction* (1968) were critical breakthroughs in their treatment of contemporary problems.

East German cinema flowered briefly after the war in Wolfgang Staudte's critical commentaries on German war guilt: *The Murderers Are Among Us* (1946), *Rotation* (1949) and *Der Untertan* (1951). Konrad Wolf's *Stars* (1959) and *I Was Nineteen* (1968) were impressive, personal views of the war years. Several self-critical films were banned in 1965, among them Frank Beyer's *Jacob the Liar*; scriptwriter Jurek Becker turned it into a bestselling novel, and Beyer finally filmed in 1974 this tragicomedy on a make-believe radio in the Warsaw Ghetto. Egon Günther, who started as a novelist, is the GDR's best filmmaker with an eye for contemporary themes; he has made *The Third* (1972), *The Keys* (1973), *Lotte in Weimar* (1974) and *The Sorrows of Young Werther* (1975).

Two factors are important in Socialist cinema. The first is a growing desire in these nationalized industries to communicate with their peoples in a direct, forthright, honest and human manner. Dialogue of this nature is often looked upon with alarm by the government, but it has grown in intensity as restrictions have been lifted on directors to attain international recognition. The second is the prevalence of religious themes reflecting the national spirit, the life of the people, and the struggle of the individual to maintain his dignity. The observation of historians Will and Ariel Durant has application here:

There is no significant example in history, before our time, of a society successfully maintaining moral life without the aid of religion. France, the United States, and some other nations have divorced their governments from all churches, but they have had the help of religion in keeping social order. Only a few Communist states have not merely dissociated themselves from religion but have repudiated its aid; and perhaps the apparent and provisional success of this experiment in Russia owes much to the temporary acceptance of Communism as the religion (or, as skeptics would say, the opium) of the people, replacing the church as the vendor of comfort and hope. If the socialist regime should fail in its efforts to destroy relative poverty among the masses, this new religion may lose its fervor and efficacy, and the state may wink at the restoration of supernatural beliefs as an aid in quieting discontent.

Since Stalinism most Socialist states have been seeking a *modus vivendi* with the peoples they rule, resulting in a friendlier approach to religion wherever the churches are still strong. In areas where religion is suppressed and poverty is known, the State's adamant position is only preparing the groundwork for a religious revival.

As Socialist cinema reflects this desire for a *modus vivendi* between state and population, so the established Western film industries are moving closer to dialogue with the audience. A 1970 editorial in *Newsweek* spoke for a changing Hollywood:

A new seriousness among today's moviemakers is undeniable and it promises at its best to produce in the months and years ahead the kind of intelligent, personal and relevant cinema Americans have admired in European filmmaking for decades. Hopefully, it will be a film industry grounded in the traditional humanism of John Ford and George Stevens, just as in France, Truffaut has carried through and updated the humanism of Jean Renoir. At least the conditions are ripe for such a flourishing. And the need is clear. "We have so many strident voices on every side," says Arthur Penn, "from the hate rhetoric of an Agnew to the wild cries of the radicals. The best we can hope for from our films is that they will talk to us about how we can live decently. People are looking for a way of coming together, and perhaps movies can aid in this search for mercy and goodwill."

IX. FAITH IN THE CINEMA
OF CARL THEODOR DREYER

Jean Renoir on *The Passion of Joan of Arc*:

His personages are of a disturbing reality, both externally and internally. When Dreyer asked Falconetti to have her head shaved to play the part of Joan of Arc in prison, he was not asking for a sacrifice to mere external truth. I think that primarily this was an inspiration for Dreyer. The sight of this admirable face deprived of its natural adornment plunged Dreyer into the very heart of his subject. This shaven head was the purity of Joan of Arc. It was her faith. It was her invincible courage. It was her innocence, even stronger than the knavery of her judges. It was the resistance to oppression and tyranny; it was also a bitter observation on the eternal brutality of those who believe themselves to be strong. It was the ineffectual protest of the people. It was the affirmation that in human tragedies it is always the poor who pay; and also that the humility of these poor people makes them closer to God than the right and the powerful could ever be. That shaved head said all this and much more to Dreyer. It was and remains the abstraction of the whole epic of Joan of Arc. What is miraculous is that this is also the case with the spectators who continue to come and purify themselves in the pure waters of Dreyer's *Joan of Arc*.

Jonas Mekas on *Ordet*:

Now, if this film means only that Dreyer is propagating nothing but a belief in miracles, as some critics have said, it would really be a limited work of art. However, this simple plot is only the surface frame. On its deeper level, or on its true level, the film transcends its plot and becomes a parable. We know parables told to children: realistic content presented through fantastic happenings. No child believes them, but everyone gets their simple moral messages: courage, endurance, or whatever it may be. *Ordet* is a modern parable, and its message — or, let us say, one of its most obvious messages — is a plea for man's faith in our time of confusion. Not a cry of desperation or pessimism, but a trembling, anguished, searching cry — a cry of a man who takes his life and his death seriously and who still believes that there must be a WORD.

The *Dutch Catechism* on faith:

Since God draws faith from the deepest core of man's being, its degree and vitality are not tied to intellectual endowments, like philosophy, for instance, which is much more dependent on them. If the way of faith was that of pure reasoning the cleverest and most cultured people would find God most easily. The less learned and the less gifted would be less enlightened than they as regards the final end of life. But the knowledge through which God is found stems rather from man's inner orientation than from his talents. "In that same hour he rejoiced in the Holy Spirit and said, 'I thank thee, Father, Lord of heaven and earth, that thou hast hidden these things from the wise and understanding and revealed them to babes; yea, Father, for such was thy gracious will' " (Lk. 10 : 21).

Dreyer's cinema bypassed the intellect for the heart. "*Gertrud* was a film that I made with my heart." His manner of directing involved two principles: first, the reproduction as close as possible of the feelings of the characters; and second, the right choice of actors to respond to this quest. This was the summation of his style. About the first:

Quite simply, I do not at all involve myself with beings — men or women — who do not personally interest me. I can only work with people who allow me to realize a certain agreement. What interests me — and this comes before technique — is reproducing the feelings of the characters in my films. That is, to reproduce, as sincerely as possible, the most sincere feelings possible. The important thing, for me, is not only to catch hold of the words they say, but also the thoughts behind the words. What I seek in my films, what I want to obtain, is a penetration of my actors' profound thoughts by means of their most subtle expressions. For these are the expressions that reveal the character of the person, his conscious feelings, the secrets that live in the depths of his soul. This is what interests me above all, not the technique of the cinema.

About the second:

You must discover what there is at the bottom of each being. That is why I always look for actors who are capable of responding to this quest, who are interested in it, who can help me with it. They must be capable of giving me, or allowing me to take, what I seek to obtain from them. But it is difficult for me to express this the way it should be — and besides, is it possible?

Carl Theodor Dreyer was born in Copenhagen on 3 February 1889 and died in the same city on 20 March 1968 at the age of 79 after a career of nearly fifty years in filmmaking. In his youth he was taught the piano and held a job briefly as an accountant before trying journalism, mostly covering trials but also reviewing theatre. It gave him the chance to study middle-class personalities, who make many memorable appearances in his films. He began in cinema in 1912 by using afternoons off to write titles at the Nordisk studio in Copenhagen; soon he was working fulltime. He was credited with twenty-six film scripts before making his first feature film, *The President* (1919). Nordisk had already seen its hey-day before the First World War and Dreyer admitted it was not a very good film, but he did manage to put some new ideas to work on the acting, decor, editing and the use of nonprofessionals to suit his sense for authenticity. He was to treat all his films in the same way.

After this melodrama about a public official who sacrifices himself for his imprisoned daughter's happiness and later commits suicide, he became interested in utilizing the language of film to tell a story. He studied Griffith, whose *Intolerance* sent him walking the streets on the night of the Nordisk screening; in the long run though he preferred the spiritual mysticism in Sjöström's and Stiller's Swedish films. If his work owes anything to any director, it is to Sjöström: the mystical elements of landscape fostered a liking for real locations and accurate decor to support the truth unveiled in the human face.

Convinced he could compete with the Hollywood market in his own way, he convinced Nordisk to attempt a minor spectacle, *Leaves From Satan's Book* (1919-1921), in line with the fashion of the day. Adapted from a popular religious novel of the day, Marie Corelli's *The Sorrows of Satan*, the film featured Satan in disguise betraying his fellow man throughout the ages: a pharisee tempting Judas, the Grand Inquisitor in medieval Spain, a revolutionary policeman in the French Revolution, a treacherous monk from Russia in Finland of 1918. It is too much an imitation of Griffith's *Intolerance* (1916); his personal touch is apparent only in the Finnish episode. All else was still wrapped in Nordisk's stylized rules of melodrama, but once in the Spanish Inquisition episode the Dreyer world appears in embryo: the intrusion on privacy, the contrasts of light and darkness, the motif of the doorway, and the forecasting of themes centering on trials, intolerance, martyrdom, witch-hunting and the defenseless female.

While Nordisk delayed releasing this small-scale spectacle, Dreyer spent the summer of 1920 in Norway filming *The Parson's Widow* (1920) for Svensk Filmindustri. Adapting a Kristofer Janson story about a true incident in the sixteenth century, he made use of an authentic museum-village near Lillehammer, with Norwegian peasants (who knew Janson) filling in on bit roles. The film utilized the acting talents of Sweden's Hildur Carlberg, who had appeared in the films of Sjöström (a Lagerlöf adaptation) and Stiller. Midway through the film Dreyer realized she was dying, and slowly he departed from his original story to give full attention to a woman he had grown deeply fond of. Instead of a comedy about the antics of a young pastor, trying to rid himself of the former pastor's widow he is forced to marry to obtain the parsonage, he made a tragicomedy on a elderly woman's loneliness in facing death. The experience made an indelible impression on the young director.

The next year he went to Berlin to make *Love One Another* (1921-1922), the story taken from the Danish novel *The Stigmatized Ones* by Aage Madelung on the horrors of the Russian pogrom of 1905. Because of the number of Russian refugees in Berlin after the revolution and the advantages of inflation (the sale of one German silent film before 1923 to Switzerland repaid the costs on the exchange market), the small Primusfilm company was able to erect a completely authentic village and employ actors from the Moscow Arts Theatre. Dreyer's ideas and experiments had already merged into a style, but he was unable to reduce the huge novel to the dimensions he preferred. Successful in obtaining the milieu he desired, he was unable nonetheless to coach spontaneous expressions from his actors to save the film.

In the summer of 1922 he returned to Copenhagen to film a popular fairy tale, Holger Drachmann's *Once Upon a Time* (1922), only the project was wasted in waiting for the construction of the sets that had been promised. He had to shoot everything in a month's time to allow the actors to return to the Royal Theatre, and he considers it his first failure. Still, the two-thirds of the print in existence shows he was able to create a breathtaking atmosphere for the unfolding of the tale. The play itself, however, provided few of the tensions and psychological climaxes he was now seeking, but in one close-up of the face of the old king, 84-year-old Peter Jerndorff, he captured again the charm and dignity that flowed through *The Parson's Widow*. It was in effect a kind of self-portrait, a signature found in his best work.

Hereafter Dreyer was totally committed to examining the mysteries of the human face. He went back to Berlin in 1923 to work on one of the 400 features made that year at the height of the inflation, an adaptation of Herman Bang's novel *Mikael* (1924) for the UFA studios. It proved to be a turning point in his career, for *Mikael* gave him the opportunity to explore freely the limits of human feeling in an intimate *Kammerspiel* atmosphere. But unlike Carl Mayer's *Kammerspiel* scripts, subjugating the plot to an examination of the instincts, those of Dreyer stayed close to the psychological possibilities of the plot and sought subtleties of expression rendered by actors carefully selected to fit the mental frame of the role. He had found his style. *Mikael* was not a film about erotic sex (as advertised in some countries on the basis of Bang's material), but about human beings stifled in a world of fashionable decay. The artist Zoret (played by Danish director Benjamin Christensen, who had just completed the atmospheric, documentary-style *Witchcraft Throughout the Ages*, 1922) suffers in the end alone, surrounded only by Dreyer's compassion, pity and understanding. This film was the direct forerunner of his masterpiece, *The Passion of Joan of Arc* (1928).

He followed with his first commercial success, *Master of the House* (or *Thou Shalt Love Thy Wife*) (1925), made in Denmark and based on Svend Rindom's popular play. For making this film, lighter in tone and tinged with realism, Dreyer as usual had every advantage: an authentic middle-class family flat was constructed especially for the set. He discovered that adapting a theatre play allowed him to purify the text to fit the needs of his cinematic style. In this story of a father acting as a tyrant in his own home (the opening scene shows him as a kind of vampire), the nanny saves the day by taking over when the wife is close to a nervous breakdown. The humanistic elements of the play allowed Dreyer to reduce the whole to a simplicity of mood rich in psychological tensions, and he edited out at the last minute scenes showing the father at work in a dismal factory at low wages. The film was enthusiastically greeted by the general public, running for months in a single theatre in Paris and thus prompting the invitation for *Joan of Arc*.

As an interlude, Dreyer returned to Norway to make *The Bride of Glomsdale* in the summer of 1925. An exercise in lyricism, it was a throwback to the glory of Swedish silent cinema, although much of Dreyer's former *The Parson's Widow* and some of Griffith (*Way Down East*, 1920) cancel out the Sjöström and Stiller elements; there is also some of the nostalgia for the recent, pastoral past that characterizes a film like Henry King's *Tol'able David* (1921). Whatever the influence, it was a little film delighting in craftsmanship. He was probably never happier than in making this little folk tale about a poor farm boy in love with a rich man's daughter, and it offered a splendid opportunity to develop the important emotional under-currents of a love story. Only the martyr is missing, the sacrifice of the self for the purity of an ideal, the tragedy of love — the elements that made his former films stand out and were to reach some kind of culmination in *The Passion of Joan of Arc* (1928), the high-water mark of the silent film.

The martyr holds a position of pre-eminence in Dreyer's cinema. His world is peopled with martyrs of various sorts, but primarily the defenseless female — for it is then that he is fully caught up in the search for the secrets in the depths of the soul. An examination of his early films shows it is essentially his interest in the subject that prompts the request of an actor to lay open his or her unconscious feelings, and further investigation confirms the suspicion that he works best when the actress is a young female. In each case — the figure of Siri in the Finnish episode of *Leaves From Satan's Book*, old Dame Margaret in *The Parson's Widow*, Hanna-Liebe as the personification of the entire Jewish community in *Love One Another*, and the artist Zoret in *Mikael* — he starts his search in the beginning detached, almost from a distant point of view, then imperceptibly he moves closer, adjusting the entire film to the response of the individual. By the time he reached *Joan of Arc* and Anne in *Day of Wrath* (1943) and *Gertrud* (1964), the stories transcended time and place and these were films dealing more with Maria Falconetti and Lisbeth Movin and Nina Pens Rode than their historical personages. *Vampyr* (1932) too can be interpreted as the hallucinatory dreams of Leone (Sybille Schmitz), and *Ordet* (1955) is striking for its daring conception of the wife Inger (Birgitte Federspiel) in the traditional male Christ role (replacing pastor-playwright Kaj Munk's Johannes as the Christ figure). *Two People* (1944), because of miscasting the only failure in his later films, is not as boring as critics contend if one considers the potentialities of the role of the adulterous wife; it is, in a sense, a parody of his style.

While working on the episode of the Finnish Uprising in 1918 as the modern addition to *Leaves From Satan's Book* (1919-1921), in which he supported the cause of liberty for Finland (said to be the reason Dreyer was never popular in the Soviet Bloc), he had already understood the power of the close-up and the importance of the spiritual message in D. W. Griffith's *Intolerance* (1916). The indications are that he was copying Griffith, but the lessons learned from Sjöström and Stiller told him that the theme could be imbued with a deeper spiritual significance by unleashing the emotions of Siri (Clara Pontoppidan) in a symbolic sacrifice against the forces of terror and war. The modern episode in *Leaves From Satan's Book* is the spiritual extension of Griffith's modern episode in *Intolerance*.

Each time it is the subject that attracted me. Here, in this Finnish story, the subject was very pleasing to me: this story of a woman who sacrifices her life for her husband and her country, in spite of everything that rises against her and the threat of her children being killed. In the end, she commits suicide. It was there that, for the first time, I used a close-up of the principal actress, in which she did what I asked of her and rendered a whole range of feelings, with a long succession of changing expressions.

The Parson's Widow (1920), the first of his minor masterpieces, demonstrates how he gradually approached his subject from afar. The first half concerns three young divinity students competing comically for the vacant parsonage, with the joke on the winner who must become the fourth husband of the residence's widow to get the position. The young parson obliges but moves his mistress into the house as maid, planning all the while an accidental death for the old witch. In the course of a number of frustrations, each quite comical as in the opening tone of the film, Dreyer's attention slowly shifts from the story line to rest solidly on the countenance of an aging woman, remembering the joy of her own first marriage and obligingly dying for the happiness of the young couple. The last walk of Hildur Carlberg as the widow around the farmstead, before taking leave of the world, is nothing short of majestic because it was really happening. From a comedy to a tragicomedy, from a farce to a martyrdom theme, is a long step, but Dreyer has lightened the widow's burden of loneliness by offering the strength of his own compassion. Her spirit is resurrected again in the costume of Mari, the parson's true love and wife.

His compassion for an isolated people, as expressed in Aage Madelung's novel *The Stigmatized Ones*, attracted him to doing a film on the Russian pogrom of 1905, titled *Love One Another* (*Die Gezeichneten* in German, after the novel's title). Although the heroine of the story, Hanna-Liebe, is rescued and finds happiness in the end in a pivotal love story between a Christian and a Jewess, it is the plight of the Jewish people that interests him most. The story wanders through a maze of intolerance and injustice, presenting a rich assortment of witches and vampires (the prejudiced school teacher and the greedy marriage broker), spies and betrayers, saints and martyrs, a full flowering of Dreyer's central theme of intolerance hidden in every pocket of social existence. *Love One Another* was the direct forerunner of his unfulfilled Jesus film, wherein he planned to exonerate the Jews as a race and put the blame on the military governor.

After the failure of *Once Upon a Time* (1922), a second primary motif of loneliness and solitude reached its proper fulfillment in *Mikael* (1924), a big success in Germany (where it was hailed as an authentic example of *Kammerspiel*) but advertised as an erotic sex film abroad for its homosexual overtones. The story of a celebrated painter (along the lines of Rodin) who is abandoned by his "adopted son" for the attentions of a princess, the old artist dies amid the clutter of fashionable, exaggerated trappings. The period is the turn of the century "when passion and exaggeration were in fashion, when feelings were willfully exacerbated; a period with a certain very false manner, which is seen in its decoration with all its outrageously supercharged interiors," a ripe setting for Dreyer to penetrate the unconscious feelings of his actors and reflect the pretense that surrounds many in the world of artists. He had discovered, with the assistance of architect Hugo Häring who zealously furnished the decors to fit his intentions, his style; it consisted in part of

a certain reflection of the period. It was, for example, the period when, in France, the monasteries were expropriated by the government. Piles of accessories that came from churches and monasteries were put up for sale, and many people bought sacerdotal ornaments, chairs, benches and other furniture. For example, I knew a Danish actress — who lived in France and was married to the composer, Bereny — who, when she moved back to Copenhagen, set herself up in an apartment filled with horrible things of this genre, all lighted up by a bunch of chandeliers. Well, all that was also part of the film's atmosphere which reflects this rich taste... which was in bad taste but which, obviously, was considered excellent at that time.

The twin motifs of loneliness and suffering martyrdom appear again in *Master of the House* (1925), a special comedy about family life and a nanny's victory over a tyrannical father. He reconstructed a middle-class flat when he found his crew could not work easily within a real one. In such sure surroundings Dreyer could exploit every detail of mood and charm, and charge the opening scenes of suffering and martyrdom with a painful poignancy by isolating the nanny in a world of selflessness, servitude and neglect. Then, as in *The Parson's Widow* (1920), he reverses the tables by shifting his attention to the father: he slowly changes from a vampire-tyrant into a lonely, pitiable human being.

With *The Passion of Joan of Arc* (1928) Dreyer began a third theme richer in scope than martyrdom and loneliness for their own sake. He embarked on an exploration into the self that demanded the utmost of an actor, a search totally unique in the cinema. Indeed, his artistic instincts led him into areas where others never dared to venture: the inner life of a person's private and emotional sensitivity. Neither the actor nor the director knew exactly what they would find at the end of their quest, and they were never certain which way the search would lead them. They worked together from both sides of the camera: Dreyer probing, the actor responding generously and openly, slowly laying bare the sheltered depths of the soul. Gradually the audience entered into a realm of cinematic life it had never experienced before: the lonely, frightened, unprotected, suffering, pitiable essence of the Maid of Orleans. Like Chaplin and Flaherty in this same period of cinema history, he worked painstakingly, letting the screen show him every step of the way. Asked in the *Cahiers du Cinéma* interview what happens when an actor does not give what he is capable of giving, he replied:

We do it over! We start over and we do everything again! Until he arrives at it. For if he is capable of giving he will always end up giving. It's a question of time and patience. With Falconetti, it often happened that, after having worked all afternoon, we hadn't succeeded in getting exactly what was required. We said to ourselves then: tomorrow we will begin again. And the next day, we would have the bad take from the day before projected, we would examine it, we would search and we always ended by finding, in that bad take, some little fragments, some little light that rendered the exact expression, the tonality we had been looking for. It is from there that we would set out again, taking the best and abandoning the remainder. It is from there that we took off, in order to begin again... and succeed.

In *The Passion of Joan of Arc* Dreyer's point of view was growing extremely subtle. That the camera was minutely observing the suffering of Joan of Arc, the defenseless maid, is obvious; but Dreyer had also entered deeply into his subject and presented the audience with his (and Joan's) view of her surroundings and the people persecuting her. As with the parson's widow and the family tyrant, both vampires stripped down to their human form, we are able to watch the perplexity of the judges rise to challenge the wisdom of their actions — until they too, particularly Cauchon, the chief judge, are completely stripped of their defenses and driven to self-doubt. Joan, a young innocent, wanting desperately to live and hoping for deliverance, is denied a sympathetic face and robbed of her last dignity: the shaving of her head. The Maid is defeated, the "witch" is taken to the stake — yet she wins her victory. The victors are left with ashes.

With *Joan of Arc* Dreyer was beginning his approach to tragedy, but in the last forty years of his life he was only allowed four more chances to prove his worth. The motifs of loneliness and suffering stemming from the isolated self made some headway in *Vampyr* (1932), the best of the horror film genre in which nothing appears to be real yet everything somehow is. A fantasy film of mood and atmosphere, its style resulted from a piece of gauze veiling the source of light; in its eery, grey abstractness a vampire (another old woman) is aided by a sinister doctor and finally defeated in the usual manner by a stake driven through the heart. It was financed by an amateur film-lover, the Baron Nicolas de Gunzburg, and its history is shrouded in the same mysterious atmosphere that pervades the film and cursed many of the participants. A financial flop when it appeared, this story of an awkward, gaunt figure (played by the baron) stumbling his way through a netherland of mists, shrieks and patched dialogue has grown in reputation with the years. *Vampyr*, set in its period, can also be viewed as a warning. In the 1930s the film industries had fallen into the hands of commercial interests or under government control, both squeezing the artistic life out of this young, still experimental medium of communication. The vendors of raw propaganda were about to vent their hatred upon mankind, and there was no room particularly for Dreyer's kind of cinema. Vampires were loose who would soon reap a grim harvest: the guardian of the vessel of humanity had issued a warning.

After *Vampyr* Dreyer went to England to work briefly for John Grierson, to Africa to begin an aborted project, and finally back to Copenhagen to return to journalism under the pen name of "Tom-men". During the war years he formalized his theories on film in a series of essays, *On Film*, lectured, and joined forces with the Danish film industry to speak out to the people under the Occupation. Danish films raised their artistic and ideological standards during this time as a form of resistance, building a spiritual bridge to the population and diverting man-power away from Nazi interests. Dreyer, the country's recognized film artist, was coaxed into making a short film for the Health Department, *Good Mothers* (1942), which opened the way for an invitation to make a feature. Pulling out of a desk drawer an old review of Wiers Jensen's *Anne Pedersdotter*, he proposed to turn the play into a film, *Day of Wrath* (1943), reflecting the spiritual problems of the day in the fear-laden environment of witch-hunting in seventeenth-century Norway (a province of Denmark at that time). It cost a little over $25,000 and proved he could work with a small budget and still obtain the results he always demanded of actors.

Anne Pedersdotter, wandering alone through her confined surroundings and peeking through windows and doors, is only a step away from *Vampyr*; her condemnation as a witch by a tribunal of judges and at the instigation of her vampire mother-in-law links *Day of Wrath* to *Joan of Arc* and the earlier silent films. Beside her is the old pastor who dies of a heart attack when he learns of his young wife's secret, erotic love, another tie to Cauchon and the pastor's widow of long ago: a tragic figure, nagged by his conscience, buried in the unutterable loneliness of the soul. In *Day of Wrath* Dreyer presented his richest assortment of characters doomed to struggle in the recesses of the soul for the last vestiges of human dignity. He offers himself in this struggle — and us.

Day of Wrath was to be the nearest Dreyer ever came to tragedy. Having to flee to Sweden soon after its completion on the pretext of selling the film for distribution there, he found himself with time on his hands and accepted an invitation from producer Carl Anders Dymling at Svensk Filmindustri (a supporter of Ingmar Bergman at the beginning of his career) to make a small film. He chose W. O. Somin's play *Attentat*, later to be entitled *Two People* (1944-1945), a financial disaster and undoubtedly the lowest point in Dreyer's career. Dymling was then at the height of his career and a refined humanist, but he could be as strong-willed as Dreyer and a clash was inevitable:

Unfortunately, the producer decided to choose the actors himself. He wanted a great career. Well, the actors in question represented the exact opposite of what I would have wanted. And, for me, the actors are extremely important. Thus, I wanted the woman to be a bit theatrical, a little hysterical, and, as for the actor for the part of the savant, I wanted a man with blue eyes, naive but completely honest, who was interested in nothing but his work. Well, they gave me an actress who was the personification of a little bourgeoise, and for the man, instead of a blue-eyed idealist, I was given an intriguing demoniac with brown eyes....

Returning to Denmark and once again without work in the Danish film industry, he tried to interest an independent American company in backing a Jesus film in the midst of the biblical spectacles (actually travelling to America and writing the script in 1949-1950). The project fell through. The Danish government then gave him a theatre to manage in downtown Copenhagen (insuring him of an income for life) and he made some short films on the side. A break came again in 1954 when the Palladium Film Company, the producers of *Day of Wrath*, decided to pay tribute to pastor-playwright Kaj Munk murdered by the Nazis during the war in 1944. Tribute had already been paid to Munk in 1943 by a production of *Ordet* in Sweden by Gustaf Molander, with Victor Sjöström in the role of the father, and poet-dramatist Rune Lindström as the miracle-working Johannes (Lindström was also the author of the folk tale, *The Road to Heaven*, filmed by Alf Sjöberg); the ten-year rights to Molander's production expired, allowing Denmark to memorialize his most famous and popular play. Dreyer had seen *Ordet* at its première in 1932 and is said to have been so impressed he again walked the streets for a night. Years later he confessed to departing from his journey toward tragedy:

I was so much happier doing *Ordet* when I felt myself very close to the conceptions of Kaj Munk. He always spoke well of love. I mean to say of love in general, between people, as well as love in marriage, true marriage. For Kaj Munk, love was not only the beautiful and good thoughts that can link man and woman, but also a very profound link. And for him there was no difference between sacred and profane love. Look at *Ordet*. The father is saying, "She is dead... she is no longer here. She is in heaven..." and the son answers, "Yes, but I loved her body too..." What is beautiful in Kaj Munk is that he understood these two forms of love. That is why he didn't separate them either. But this form of Christianity is opposed by another form, a somber and fanatic faith.

Dreyer turned *Ordet* into his definitive statement on intolerance of all kinds, not just the religious intolerance that is at the root of the play. Since *The President* (1919), in which he depicted his fellow journalists gorging themselves at a banquet, and the French Revolution episode in *Leaves From Satan's Book* (1919-1921), in which children play a game of trial and persecution against a background of larger injustices, he had sought to expose intolerance in every corner of society. After the Spanish Inquisition episode in *Leaves From Satan's Book*, the 1905 pogrom in *Love One Another* (1921-1922), the persecution of young, defenseless females as witches in *The Passion of Joan of Arc* (1928) and *Day of Wrath* (1943), it was not surprising that he looked upon religious differences as one of the primary causes of intolerance in the world. Like Munk, he felt that the only way to combat it was with a sign of love and renewed faith in man. The common man must face the contradictions in his own soul and make a choice for the good in life, an affirmation, a credo. As in St. Luke's account of the prayer of Jesus: "I thank thee, Father, Lord of heaven and earth, that thou hast hidden these things from the wise and understanding and revealed them to babes" (Lk. 10 : 21) — Dreyer left the believing up to children, whose faith is pure and unsoiled. It is a child therefore who works the miracle in *Ordet*.

His last film ten years later, *Gertrud* (1964), was a final return to tragedy based on Swedish playwright (and contemporary of Strindberg) Hjalmar Söderberg's central theme, "the desire of the flesh and the incurable loneliness of the soul." Although in line with his own theme of intolerance, Gertrud does recognize (contrary to the playwright) that her lover must live too for his work but doesn't want to take second place in any case; she ends her life in self-delusion.

Before his death Dreyer was given the funds to begin his long-cherished *Jesus* film, with the military in the role of the villains. He had said that he hoped to arrive finally at tragedy in its fullest sense with the film about Christ, and with a script he had prepared on *Medea*. Faulkner's *A Light in August*, to be filmed in America, also lay in waiting.

Of all the tributes paid to Dreyer, Jean Renoir's is the most fitting:

The spreading of the knowledge of man by artists is even more formidable than nuclear fission; it is a sin which can only be pardoned if the sinner is a genius. This is the sin of Dreyer. God will forgive him for it was He who bestowed upon him his extraordinary perception.

The cinema of Dreyer has often been compared with that of Robert Bresson, prompted apparently by the slow solemnity with which both unfold their images. In fact, they couldn't be further apart in attitudes, goals and manner of filming. Bresson works only with nonprofessionals; Dreyer uses nonprofessionals for bit roles, but relies primarily on actors to work with him in baring the recesses of the soul. Bresson accepts the soul as the vessel of God's grace and from this standpoint interprets the tragedies that prove God's love; Dreyer, an agnostic, is moving toward tragedy in his quest to unveil the secrets of the soul. Bresson is an insider looking out; Dreyer an outsider looking in.

X. THE FILMMAKER
AS BIBLICAL THEOLOGIAN

When he undertakes the study of human affairs the historian commits himself, by the act, to becoming a theologian, too.

TOYNBEE.

I am very much attached to Nazarin. He is a priest. He could as easily be a hairdresser or a waiter. What interests me about him is that he stands by his ideas, that these ideas are inacceptable to society at large, and that after his adventures with prostitutes, thieves, and so forth, they lead him to being irrevocably damned by the prevailing social order.

BUNUEL.

Bunuel's *Nazarin* is ready-made for theological dialogue. The director is one of the leading modern filmmakers with an intense interest in human affairs. The film is an interpretation of the life of Christ. Few better examples exist in modern art and literature of the biblical message directly challenging Western man on his own terms. *Nazarin* is a man in search for himself — for the power to believe, for a final right to hope and love.

In *Man's Search for Himself* Leo Scheffczyk goes beyond the view of regarding the Bible simply in its traditional function of revelation. Like the modern artist, he views God's way of making himself known to the world as man's search for himself.

Scheffczyk begins by noting that the Old Testament had not yet discovered individual man. The first description of man pictures him essentially as the creation of God. Considered against the background of the surrounding pagan world and the Babylonian creation myths, God stands above these myths in that he is not a part of the cosmic reality. He is in a position of absolute transcendence over man. Man depends upon his creator, and in this way he is somewhat liberated from fear of the world. God has created him: God will take care of him. Man feels he is wanted.

Genesis leaves no doubt that only man stands immediately before God. The people Israel are singled out by special election for divine help and guidance. Man is not a law unto himself, but made in the image and likeness of his creator (Genesis 1 : 26). Man's unique dignity is underlined. The words of the eighth psalm echo this dignity in its greatness, and give a full insight into the make-up of Old Testament man. But exactly what this "image and likeness" was, the Old Testament doesn't say. And it could not be fully developed until the arrival of the perfect human image of God, Jesus Christ, the God-man.

A second element of the creation story differentiating it from pagan mythologies is the act of creating through words. This again is echoed in Psalm 147 : 15-20, in which his word accounts for the subsequent preservation of the world. The creative power of God's word is fundamental to the Old Testament, expressed over and over again. Isaiah gives it added depth when he says the word "shall not return to me fruitless without accomplishing my purpose or succeeding in the task I gave it" (Isaiah 55 : 11). In this context the word takes on the appearance of a ray of light, and the wonders of nature are a mirror radiating the word back to its author. But mindful again that only he is created in God's image and likeness, man becomes the only proper response to God's word.

The Old Testament is rich in references to man being addressed by God, and called to give an account of himself. Often, when man has sinned, he is summoned in divine anger. He is told to take the word of God to heart, and when God makes a new covenant with man, God writes it in man's heart (Jeremiah 31 : 33). There stands a continual redeeming intercourse between God and man.

A third element coming out of the creation story is the essential make-up of man as "matter" and "spirit," or "body" and "soul" (Genesis 2 : 7). Hebrew thought regarded man as a unity of the two, without any suspicion of dualism: "soul" or "spirit" means he is living, and "body" or "matter" means he is transitory. Thus sin was not something deriving from the tension between body and soul, but rather the whole man resisting the will of God. This unified vision of man eliminated any notion of the immortality of the soul, but at the same time the Jewish nation cannot be accused of espousing materialism. The people Israel looked upon earthly existence as a rich complex of values in which the spiritual was never separated from the material. A "spirituality of life" evolved, and the reward of the just man was to be his final resurrection from the dead (2 Maccabees 7 : 9). This was not basically the same as the Christian concept of the immortality of the soul, for the Hebrew was unable to come to grips with the problem of suffering (which could have been eased greatly by the concept of the immortality of the soul). Out of this excruciating frustration came the great dramatic poem of the Old Testament, the Book of Job. It simply asks the question "why?"

Job is the classic figure of Old Testament man. Knowing himself addressed by God, he finds himself unable to respond in his frustrated state of sin (and the resulting suffering meted out by God). A tension manifests itself between devotion to God and a mounting despair, a tension so striking one senses within it the kernel of hope. Surely God will save man from an existence torn by sin and suffering (Job 19 : 25).

This is the picture of Old Testament man three to five centuries before Christ, on the threshold of salvation.

The New Testament follows the Old Testament line in the essential points and brings it to completion. It pictures man as fully dependent on God and recognizes that with God "all things are possible" (Mark 10 : 27 — Genesis 18 : 14). The Sermon on the Mount outlines man's universal rule of conduct, and the necessity of being totally dedicated to God (Luke 17 : 10). Jesus Christ himself, from his infancy, gives the highest example of a life dedicated to God (Luke 2 : 49). Secondly, man's relationship to God is personal and through dialogue (Matthew 4 : 4 — Deuteronomy 8 : 3), with the only begotten Son of God identified as his Word (John 1 : 1-14). Thirdly, the concepts of "flesh," "spirit," and "soul" are identical with the Old Testament in that they refer to the *whole* man (1 Thessalonians 5 : 23; Hebrews 4 : 12 — Genesis 2 : 7; 6 : 12-13). The difference is that Paul has changed the concepts around: "flesh" now refers to man's sinful nature; "spirit" means the power of God sanctifying the baptized man; and "soul" is that which is in opposition to "spirit" (Galatians 5 : 17-21: "spirit" and "flesh"; 1 Corinthians 2 : 14: "soul"). All the essential characteristics of Old Testament man are brought to completion. Man is now stamped by redemption through Jesus Christ.

More striking is the atmosphere in which the New Testament speaks and thinks about man, in contrast to the formal legalism of Old Testament texts relating to God. A dissipating interest and listlessness crept into religious practices, while the hairsplitting of the Pharisees over the meaning of the law led to a diminishing morality. This is reversed in the Synoptic Gospels where God takes a keen interest in the affairs of man, and the mystery of incarnation is opened up as a proof of his love. The relationship of father-son is introduced between God and man, signifying a much deeper bond than just dialogical (Parable of the Prodigal Son: Luke 15 : 11-32). The Synoptic Christ is as far removed from the problems of Job as light from darkness. Even the moment of Christ's death is accepted with absolute confidence as God's will and in union with his love. The belief in eternal life with the promise of resurrection dispelled the shadow of suffering.

Paul's own dynamic conversion and his forceful rejection of Jewish legalism as rigid and enticing to sin (Romans 7 : 7-13) pointed to a new freedom, a "putting on of the new man" (Ephesians 4 : 23-24). This new freedom implied a profound attachment to God, and a release from the enslavement of sin (Romans 7 : 14). It broke out in a cry of adventure in the experience of spiritual newness: "the freedom of the glory of the sons of God" (Romans 8 : 21). Even while admitting that the sinfulness of the world and the flesh may still attack man and draw him back, he still looks upon his own Christian existence and relapse as a contradiction in terms. The new being in Christ, to Paul, is only a task to be carried out in God's grace (Philippians 2 : 12-13). It is the complete joy of the spirit, or specifically, of the Holy Spirit (1 Thessalonians 1 : 6).

Man experiences the newness of his existence primarily in an encounter with Jesus Christ, the God-man. Christ, in a sense, is taking hold of the person (Philippians 3 : 12), and Paul never tires of announcing that the life of the redeemed man is lived in personal intercourse with the Lord (and through Christ with God). Christlikeness is now God's likeness, and man's original likeness to God requires a Christ-like stamp to be authentic. At the same time, love of one's neighbor is the criterion by which is measured the genuineness of love for Christ (1 Corinthians 11 : 17-34). Therefore, "being in Christ" is the true completion of humanity.

This fulfillment is realized anew in every act of faith, putting man in a position of always looking into the future with expectation (Romans 8 : 23). The greatest treasures are simply not of this world, so man must prepare for them through his pilgrim's progress on earth. In this sense, man's earthly existence is something to be transcended. In the early church this pilgrim character generally resulted in the Christian putting a space between himself and worldly goods, often displaying a scorn for the things of the world. But the Johannine Christ puts the world back into place again in his farewell discourse to his apostles (written after Paul's letters), in which he prays that the Father will not take his disciples out of the world but protect them from its evil (John 17 : 15). A positive approach toward the world is the mark of the Christian.

Paul confirms this too in his own way when he says "everything belongs to you, and you to Christ" (1 Corinthians 3 : 22-23). The Christian is superior to the world, but at the same time using it. Throughout First Corinthians, it is also evident Paul is purposely creating a tension between existence in this world and expectation of the next. This heightened the thirst for the new being in Christ. As a last word of advice Paul always ends on a note of Christian hope (Romans 15 : 13; 2 Corinthians 5 : 6). It is absolutely essential for Christian progress and the life of the believer. It is the key to the resurrection of the dead and eternal life. Hope transforms the believer into a man with a tremendous future. Indeed, he goes so far as to hint that only a man who is sure of a positive future can exist as a human being. For the Christian has no fear. He lives now in a world filled with God's power leading him to God himself. Man has found his identity.

Scheffczyk uses this hope-centered interpretation of biblical truth as an avenue into the despair and pessimism of existentialist philosophers Sartre, Heidegger and Jaspers, as well as the literature of Franz Kafka, Thomas Mann, Ernest Hemingway and Thomas Wolfe. By mirroring man's frustrated need to communicate in biblical man's search for himself, he confronts the negative aspects of existentialism with the positive Christian message.

It is only a short step from modern philosophy and literature to the contemporary filmmaker. The major films in Fellini's important religious cycle — *La Strada* (1954), *Nights of Cabiria* (1957), *La Dolce Vita* (1959) — catch this note of despair in the personages of Zampano, the circus brute, Nazzari, the actor, and Marcello, the reporter, lost people still clinging to a shred of hope and recognizing it when they see it. The lingering faces and personalities of Gelsomina, Cabiria and the young teenager waving from across an abyss are attempts to communicate at the end of these films, providing motifs for theological dialogue and an interpretation of the Christian message of hope. Fellini is saying — and repeats it in his later, autobiographical films, *Eight and a Half* (1963) and *Juliet of the Spirits* (1965) — that man is unfulfilled in today's existence and longs for redemption.

Pasolini's oft-repeated passion for life, for reality, for the physical, existential reality about him is the contact point for the theologian. As a professed existentialist, his notion of being open to the limits brings him close to the biblical message of hope in his early films, and places him never very far away in the best of his later ones. *Accattone* (1961) ends with the petty thief crawling into a ray of light for a useless death, an image repeated in an art-inspired crucifixion at the end of *Mamma Roma* (1962). The crucifixion is parodied in the *La Ricotta* episode of *Rogopag* (1962), but this only adds more meaning to the nature of the event. *The Gospel According to St. Matthew* (1963-1964), even in conceding its social message, also draws power from a transcendental reality. Pasolini's canonization of profane love in *Teorema* (1968), on the surface conceived as a parody of Christian virtue, finds his intentions again contradicted by deed. Before his tragic death Pasolini appears to have abandoned his philosophy altogether; for a time he best exemplified Paul Tillich's statement: "Existentialism has been a windfall for Christian theology".

Similarly, Bunuel's dry sarcasm, "Thank God, I am an atheist", is already a contact point. His atheistic humanism projects an image of man tagged as a perversion of Christian man, much in the order of Sartre. Yet precisely because it is so radical, the contours of the original image remain visible and recognizable. Bunuel's *Nazarin* (1958), as well as Dreyer's *Ordet* (1955), reach to the heart of the Christian experience today.

They are both humanist directors who have seldom, if ever, compromised their positions, and they equate human love for the most part with personal liberty. Their careers to a degree complement each other. Bunuel's acid observation in *Un Chien Andalou* (1928), his surrealist fantasy, imply that religion and moral conventions lead to cruelty, superstition and ignorance, a position that is also reflected in the purity of Dreyer's *The Passion of Joan of Arc* (1928). Bunuel's frontal attack on the church and the bourgeoisie in *L'Age d'Or* (1930) (leading to riots and government censorship) finds its moral base in the documentary *Land Without Bread* (1932), in which superstitious parents prevent their children from even eating bread; both sensitivities are echoed in Dreyer's themes of intolerance. Further, Bunuel's documentary on poverty in Spain demonstrates that reality is more terrifying than dreams, roughly the same message in Dreyer's *Vampyr* (1932) of the same year. Neither director could find work again until the war: Bunuel edited newsreels for the Republican Government in the Spanish Civil War, while Dreyer joined the resistance efforts of the Danish film industry to make *Day of Wrath* (1943).

Beyond this, Bunuel was exceptionally good at reflecting the thinking and emotions of various classes of people when the subject interested him, utilizing the symbols of obsession — feet, dreams, sounds, music, cripples, children, religious ornaments, objects of superstition, sexual motifs — in a private war against the sentimental, commercial elements in the cinema. Although Bunuel saves his saltiest images for attacks on the Catholic Church, his understanding of the human condition and the intolerant attitudes of man to his fellow man in every walk of life endears him to the modern theologian.

Humanism in its most radical terms permeates the most successful films of his early Mexican period, *Los Olvidados* (1950) and *Ascent to Heaven* (1951), which dealt primarily with the problems of the poor in Mexico City and village life in the vein of *Land Without Bread*. It is difficult to forget images in *Ascent to Heaven*, like the little girl dead in her coffin (a direct tie to *Land Without Bread*) or the man with a peg-leg stuck in the stream; the best of his films contain such unforgettable images.

From *The Adventures of Robinson Crusoe* (1952) on it is the emotional life of his central characters that makes Bunuel's films intriguing. The figure of a conventionally moral man faced with his sexual hang-ups on a deserted island reappeared again in *El* (1952), about the moral character of a 40-year-old "celibate" devoted to the church, fantasies repeated again in *Practice of a Crime* (1955).

Mexican co-productions with France on the theme of revolution — *That Is Called the Dawn* (1955), *Death in the Garden* (1956), and *The Fever Reaches El Pao* (1959) — offer many fine character portraits: the exposure of a right-wing conservative in the role of the police inspector, the revelation of human failings in a "liberal" Mexican priest, and the marred but convincing exposé of the faults of the liberal Left in the figure of a reformer. *Nazarin* (1958), made in the middle of the "revolutionary" cycle, rips a hole in the social doctrine of the priest-worker movement. *The Young One* (1960), made just after, is a treatise on the prejudices of the Protestant conservative. In each of these films, Bunuel takes his position with humanity against the attitudes of prejudiced thinking and intolerable restrictions of liberty.

The most significant period of his career is the cycle on religious themes: *Nazarin* (1958), *Viridiana* (1961), *The Exterminating Angel* (1962), *Simon of the Desert* (1965), and *Tristana* (1970), beginning and ending with the mystical novels of Spain's Benito Pérez Galdós. Pérez Galdós marks the beginning of modern Spanish literature at the turn of the century and, like Cervantes, imbues his novels with a broad vision embracing the history of the Spanish nation. From this standpoint *Nazarin* cannot be interpreted as symptomatic of Bunuel's break with the Catholic Church; it is a modern view of the biblical roots of Western man's cultural tradition.

In Ingmar Bergman's *Winter Light* (also known as *The Communicants*) (1962) biblical man's search for his own identity culminates in a new awareness of his own existence. The director was greatly satisfied with the results achieved in the film, in which a non-believing Swedish pastor is confronted by the death of God about him, but in the midst of his own disbelief continues to praise God's name. One of the most autobiographical of modern filmmakers, Bergman invited a dialogue partner, journalist-director Vilgot Sjöman, to trade thoughts during the production. The dialogue sessions are recorded in *L 136*, Sjöman's diary of the Bergman film. The conversation on Thursday, 10 August 1961:

He settles back comfortably in his chair in his room at Svensk Filmindustri, with a searching smile:

"Well, do we go ahead with it?"

"Yes, surely."

I can hear myself how this "Yes, surely" sounds. This hovering, ill-defined, lack of enthusiasm that is me; which is exactly the opposite of his sudden choices between hot and cold (he is either gripped by enthusiasm for something or spits it viciously away). I take a deep breath and begin to list, as planned, everything that I like about the script; but all this he waves impatiently away, anxious for what is to come, the objections, the criticism.

"When Tomas meets the fisherman for the first time and then when he meets Märta... I don't know, but isn't there a bit too much of yourself in the dialogue still? In *Through a Glass Darkly*, there you manage to objectivize yourself much more...."

A shake of the head.

"There's far less of myself in Tomas than you think. Really I have only one thing in common with him, this showdown with an old concept of God; and the glimpse of a new, much more difficult to capture, difficult to explain, difficult to describe God. Otherwise he's not me.... Anything else?"

"The end. You never feel 'the pulsing of a new faith' in Tomas. He just goes in to take Mass...."

"Exactly. He's the beast of burden who just pushes on. Too weak to be of any use in God's work. God can't put any force in him — but He can in Märta who takes over as defender of the faith in the end, you see that?"

I hesitate. I've been reading the film script for two days now, back and forth, but all my jottings show that I have understood Märta to be an unbeliever throughout the film.

"Yes, but what about her *commendatio*?" says Ingmar. "Right at the end?"

Bang! My own religious phobias had played me such an intellectual trick that I had not even noticed it *was* a *commendatio*. I had merely been painfully embarrassed by her genuflection and mumbling about "the gift of faith."

The final scene in the sacristy and church in Bergman's script for *Winter Light*:

Tomas pours out a glass of water and takes two more of Märta's aspirin tablets.

Algot (the sacristan) goes over to the door to look.

Tomas: Well?

Algot (sadly): No, only Miss Lundberg sitting out there. (Apologetically.) Well, of course, that's not to say "only."

Tomas: What shall we do?

Algot: Don't ask me, Vicar. I can see well enough you're really bad, and we certainly won't be a crowd. But, well... don't ask me.

He looks at the floor and the wall, scratches some unevenness in the plaster with his fingernail, looks apologetically at his watch.

Algot: It's time to start the service bell. People usually stir their stumps when they hear it. I mean, if there's anyone coming up the road.

He hurries down the aisle and bows politely to Märta, who doesn't even look in his direction. Then the bells are set in motion, tolling out once again through the twilight and the icy wind.

Märta is overcome with violent emotion. To master an unusual and powerful shuddering she clasps her hands, presses her arms tightly against her sides, deeply bows her head.

Märta (slowly with pauses): If I could only lead him out of his emptiness, away from his lie-god. If we could dare to show each other tenderness. If we could believe in a truth.... If we could believe....

Tomas gets up out of his chair, stands shivering in the middle of the room. The service bell ends with a few resounding clangs. The twilight has begun to deepen into darkness. Algot peers in through the sacristy door.

Tomas: Well?

Algot: Well, of course, Miss Lundberg's still there. And someone might still come in during the first hymn.

Tomas (looks at Algot).

Algot: So. A service?

Tomas (nods): Yes.

Algot looks at Tomas in surprise. Makes a sign to Blom on the organ gallery, who immediately intones a hurried prelude.

Algot steps into the church and sits down close to the aisle, supporting the organist's rather melodious bass with vague mumbling song.

During the hymn Tomas goes up to the altar, kneels, rises, turns a pale and anxiety-filled face to his congregation.

Tomas: "Holy, holy, holy, Lord God Almighty. All the earth is full of his glory...."

Bergman looks for a dialogue partner through all of his important films of the 1950s: *Summer Interlude* (1950), *Sawdust and Tinsel* (1953), *The Seventh Seal* (1956), and *Wild Strawberries* (1957), those "etudes" leading up to the trilogy on God — *Through a Glass Darkly* (1961), *Winter Light* (1962), and *The Silence* (1963) — that stands at the heart of his work. *Cries and Whispers* (1973), his Passion film, is the epilogue, a requiem for the old belief.

Robert Bresson, the only tragedian working in cinema today, differs from other religious filmmakers in that he is a professed believer. His films manifest an outpouring of grace and deal with questions of evil and salvation. His domain is love.

The key to Bresson's cinema is his interpretation of the traditional Christ figure in Western art and literature. In an article written in 1964, Robert Detweiler revealed some interesting aspects of the modern use of "Christ and the Christ Figure in American Fiction." He pointed out four basic structural avenues — sign, myth, symbol and allegory — in the use of the Christ figure in literature, selecting as examples John Steinbeck, Ernest Hemingway and William Faulkner, among others. The same type of study could prove useful in cinema.

Detweiler asserts that the Christ figure as *sign* carries the least connotative quality in itself, having to rely entirely on the meaning of the object signified. The Christ figure is not a figure at all, but a mold to fit the Christ of tradition in simplified terms. It is usually presented as an object of Christian propaganda. The Christ figure as *myth* leans on the cultural significance of Christ without turning to the questions of belief or historical truth. Christ is usually depicted as a hero, the embodiment of the moral man, or the redeemer on the supernatural level. The Christ figure as *symbol* concentrates on the primary significance of Christ for the Christian faith, his role as redeemer, adapted to the problems of this world. It carries in it a note of optimism and witness to the faith. The Christ figure in *allegory* follows the main thread of the Christ story, while disguising it through a surface narrative and relying on the viewer to provide the necessary continuity. The figure is strong enough to exist by itself, but points to a meaning far beyond this existence for its ultimate truth. It relies upon the participant's keen familiarity with the Christ story and his ability to perceive the fundamental idea.

In the visual world of cinema the application of the Christ figure is common, and a number of uses can be easily differentiated. The four categories can be broken down to analyze the key "Christ" films of prominent directors already discussed. Needless to say, these films are the objects of much dispute among secular and religious critics. The application of these categories may dispel some of the confusion.

Bunuel's *Nazarin* (1958) works its magic in the area of sign. He does not directly espouse the purity of Christ's message in life and mission, but blesses the foolhardiness of people who follow in Christ's footsteps. The social-gospel Jesus-imitation flowered in popular literature at the turn of the century, from which period the mystical novel of Benito Pérez Galdós is adapted to revolutionary Mexico in 1900 to comment indirectly on the fervor of the priest-worker movement in France in the 1950s. Bunuel objectively views both Christ imitations (Nazarin and the modern priest-worker) as commendable but ill-conceived in the world such as it is. By treating the figures as signs he maintains intact his own reputation as atheist but humanist.

Pasolini's *The Gospel According to St. Matthew* (1963-1964) approaches the Christ figure as myth, on the grounds that such is the faith of the population of Southern Italy (where the film was made and for whom it was directed). Far from interpreting the gospel message, the poor Southern Italian looks upon Christ as a legendary, heroic figure, the archetype of the good man who suffers and dies for his ideals. Pasolini worked within the frame of the Christian mythos, retaining the freedom to channel the social and revolutionary elements of Matthew's gospel into a demonstration against church authorities. As a Marxist, existentialist and atheist, he is concerned with the Christian mythos as the foundation of experience. The Christian faith itself is bypassed.

Bergman's *Winter Light* (1962) places the Christ figure in a church setting as a symbol among symbols. The crippled sexton, hidden among an assortment of religious trappings (including a huge crucifix of the suffering Christ), stands out in an otherwise secular world because of his key redemptive role. Throughout the excruciating events of the day God is effectively being declared dead, until the cripple puts everything back into place again by echoing symbolically the death of Christ on the cross: "Vicar, that must have been terrible suffering!" The pastor's mistress also echoes this sacrifice, Christ's abandonment, with the passionate plea, "If we could believe...," to close the gap left by the pastor's unbelief. Thus the ray of light in winter.

Bresson's *Au hasard, Balthasar* (1966) works on the level of allegory drawing its strength indirectly from the Christ figure. The complex relationship of the girl Marie and the drunkard Arnold to the donkey Balthasar, a beast of burden figuratively carrying the cares of the world, presumes on the Christ figure to give it meaning and depth. Without this relationship, the story limps badly. With it, Bresson is able to comment on the human condition, widen his vision to a study of the seven deadly sins, and set the sacrifice and death of his three main characters in proper focus. What makes the film an allegory is the central, underlying current of redemptive grace, bestowing on the trio a certain tragic nobility of purpose (no matter what evil they do). Bresson has imbued his story with a deeper sacrificial meaning, the tragedy of love.

About *Balthasar*, Bresson has said:

The film started from two ideas, from two schemata, if you will. First schema: the donkey has in his life the same stages as does a man, that is to say, childhood, caresses; maturity, work; talent, genius in the middle of life; and the analytical period that precedes death. Well. Second schema, which crosses the first or which starts from it: the passage of this donkey, who passes through different human groups representing the vices of humanity, from which he suffers, and from which he dies. There are the two schemata, and that is why I spoke of the vices of humanity. For the donkey cannot suffer from goodness, or from charity, or from intelligence.... He must suffer from what makes us, ourselves, suffer.

Balthasar is Bresson's central film, seven years in planning and everything original from beginning to end. Working slowly, he left behind the limitations of religious propaganda in *Les Anges du Péché* (1943) and the existential fatalism of *Les Dames du Bois de Boulogne* (1944) to examine the phenomenon of faith in the adaptation of Georges Bernanos's *Diary of a Country Priest* (1950). In this unique cinematic journey into the nature of the spiritual life, Bresson developed his style and basic approach to the cinema:

Here I add another thing that I have not yet said and that is important: the great difficulty is that my means are exterior means, and that therefore they are in relation to appearances, all appearances, the appearance of the person himself as well as the appearance of what surrounds him. So the great difficulty is to remain in the interior, always, without passing to the exterior; it is to avoid the sudden occurrence of a terrible disconnection. And that is what happens to me sometimes, in which case I try to repair the fault.

The films made between *Diary of a Country Priest* (1950) and *Balthasar* (1966) — *A Condemned Man Escaped* (1956), *Pickpocket* (1959), and *The Trial of Joan of Arc* (1961), a total of five films in fifteen years — form a remarkable study of the individual isolated but surrounded by a protective net of God's grace. *A Condemned Man Escapes* relives Bresson's own experiences in prison during the Occupation, recording the true story of another resistance fighter escaping just before his planned execution. *Pickpocket* picks up the thread of a criminal pursued by his fate, until in the end he turns and meets it. Both have a transcendent quality directing the action through to something beyond which signifies liberation, a quality that is also felt in the rigorous attention to the historical facts in *The Trial of Joan of Arc*, a saint.

Bresson turned to tragedy in *Mouchette* (1966) and the two Dostoievsky stories, *Une Femme Douce (The Gentle One)* (1969) and *Four Nights of a Dream* (1971) (based on *White Nights*). In *Mouchette* (along with *Diary of a Country Priest*, the core of his work), the suicide hinted at in the fate of Marie in *Balthasar* is carried out in one of the strongest and most daring endings in cinema history: a young girl of fifteen ends a life that holds out no more possibilities of love. *Une Femme Douce* proceeds to question whether modern society can comprehend the truth in such an act, not to say its purity. *Four Nights of a Dream* goes deep into another form of withdrawal: dreams, in which the young tragically escape reality. Considering the philosophy of the pop culture and drug scene today, it is Bresson's most timely film. *Lancelot du Lac* (1974) is an apologia for erotic love.

Bresson's films, more than any others, require dialogue. In discussing Bresson, one discusses Pascal and Dostoievsky, the Jansenists and the Inquisition. But one also discusses oneself.

I put the Question.... The Question that will bring out the response. But we live, we put questions, and, perhaps, we ourselves give responses. But it is certain that this manner of work is a questionnaire. Only it is a questionnaire in the unknown, that is to say: give me something that will surprise me. That is the stratagem.

Bresson's Question is at the heart of modern cinema: he is requesting a religious response, seeking theological dialogue. Without an answer from the theologian, his cinematic images remain buried and confusing to the critical and general public. Indeed, the theologian does a great disservice to himself and the filmmaker by turning his back on this "questionnaire in the unknown," by resisting surprise and challenge. In short, he must learn to look *beyond the image* for fresh avenues of spiritual expression in an increasingly conformist world.

BIBLIOGRAPHY

FILM HISTORY, THEORY, AND CRITICISM

Agee, James. *Agee on Film* (New York: McDowell Obolensky, 1958).

Agel, Henri, and Ayfre, Amédée. *Le Cinéma et le sacré* (Paris: Editions du Cerf, 1961).

Anderson, Joseph L., and Richie, Donald. *The Japanese Film* (New York: Grove Press, 1960).

Andrew, J. Dudley. *The Major Film Theories* (New York: Oxford University Press, 1976).

Arnheim, Rudolf. *Film as Art* (Berkeley: University of California Press, 1957).

Ayfre, Amédée. *Cinéma et mystère* (Paris: Editions du Cerf, 1969).

— *Le Cinéma et sa vérité* (Paris: Editions du Cerf, 1969).

— *Conversion aux images?* (Paris: Editions du Cerf, 1964).

Balazs, Béla. *Theory of the Film: Character and Growth of a New Art.* Translated by Edith Bone (London: Dobson, 1952).

Barnouw, Erik, and Krishnaswamy, S. *Indian Film* (New York: Columbia University Press, 1963).

Bazin, André. *What Is Cinema?* Selected and translated by Hugh Gray (Berkeley: University of California Press, 1967).

— *What Is Cinema?*, Vol. II. Selected and translated by Hugh Gray (Berkeley: University of California Press, 1971).

Ceran, C. W. *Archaeology of the Cinema* (London: Thames and Hudson, 1965).

Eisenstein, Sergei. *Film Form: Essays in Film Theory.* Edited and translated by Jay Leyda (New York: Harcourt Brace & Co., 1949).

— *The Film Sense.* Edited and translated by Jay Leyda (New York: Harcourt Brace & Co., 1942).

Ford, Charles. *Le Cinéma au service de la foi* (Paris: Présence Plon, 1953).

Furhammar, Leif, and Isaksson, Folke. *Politics and Film* (London: Studio Vista, 1971).

Griffith, Richard, and Mayer, Arthur. *The Movies* (New York: Bonanza Books, 1957).

Hampton, Benjamin B. *History of the American Film Industry* (New York: Dover, 1970).

Huff, Theodore. *Charlie Chaplin* (New York: Henry Schuman, 1951).

Jacobs, Lewis, ed. *The Documentary Tradition* (New York: Hopkinson and Blake, 1971).

— ed. *The Emergence of Film Art* (New York: Hopkinson and Blake, 1969).

— ed. *The Movies as Medium* (New York: Farrar, Straus & Giroux, 1970).

— *The Rise of the American Film* (New York: Teachers College Press, 1969).

Kael, Pauline. *I Lost It at the Movies* (Boston: Little, Brown and Co., 1965).

— *Kiss Kiss Bang Bang* (Little, Brown and Co., 1968).

Kracauer, Siegfried. *From Caligari to Hitler: A Psychological History of the German Film* (Princeton: Princeton University Press, 1947).

— *Theory of Film: The Redemption of Physical Reality* (New York: Oxford University Press, 1960).

Lindsay, Vachel. *The Art of the Moving Picture* (New York: Liveright, 1970).

Lord, Daniel. *Played by Ear* (New York: Image Books, 1959).

MacCann, Richard Dyer, ed. *Film: A Montage of Theories* (New York: E. P. Dutton & Co., 1966).

— ed. *Film and Society* (New York: Charles Scribner's Sons, 1964).

Mast, Gerald, and Cohen, Marshall, eds. *Film Theory and Criticism: Introductory Readings* (New York: Oxford University Press, 1974).

Metz, Christian. *Film Language: A Semiotics of the Cinema.* Translated by Michael Taylor (New York: Oxford University Press, 1974).

Mitry, Jean. *Esthétique et psychologie du cinéma,* two volumes (Paris: Editions Universitaires, 1963-65).

Munsterberg, Hugo. *The Film: A Psychological Study* (New York: Dover, 1970).

Niver, Kemp. *Motion Pictures from the Library of Congress Paper Print Collection 1894-1912* (Berkeley: University of California Press, 1967).

Perkins, V. F. *Film as Film* (Baltimore: Penguin Books, 1972).

Potamkin, Harry Alan. *The Compound Cinema: The Selected Writings of HLP.* Edited by Lewis Jacobs (New York: Teachers College Press, 1977).

Powdermaker, Hortense. *Hollywood, the Dream Factory* (Boston: Little, Brown and Co., 1960).

Pudovkin, Vsevolod I. *Film Technique and Film Acting.* Edited and translated by Ivor Montagu (New York: Grove Press, 1960).

Robinson, W. R., ed. *Man and the Movies* (Baton Rouge: Louisiana State University, 1967).

Rotha, Paul. *Documentary Film* (London: Faber and Faber, 1952).

— with Richard Griffith. *The Film Till Now* (New York: Twayne, 1960).

— *Rotha on the Film* (Fair Lawn: Essential Books, 1958).

Sadoul, Georges. *Histoire générale du cinéma,* five volumes (Paris: Editions Denoël, 1946-54).

Sarris, Andrew. *The American Cinema: Directors and Directions 1929-1968* (New York: Dutton, 1969).

Sharp, Dennis. *The Picture Palace* (London: Hugh Evelyn, 1969).

Talbot, Daniel, ed. *Film: An Anthology* (Berkeley: University of California Press, 1970).

Tudor, Andrew. *Theories of Film* (London: Secker and Warburg, 1974).

Wolfenstein, Martha, and Leites, Nathan. *Movies, a Psychological Study* (Glencoe: The Free Press, 1950).

Wollen, Peter. *Signs and Meaning in the Cinema* (London: Secker and Warburg, 1974).

Young, Vernon. *On Film: Unpopular Essays on a Popular Art* (New York: Quadrangle/The New York Times Book Co., 1972).

Youngblood, Gene. *Expanded Cinema* (New York: Dutton, 1970).

THEOLOGY AND CINEMA/CULTURE

Altizer, Thomas J. J. *Toward a New Christianity* (New York: Harcourt, Brace, 1967).

Ayfre, Amédée. *Le Cinéma et la foi chrétienne* (Paris: Librairie Arthème Fayard, 1960).

Barth, Karl. *The Faith of the Church* (New York: Meridian, 1958).

Bazin, André. *Jean Renoir*, Translated by W. W. Halsey and William H. Simon (New York: Simon and Schuster, 1973).

Berdyaev, Nicolas. *Truth and Revelation.* Translated by R. M. French (New York: Collier Books, 1962).

Berger, Peter. *A Rumour of Angels* (New York: Doubleday, 1969).

Bergman on Bergman. Interviews with Ingmar Bergman by Stig Björkman, Torsten Manns, and Jonas Sima, translated by Paul Britten Austin (London: Seckar & Warburg, 1973).

Bloch, Ernst. *Das Prinzip Hoffnung*, three volumes (Berlin: Aufbau Verlag, 1959-60).

Bogdanovich, Peter. *John Ford, Interviews* (London: Studio Vista, 1967).

Bonhoeffer, Dietrich. *Letters and Papers from Prison.* Edited by Eberhard Bethge, translated by Reginald H. Fuller (New York: Macmillan, 1952).

Brantl, George, ed. *The Religious Experience*, two volumes (New York: George Braziller, Inc., 1964).

Brunner, Emil. *Christianity and Civilization* (New York: Charles Scribner's Sons, 1949).

Buache, Freddy. *The Cinema of Luis Buñuel.* Translated by Peter Graham (London: The Tantivy Press, 1973).

Buber, Martin. *I and Thou* (New York: Charles Scribner's Sons, 1957).

Bultmann, Rudolf. *Existence and Faith* (New York: Meridian, 1960).

Butler, Ivan. *Religion in the Cinema* (New York: A. S. Barnes, 1969).

Calder-Marshall, Arthur. *The Innocent Eye: The Life of Robert J. Flaherty* (London: W. H. Allen, 1963).

Cameron, Ian, ed. *The Films of Robert Bresson* (London: Studio Vista, 1969).

Cox, Harvey. *The Secular City* (New York: Macmillan, 1965).

— *The Feast of Fools: A Theological Essay on Festivity and Fantasy* (New York: Harper & Row, 1969).

Cutler, Donald R., ed. *The Religious Situation,* two volumes (Boston: Beacon Press, 1968-69).

Dawson, Christopher. *Enquiries into Religion and Culture* (New York: Sheed and Ward, 1936).

Dewart, Leslie. *The Future of Belief* (New York: Herder and Herder, 1966).

— *The Foundations of Belief* (New York: Herder and Herder, 1969).

Durant, Will. *The Story of Philosophy* (New York: Simon and Schuster, 1953).

Eliade, Mircea. *Cosmos and History: The Myth of the Eternal Return* (New York: Harper Torchbook, 1959).

— *Patterns in Comparative Religion* (New York: Sheed and Ward, 1958).

— *The Sacred and the Profane* (New York: Harcourt, Brace, 1959).

Eliot, T. S. *Christianity and Culture* (New York: Harcourt, Brace, Harvest Book, 1960).

Fromm, Erich. *Psychoanalysis and Religion* (New Haven: Yale University Press, 1950).

Gibson, Arthur. *The Silence of God* (New York: Harper and Row, 1969).

Guarner, José Luis. *Roberto Rossellini.* Translated by Elisabeth Cameron (London: Studio Vista, 1970).

Hamilton, William. *The New Essence of Christianity* (New York: Association Press, 1961).

Huizinga, Johan. *Homo Ludens: A Study of the Play Element in Culture* (Boston: Beacon Press, 1955).

Hurley, Neil P. *Theology through Film* (New York: Harper & Row, 1970).

Ivens, Joris. *The Camera and I* (New York: International Publishers, 1969).

James, William. *Varieties of Religious Experience* (New York: Modern Library, 1936).

Jaspers, Karl, and Bultmann, Rudolf. *Myth and Christianity: An Inquiry into the Possibility of Religion without Myth* (New York: Noonday, 1958).

Jung, Carl Gustav. *Modern Man in Search of a Soul.* Translated by W. S. Dell and Carl F. Baynes (New York: Harcourt, Brace, Harvest Book, 1963).

— *Psychology and Religion* (New York: Pantheon, 1958).

Kierkegaard, Soren. *Fear and Trembling* and *The Sickness unto Death* (New York: Doubleday Anchor Book, 1954).

Lynch, William. *Christ and Apollo* (New York: Sheed and Ward, 1960).

Marcel, Gabriel. *Man Against Mass Society* (Chicago: Henry Regnery, Gateway Edition, 1962).

Maritain, Jacques. *Approaches to God.* Translated by Peter O'Reilly (New York: Macmillan, 1964).

— *Art and Faith: Letters between Jacques Maritain and Jean Cocteau* (New York: Philosophical Library, 1948).

Marty, Martin E., and Peerman, Dean C. *New Theology,* Volumes 1-12 (New York: Macmillan, 1964-76).

May, Rollo, ed. *Symbolism in Religion and Literature* (New York: Braziller, 1960).

Metz, Johannes Baptist. *Zur Theologie der Welt* (Mainz: Matthias Grünewald Verlag, 1968).

Milne, Tom. *The Cinema of Carl Theodor Dreyer* (New York: A. S. Barnes, 1971).

Moltmann, Jürgen. *Theology of Hope* (New York: Harper, 1967).

Müller-Schwefe, Hans-Rudolf. *Technik und Glaube* (Göttingen: Vandenhoeck & Ruprecht, 1971).

Niebuhr, H. Richard. *Christ and Culture* (New York: Harper Torchbook, 1956).

Nietzsche, Friedrich. *Thus Spoke Zarathustra* (New York: Modern Library, 1937).

Novak, Michael. *Belief and Unbelief* (New York, Macmillan, 1965).

Ong, Walter. *The Presence of the Word* (New Haven: Yale University Press, 1967).

Otto, Rudolf. *The Idea of the Holy* (New York: Oxford Galaxy Book, 1958).

Pascal, Blaise. *Pensées* and *The Provincial Letters* (New York: Modern Library, 1941).

Pieper, Josef. *In Tune with the World: A Theory of Festivity*. Translated by Richard and Clara Winston (New York: Harcourt, Brace, 1965).

Rahner, Hugo. *Man at Play* (New York: Herder and Herder, 1967).

Robinson, John A. T. *Honest to God* (London: SCM Press, 1963).

Santayana, George. *Poetry and Religion* (New York: Harper Torchbook, 1957).

Scheffczyk, Leo. *Man's Search for Himself* (New York: Sheed and Ward, 1966).

Schillaci, Anthony. *Movies and Morals* (Notre Dame: Fides, 1968).

Schrader, Paul. *Transcendental Style in Film: Ozu, Bresson, Dreyer* (Berkeley: University of California Press, 1972).

Scott, Nathan A. *The Broken Center: Studies in the Theological Horizon of Modern Literature* (New Haven: Yale University Press, 1968).

Solmi, Angelo. *Fellini*. Translated by Elisabeth Greenwood (London: Merlin Press, 1967).

Sontag, Susan. *Against Interpretation* (New York: Farrar, Straus & Giroux, 1966).

Stack, Oswald. *Pasolini on Pasolini: Interviews with OS* (London: Thames and Hudson, 1969).

Teilhard de Chardin, Pierre. *The Divine Milieu* (New York: Harper, 1960).

— *The Phenomenon of Man* (New York, Harper, 1959)

Tillich, Paul. *The Courage to Be* (New Haven: Yale University Press, 1963).

— *Theology of Culture* (New York: Oxford University Press, 1959).

Toynbee, Arnold J. *Christianity among the World Religions* (New York: Charles Scribner's, 1957).

Vahanian, Gabriel. *The Death of God: The Culture of Our Post-Christian Era* (New York: George Braziller, 1966).

van Buren, Paul M. *The Secular Meaning of the Gospel* (New York: Macmillan, 1963).

Wall, James M., ed. *Three European Directors* (Chicago: William B. Eerdmans Publishing Co., 1973).

Whitehead, Alfred North. *Symbolism: Its Meaning and Effect* (New York: G. P. Putnam's Capricorn Books, 1959).

Wittgenstein, Ludwig. *Philosophical Investigations* (Oxford: Blackwell, 1958).

Zahrnt, Heinz. *The Question of God: Protestant Theology in the Twentieth Century*. Translated by R. A. Wilson (London: Collins: 1969).

INDEX OF FILM TITLES

INDEX OF NAMES

PRINTED IN SWITZERLAND

WITHDRAWN